THE term " Central Asia
loosely. Its true bound
define them, should encl(
within the region limite
Karakorum and the Kunlun ranges on tne suuui ;
the Syr Darya and the Tian Shan mountains on
the north ; the Gobi Desert on the east, and the
Kizil Kum on the west. This is the kernel of the
nut. Tibet is an entity to itself, and is not Central
Asia, nor is Dzungaria—the region to the north of
the Tian Shan. East and west, it is true, the boun-
daries are somewhat vague, there being no special
land features to decide them. But it may be said
that the Gobi Desert is not " Central Asia " nor is
the Caspian Sea. In my opinion, *Central* as opposed
to *Middle*, should be reserved for the innermost core
of the Continent.

The only moot point seems to be Northern
Afghanistan, ancient Bactria, present-day Afghan
Turkestan—the region between the Hindu Kush and
the Oxus. A good case can be made out for including
this area in Central Asia, although it is generally
acknowledged that Afghanistan, as a whole, lies
within the so-called " Middle East." But ethnographically and biologically Afghanistan *north* of the
Hindu Kush is purely Central Asian.

But even this broad definition is open to criticism.
For instance, the oasis of Hami might complain that
she is only just included in the extreme north-east
corner of this " Central Asia," whereas she is actually

the very bull's eye of the whole Continent. Again, there are some to whom the term has a political, rather than a geographical savour, " Central Asia " to them means the lands of the Amir Nasrulli, the Emperor Baber, Yakub Beg—and no more.

The Russians, it should be noted, use " Middle Asia " for their own territory—the Turkmen, Uzbeg, Kirghiz and Tadjik Republics, and reserve " Central Asia " for Chinese Turkestan.

The majority of the names on our maps of Central Asia have originated from Russian sources ; that is to say they are the English transcription of the Russian which are in turn the Russian transliteration of the native names—Mongol, Aryan, or a composition of the two. The result is not very satisfactory. However, the Permanent Committee on Geographical Names for British Official Use has made a start, and produced two General Lists of Asiatic Names. But Asia is a large continent, and in these two lists, there are not more than fifty place-names that belong to Central Asia. Since the map of this region, which has been drawn especially to illustrate the present volume, is based on the British Council Map of Europe and the Middle East, I have decided to use its spelling for the place-names, in spite of the fact they are not consistent with the system used by the Permanent Committee on Geographical Names. This decision has forced me to retain the K in place of Q, in all place-names and proper-names throughout the text, for the sake of uniformity.

I do not hold the view that a book illustrated with " photographs taken by the author " has any special merit. The pictures should emphasize the written words of the text, their origin is immaterial.

THE TURQUOISE TARN

BEYOND THE CASPIAN

A NATURALIST IN CENTRAL ASIA

CHECKED - 1963

BY

DOUGLAS CARRUTHERS

F.R.G.S., F.Z.S.

GOLD MEDALLIST OF THE ROYAL
GEOGRAPHICAL SOCIETY

ILLUSTRATED WITH TWENTY-TWO
FULL-PAGE PLATES, OF WHICH
SIX ARE COLOURED

OLIVER AND BOYD

EDINBURGH: TWEEDDALE COURT
LONDON: 98 GREAT RUSSELL STREET, W.C.

1949

THE HYDERABAD BOOK DEPOT,
GUNFOUNDRY, HYDERABAD-DN.

All the photographs in this volume, with two obvious exceptions, are of my own taking, but if I could find better ones I would not hesitate to use them. Where my films failed, Mr Roy Beddington came to my aid, and has succeeded so well in translating my own rough sketches and descriptions into picture form, that they tell the tale more vividly than I, or my camera could have done. My gratitude to him is unbounded.

I am much indebted to the Society for Cultural Relations between the Peoples of the British Commonwealth and the U.S.S.R. for permission to include several examples of how the Russian artistic eye sees bird and animal life. Those in the text on pages 63 and 114, are by C. Flerov; the coloured plate opposite page 86, is by V. Vatagin, and has been reproduced by the courtesy of the Editor of *L'Oiseau et la Revue Francaise d'Ornithologie*.

Times have not been easy for the production of a book of this nature, requiring a certain amount of research, and access to literature on a variety of subjects in many languages. War-conditions, followed by post-war restrictions ; dispersed libraries, libraries destroyed or damaged, or in possession of only a portion of their belongings ; valuable foreign sources of knowledge withheld from us ; Museums evacuated or partly destroyed ; all these factors have reduced my chances of making this book as comprehensive as I should have liked to do, and increased the labour of making one at all. Had it not been for the help given to me by various old friends, I should not have been able to incorporate some valuable material.

Dr David Bannerman, who contributes the

Foreword, the late R. I. Pocock, F.R.S., Mr N. B. Kinnear, Mr T. C. S. Morrison-Scott, and Mr J. L. Chaworth-Musters were my mainstay at the British Museum (Natural History), and I owe to each of them a great debt of gratitude. For a continuous and liberal supply of books, which I could study at my leisure in the country, I have to thank Mr G. B. Stratton, Librarian of the Zoological Society ; Mr W. R. Woodrow of the Royal Geographical Society ; Miss R. O. Wingate of the Royal Central Asian Society ; Mr C. J. Purnell of the London Library ; Miss P. M. Thomas of the Zoological Museum, Tring ; and Major H. G. K. Molineux for a presentation copy of his invaluable *Catalogue of Birds of the Western Palæarctic Region.*

From America I received support from Dr Roy Chapman Andrews, while Professor Ellsworth Huntington of Yale University kindly supplied me with literature from his own library.

To the Editors of the *Times of India, The Field, Country Life,* and the *Geographical Magazine,* I am indebted for permission to use material which has already appeared under my name in their respective publications ; and to Messrs Hutchinson and Co. for the use of the illustrations opposite pages 132 and 224, which have previously appeared in my *Unknown Mongolia.*

Lastly, my special acknowledgments are due to Messrs Oliver and Boyd for the care which they have lavished on the production of this volume in most difficult times.

FOREWORD

To follow in the footsteps of the late Lord Curzon of Kedleston, Viceroy of India, and write a Foreword to one of Mr Carruthers' books, is a task which should make a braver heart than mine shrink from the attempt. It is an honour of which I am entirely unworthy, but having known and greatly admired the author of *Unknown Mongolia* from my Cambridge undergraduate days, and seen something of the beautifully prepared collections which he has sent back to the British Museum (Natural History), over a period of forty years, I can write from an angle which was denied even to the distinguished President of the Royal Geographical Society. Would that I had Lord Curzon's gifted pen to do justice to my subject.

There can be few Englishmen with a better claim than Mr Douglas Carruthers to write with knowledge, sympathy, and understanding of the countries and peoples " Beyond the Caspian," for the author of this book is not only a distinguished traveller and naturalist, who, at an early age was awarded the Gold Medal of the Royal Geographical Society for his successful explorations, but is to-day an acknowledged authority on that region.

In one of his earlier books Mr Carruthers tells us that as a boy he had three great desires, to cross what was still called " darkest Africa," to see rock-hewn Petra, and to reach that strange capital at the back of the world—remote Bukhara. By the age of twenty-six all three ambitions had been fulfilled, but that merely stimulated his desire for more adventurous travel, and in the years which followed, up to the outbreak of the first world war, journey succeeded journey in almost ceaseless procession.

From his early days Mr Carruthers equipped himself to be an explorer-naturalist above the ordinary. Not only was he fully qualified as a surveyor and geographer, but in the scientific preparation of museum specimens, both birds and mammals, it would be difficult to find his equal. Moreover in his writings he is the fortunate master, as Lord Curzon pointed out, of " a very clear, agreeable, and scholarly style " as the reader of this book will soon discover.

The year 1904 found him in Syria, attached to the Museum of the American University at Beirut to which already valuable collection he added 323 bird skins and 19 mammals, as well as mounting over one hundred specimens for the show cases. But no museum could hold so restless a spirit for long, and on the expiration of his engagement there he set out with a companion to explore the Syrian Desert beyond Damascus, thus laying the foundations of his love of desert places which have lasted a lifetime. The 155 animals and birds which were obtained on that first trip proved Mr Carruthers to be a first-rate collector, and thus began a connection with the Zoological Departments of the British Museum which was to last for many years.

At the close of the Syrian adventure, Carruthers was invited to join the select band of naturalists sent out by the British Museum to explore Ruwenzori, that great range of mountains in Equatorial Africa known as " the Mountains of the Moon," which in those days offered an unrivalled field for scientific investigation. No official expedition was more successful and that happy result was due in no small measure to the author of this book, who, with his companions, set a standard in collecting which it would be difficult to surpass. The many specimens which Mr Carruthers personally prepared over forty years ago, are in perfect condition to-day, and are some of the best made skins in the National Collection.

On the completion of the Ruwenzori Expedition, accompanied by A. F. R. Wollaston, he set out to cross Africa from East to West, and thus fulfilled the second of his youthful ambitions. The story of what at that time was an adventurous journey from Uganda to the mouth of the Congo, by way of the Mfumbiro Volcanoes, was told in a fascinating book *From Ruwenzori to the Congo* by his companion. But the damp Congo forest held no allure for Carruthers and, as he later confessed, an indescribable obsession overcame him for the sunlit open spaces and to be quit of " the dismal depths of that sodden jungle."

So Carruthers turned his back on Africa, never to return, and 1907-8 found him far away in Russian Turkestan, hunting and collecting. An exceptionally fine series of specimens, numbering 522 birds and 123 mammals, was eventually received at the British Museum as a result of his labours. Among the birds were many rare pheasants, mountain finches and chats, while of the mammals five were new to science, including a vole named in his honour *Pitymys carruthersi*. His work lay first in the desert to the west of Bukhara and to the north-west of Samarkand and later in Eastern Bukhara, where, on the borders of

Afghanistan lie some of the highest mountains in Central Asia.

In January 1909 Carruthers was again in Damascus laying plans for what was probably the most daring adventure of his life to penetrate to the heart of Arabia in search of the Oryx—that elusive and beautiful antelope whose sanctum was guarded by treacherous tribes always at war with one another. How his difficulties were overcome and the prize eventually secured has been narrated in *Arabian Adventure* (*1935*). Although the Unicorn of the Old Testament—if indeed it is identical with the Oryx—was the successful goal, much else was accomplished on this Expedition. Taima was visited and fully described and the sands of the Great Nafud penetrated "a desert world of new and dreadful aspect."

" The colour of the sands from a distance," wrote Carruthers " is pure carmine in a low morning light, changing under the mid-day glare to white, and at dusk they appear wine-red and of an intangible velvety texture. But at close quarters the sands are every shade of yellow and red, blending softly into an amazing mixture for which one can find no name."

I quote that paragraph from *Arabian Adventure* to show, as readers of *Beyond the Caspian* will discover, that Mr Carruthers has an eye for desert beauty, as well as for hard scientific facts, in which one's imaginations can find no room for play. For his survey work and explorations in Arabia Carruthers received on his return home the award of the Gill Memorial from the Royal Geographical Society.

There followed two years mostly spent in Siberia, Mongolia and Chinese Turkestan, during which

Carruthers set the seal upon his reputation as a great explorer-naturalist. In company with J. H. Miller and M. P. Price, he spent the first eight months in the Upper Yenesei regions and in Mongolia, the next eleven with Miller, travelling through Dzungaria, finally crossing Turkestan to India, arriving home in December 1911. Mr Carruthers was the first Englishman to undertake serious exploration and survey work in North-West Mongolia while in the Upper Yenesei basin he had no forerunners. The collections which he sent home to the British Museum were of exceptional interest and rarity. The mammal collection numbered 186 and included 16 undescribed species, a new Suslik *Citellus carruthersi* being named in his honour. The bird collections, numbering some 247 beautiful skins, were unfortunately never worked out and thus was lost to the British Museum a number of types which would have enriched the value of the National Collection had a prompt report been issued.

The results of that great expedition, during which vast tracts of country were accurately mapped for the first time, were embodied in two volumes entitled *Unknown Mongolia* (1913). In a foreword to that work the late Lord Curzon of Kedleston pays high tribute to the author, predicting that the book will long remain a classic on its subject—a prediction which has been amply fulfilled.

In 1912 Douglas Carruthers was awarded the " Patron's Medal " of the Royal Geographical Society for his outstanding work on several expeditions with special relation to his explorations in Mongolia, and well he deserved that signal honour bestowed upon him with the approval of His Majesty the King.

Early in 1913, in company with G. Fenwick-Owen, he directed his steps towards Asia Minor, a country concerning the natural history of which we know singularly little. While in Turkey he covered the regions of the Eastern Taurus : Aleppo—Marash—Kayseri—Ankara, but his journey was more in the nature of a reconnaissance than a serious expedition.

War clouds were already gathering in Europe and for the time being any exploration work or collecting in Asia Minor was out of the question.

Willing to serve his country in any capacity in which he was needed Mr Carruthers was selected on the outbreak of war to compile the maps of the Middle East for the War Office, especially those of Arabia. This work brought him into close touch with Lawrence who supplied data for incorporation in the compilations and with other " Arabian " officials and explorers. All Captain Shakespear's and Gertrude Bell's surveys, and some of St John Philby's, passed through his hands, and he was responsible for their final publication. Six long years were devoted to this task and though the work was unspectacular, it was as can be imagined, of the utmost national importance. In 1916 Carruthers was elected an Honorary Secretary of the Royal Geographical Society, a position he filled with distinction until 1921.

On the termination of the first world war his many friends had hoped that Carruthers would return to conquer more fields in which he had already achieved so much, but it was not to be. We must comfort ourselves with the thought that what has been lost by his decision to withdraw from active exploration, has been gained in the realm of literature. His articles published in the *Geographical Journal* (1922) on "Captain Shakespear's Last Journey" were described by D. G. Hogarth as in themselves valuable contributions to our knowledge of Northern Arabia and it was fitting that in 1929 he should be asked to edit for the Hakluyt Society *The Desert Route to India*, contributing a scholarly introduction to the "Journals of four travellers by the Great Desert Caravan route between Aleppo and Basra (1745-1751)." Six years later he wrote *Arabian Adventure—to the Great Nafud in search of the Oryx*, following that by editing and republishing *Northern Najd*, or the *Travels of Carlo Guarmani in Arabia*, originally published by the Arab Bureau, Cairo, for official use only, and later sumptuously reproduced by the Argonaut Press. As the reviewer of that work in the *Times Literary Supplement* pointed out, no one was better qualified than Douglas Carruthers to annotate that interesting book and his introduction and notes—to use the reviewer's own words—drawn from a wide field of activity and learning, are a great part of the value of the production.

Now he has given us *Beyond the Caspian* in which he allows us to glimpse a land to which few Englishmen have ever penetrated, writing with intimacy of the birds and beasts it was his fortune to encounter when traversing the deserts, or exploring the mountains, of this far away corner of the earth. In order to bring his knowledge up to date, Carruthers set himself the laborious task of translating and reading everything that has been written on Russian Turkestan until he became a thorough master of his subject, showing the same patience and care for detail in that rôle which marked out his work in the field. Reference to the Bibliography will show how extensive these writings are.

One does not look for humour in a serious book of travel, but there are flashes hidden in these pages—for those with discerning eyes—which would make Noel Coward himself green with envy.

In this Foreword, which falls far short of what I had desired, I have attempted to give the reader of this volume a *background* to the narrative which it contains, so that whoever may peruse its pages may realise with what authority Mr Carruthers writes of the countries, peoples, animals and birds which he describes so vividly. It has given me great pleasure to make this small contribution to his book as it has afforded me an opportunity to express in some measure appreciation of the benefits which Mr Carruthers work has bestowed upon the Science of Geography, and in particular upon the British Museum (Natural History) whose collections have been so greatly enriched by his labours.

Readers of *Beyond the Caspian* will be grateful to him for an opportunity to turn their thoughts for a while from this troubled world and to travel in his company to Samarkand, to Bukhara, and to the distant lands which he loves so well, and on which he must be reckoned an outstanding authority.

Mr Carruthers has a fascinating tale to tell of his wanderings beyond the Caspian, told with the simplicity and charm of an accomplished writer and a true naturalist.

DAVID A. BANNERMAN

CONTENTS

ILLUSTRATIONS

COLOUR PLATES

BLACK AND WHITE PLATES

ILLUSTRATIONS

MAP

Where the human race was cradled
  Rocked in mighty Oxus' arms,
Samarkand and old Bukhara
  Ravish with their charms.

Jenghis Khan and Alexander,
  Conquerors of old,
Gazed upon your wealth in wonder
  Scatterer of Gold !

Teeming life 'mid barren desert,
  Rock and sand and snow ;
Land of paradox and promise
  Where the roses blow.

Range on range that beckon onward,
  Plains where trod the Tartar horde,
Poet's theme and traveller's story—
  World yet unexplored !

INTRODUCTION

THE title I have chosen for this book is both fact and fancy, for although the principal chapters in it do relate to those spacious regions beyond the Caspian Sea where Europe merges into Asia, others do not. But still the title serves, for it has a symbolic meaning in addition to its geographical one.

Perhaps I should begin by saying at once that the chapters which follow do not describe contemporary conditions in those Soviet Republics which occupy the regions beyond the Caspian. I have nothing to say about recent industrial developments in Transcaspia, nor of racial readjustment in High Tartary, and I do not mention air-lines or motor-routes across Central Asia. Should the reader expect to hear how the medieval mountaineers of Eastern Bukhara have reacted to Soviet jurisdiction, or to what extent obsolete Oriental societies have adapted themselves to the New World, he will be disappointed ; he must look elsewhere—there are many handbooks on the subject. But I can tell of things which have been able to withstand the avalanche of war and revolution, and which are to-day as they were before those things happened : also I can reveal a good deal on my own special subject which is not known, at any rate outside Russian literature. For these regions have stood beyond the range of even the ubiquitous Englishman, and no other one to my knowledge has been privileged to live openly, and travel freely, as long as I was allowed to do under Russian rule *north* of the Oxus.

I believe it to be the onus on every man to add, if he can, his jot to the sum total of human knowledge. Justification, then, if such is necessary, lies in the fact that my sketches of travel cover fresh ground, and do not repeat what has already been told.

Before me, on my table, lie several rather dirty and much worn quarto note-books. Each holds a hundred pages, and every page is crammed on both sides with closely written manuscript, in indelible pencil, luckily, for they show signs of having been under water. They are entirely legible, although they were written chiefly in the night-watches, by the light of a flickering candle, in tent, cave, hut or hovel, at the end of long and tiring days. They represent my daily experiences over several years wandering beyond the Caspian. There are no gaps, although written sometimes, when time was short and physical strength at low ebb, in a sort of spurious shorthand. The most exciting episodes, the most awkward moments, and the longest but most eventful days may on occasion be condensed within a few lines, but the full story is there.

" First impressions are always the most interesting, and even a day or two's delay causes one to think a circumstance or observation of less importance, and then it is forgotten." So I proceeded to put down everything that appealed to me in Nature, whether it was bird or beast, forest or flower, winter's storm or summer's heat, not omitting glances into the past, when history chanced to make a barren landscape alive with romantic figures or where prehistoric periods had entirely altered the scene. The Caspian deserts, for instance, assume a new and greater interest as an erstwhile Asiatic Mediterranean, while the dreary steppes come back to new life when seen as the fairway of the human tides that have flowed from Asia into Europe. These things appeal to me more than the aspect of the same region as a potential cotton-growing and oil-producing area, or as a deposit of artificial manures.

The incentive to write a book is, or should be, created by two very natural desires—to pass on to others the information one has so hardly come by, and to share with them the enjoyment of things which they cannot see. In this case there is a third factor, namely—that a' happier and more permanent understanding between this country and Russia is highly desirable, and how can this be achieved better than by an interchange of knowledge about the two countries?

Parts of this book may appear to be scattered thoughts and enthusiasms, but that is the result of having an insatiable appetite for a varied diet. If there is a lack of cohesion, it is because I believe that a great variety of interests is one of the major sources of happiness. It will be noted, and probably brought up against me, that the so-called human element is lacking. I do not attempt to recall the departed glories of those strange capitals at the back of the world, Bukhara and Samarkand, and there is no conversation and back-chat with native guides, local hosts and fellow wayfarers, running continuously through my narrative ; one learns more by keeping one's ears open, but one's mouth shut ; while living alone tends to make one taciturn and unsociable. Even the ancient cities of Tartary savoured somewhat of civilisation, and I would away from crowded bazaars to less frequented places. This, perhaps, explains the judgment once passed on me by a

3

travelling companion : "Out in camp he's extra-
ordinarily good, but in town he's impossible." In
other words, my tale is of the veritable wilderness,
and of the "herds of Pan," of things which change
not, nor are subject to the caprice of Man. The
slow grist of ages, the infinite course of evolution,
is their only concern. "What we know is but little ;
what we do not know is immense," is only too true ;
but the trouble is we are far too apt to jump to the
conclusion that we know more than we actually do.
I often recall to myself a conversation I once had with
an eminent judge who was trying to decide to what
interest he would devote himself upon retirement.
He considered ornithology, but decided finally on
wild flowers, because birds had already been "done."
Done ! when there is so much to be learnt about our
commonest companions of the hedgerow and the
garden. This applies to Central Asia in a very marked
degree. When I arrived in Samarkand and looked
round I felt somewhat overawed by the prospect—
such a wide range of opportunity lay spread around
me. As a field naturalist, I foresaw years of fascinating
and useful work ahead of me, if not indeed a life's
labour, and I planned accordingly. I would work
from the Caspian eastwards, while the British
Museum's other collectors were operating from Pekin
westwards ; anon we would join up in the heart of
the continent, having investigated its fauna in
passing. That might be five or ten years hence. But
the fauna of the country was a small consideration
compared with other possibilities which discovered
themselves to me. There were the flowers and the
fruits of a land wealthy in both. There were the
unclimbed mountains—dozens of them, from 24,000

4

feet downwards.   There were the ancient sites and remains awaiting the arrival of trained archæologists. If it was the " unknown " which appealed, here was opportunity unbounded.   But my own work, as a naturalist, was clearly defined, and even if I could only scratch the surface, the prospect was brilliant.

There are some of us to whom " free air astir to windward " is almost essential.   It is a desire inexplicable to those who have never felt it, ineradicable in those who have.   I was lucky.   My new home stretched from the Caspian to Mongolia, from Siberia to India.   My playground was the Gobi desert and the Hungry Steppe ; my garden the flower-strewn Heavenly Mountains and the rose-encumbered gorges of Bukhara.   My park wall comprised the Hindu Kush, the Pamirs and the Altai.   My chase held the giant wild ram, the heraldic beast of Central Asia— " primeval patriarch, perhaps, of all the flocks on earth," besides the world's biggest ibex, stags, and roe-deer :   there were tigers and wild asses.   The river-valleys swarmed with pheasants and the open plains with partridges ; myriads of wildfowl crowded the lakes in winter.   For three years I had the run of it all, but three years was not enough.   When I left Central Asia, I registered a vow on the summit of the Karakorum Pass that I would return ; but although my cartridges awaited me in Samarkand and my tents in Kuldja, I was never to make use of them again.

> For he remember'd his own early youth,
> And all its bounding rapture ; as at dawn,
> The Shepherd from his moutain-lodge descries
> A far bright City, smitten by the sun,
> Through many rolling clouds. . . .

CHAPTER I

THE VALE OF SAMARKAND

BEYOND the Caspian lies a desert, not perhaps the desert of one's imagination, for although some parts of it are as hopelessly sterile as any on earth, others have been reclaimed or are reclaimable : Eurasia, where a long-dead Asia is being rapidly rejuvenated by a virile Europe. Beyond the desert rise the mountains, the first outlying ranges of that vast uplift, which appears to fill the bulk of Middle Asia ; a mountain world so great that such giants as the Tian Shan and the Himalaya are mere offshoots of it, so extensive that it has profoundly influenced the histories of remote and irrelative regions such as China, Hindustan, Persia and Siberia, if not indeed of the whole world, should theory prove true that it was indeed the cradle of the human race.

In the western declivities of these mountains, three historic rivers have their origin—the Oxus, the Syr, and the Zarafshan. These three, and the most important in many ways is the least of them, the Zarafshan, for this river dedicates itself to the use of man and thereby wins fame, for it is the creator of the great and renowned cities of Samarkand and Bukhara. Bukhara is a city of the plains, low lying, desert encircled ; but Samarkand stands high, tucked away under the foothills of the mountains, embedded in a veritable Garden of Eden, in a land literally flowing with milk and honey, where all the fruits of the earth seem to grow in profusion and to perfection, where man finds life easy and the climate is perfect.

Samarkand has an atmosphere and character of its own, and superior to those of any other Eastern city of my acquaintance. It is a beautiful city in beautiful surroundings, a pleasure city as it were, created especially for some super-man, in fact, Timur's throne. Its atmosphere is entirely æsthetic and academic. It exudes—or rather did exude—art, learning and religion. That is its charm. Samarkand stands aloof from the noisy, vulgar world ; uncontaminated by commerce and free from the ignoble influence of trade. Even in its decline Samarkand is like some fair lady looking out from the seclusion of her garden on to the wilderness around her.

Although once upon a time a great emporium of trade, and without doubt a port of call on the northernmost of the three Silk Routes, it certainly does not give one the impression of being, or of ever having been, a caravan city. The atmosphere and character of a true caravan city linger on, even when the city itself has died a natural death from a diverted trade. But Samarkand does not give one that feeling.

It has been customary to speak loosely of Samarkand as being a " half-way house for trade between East and West," and so on. But was it ? Was it not Bukhara that caught the trade ? Bukhara, on which every road in Asia was said to converge, Bukhara of the plains, not Samarkand under the mountains ? Bukhara was the City ; Samarkand the West end. Bukhara did the work ; Samarkand got the glory. Again, if you come and study the problem " on the spot " (as Stein so often advised arm-chair archæologists to do), if you stand aloft on Kemkutan * and look at the geographical situation

* A 7000 ft. summit on the hills, 10 miles to the south of Samarkand.

7

of Samarkand in relation to its surroundings, you will notice that Samarkand is at the mouth of a valley that has no exit—except by the entrance to it ; also that it is, or rather was, on the very outside fringe of the settled world, on the frontiers as it were, of Barbarism. Compare Samarkand with Kashgar, Balkh, Baghdad, Aleppo or Damascus, and you will find it is not in the same category.

In the heart of Samarkand is a great public square, said to be one of the noblest in the world, and from its corners spring four slender minarets. The summit of one of these I used to frequent almost daily during my years' sojourn in those parts. It became a habit with me, for from its vantage point I was granted as fair a prospect of Allah's bounty as could possibly be imagined. · Small wonder that travellers and poets have vied with each other throughout the. ages in their efforts to extol the beauties, the delights and the splendours of this Elysium.

Set in a landscape of perfect proportions, belonging neither to the mountains nor to the plains, in the folds of the hills, which are themselves near enough to form a background, yet not so near as to shut it in, stands Samarkand. Much character in little space applies most suitably, for whatever may have been the extent of the Greek Maracanda, or of the city demolished by the Mongols, Timur's town was comparatively small, and the present day Samarkand is smaller still. But the brilliance of it compensates for size, and quality for quantity.

No air of decay hangs over the place ; no dust of Time clings to it. This is no Damascus, city built on city, inhabited since the days when nomadic man first settled. Samarkand is comparatively new, and looks it.   Old Afrosiab, which was probably a very ancient settled site, lies away to the north, well outside the present city's precincts.

Samarkand looks new because its monuments fall to the ground before they even reach the stage of looking ancient.   If the truth be told, Samarkand's " face is her fortune " ; her foundations are on clay, her ornamentation will long outlast the fabric to which it is attached, and none of it will last very long.

One could see that the monuments were very much on the decline, and that even a few years would leave their mark on their already ruinous condition.   I saw them in a state the worse for an earthquake which occurred a few years before.   Curzon had seen them prior to this.   It is a pity we have no first-hand description of Samarkand left to us by those emissaries to Bukhara early in the nineteenth century, Moorcroft, Burnes, Stoddart, and Conolly.   But Bukhara, the capital, was their goal and not one of them even set eyes on Samarkand.

A lot of history had been enacted within my view from the summit of the minaret ; Greeks and Persians had come thus far from the West, Chinamen and Mongols from the East, Russians from the North, but nobody from the South.   Central Asia had sent invaders over the mountain barriers into Hindustan, but there had never been reflex action.   Samarkand is indeed a place for those who like to dream dreams, and its atmosphere is such that it is not difficult to see it as it was when the now empty steppe was alive with moving, if ephemeral, hosts of migrating peoples ; when the city itself was the hub of half the universe ; when emissaries came hither from all countries, Christian and infidel alike, and when the great

MINARET AND FLUTED DOME

Tamerlane might be setting out at any moment he pleased to annex another kingdom.

Below me is spread the historic Vale. The broad belt of cultivation, the renowned Zarafshan flowing over its shingly bed, the painted minarets, and turquoise domes agleam above the poplars, and beyond again the steppe, backed by tawny hills, and blue, more distant mountains. The steppe is near enough to the cultivation to be its neighbour, and if you let your fancy play you can easily picture it peopled by the Tartar hosts which followed their chieftain, as closely as they could, but would not enter the noxious oasis. As sailors love the sea, so those nomads loved their own free steppes. There in the open they pitched their town of tents, in ordered ranks—" like streets," so a contemporary visitor asserted, fifty thousand of them, shops and all. In those days the Valley must have presented a grand spectacle, thronged with such vast concourses of nomadic clans gathered from the four corners of Asia.

Timur chose the site well. He could reside in his capital, surrounded by a fair and fruitful garden, and yet be within sight and reach of his natural home— the open steppe, which to him meant the ways and means to conquest. A complex character he must have been. The ruthless destroyer of so much human life, the creator of so much beauty. A nomad by nature, yet he never succumbed to the snares and luxury of a sedentary life, but retained such vitality that at the ripe age of seventy he was able to plan, and embark upon, the conquest of Cathay. A mighty figure : by far the most heroic Central Asia has produced. And there he lies beneath that great green block of jade—in the beautiful little mausoleum which he himself built for his guide, philosopher and friend, and by whose side he desired to be laid to rest when his time came.

Being untutored in local history and Moslem architecture in no way detracted from my sense of enjoyment, nor lessened my ability to comprehend the real beauty of all that surrounded me. In fact, it probably allowed me a freedom of approach forbidden to the student and the expert in such matters. The authorities, Curzon, Stein, etc., had passed their verdict : Samarkand's " incomparable monuments are not surpassed even by the combined reminiscences of Lahore, Delhi and Agra," and that still, even in their ruin, they are " the wonder of the Asiatic continent." High praise indeed, but justifiable. Those examples of Timurid architecture beyond the Oxus, such as at Meshed and Herat, may or may not be finer : few experts, if any, have seen the lot, or been in a position to compare them. But the mausoleum where the Amir—Timur—lies is a gem above price, and must be without equal. It is far more impressive than those great edifices erected in memory of lesser men. Impressive because of its very simplicity and unostentation. On the other hand that mighty fabric which Timur caused to be built, called Bebi Khanum, is without doubt a superb creation, imposing in its immensity, and magnificent even now in its crumbling decay. Dwarfing all else in Samarkand, it is the grandest but most forlorn. To see it to the best advantage one should go beyond the city's precincts, out to the waste place where old Maracanda stood. One should go at even, when the sun sinks low, and watch the pageant as it passes out over the Kizil Kum desert. One should wait till the

great turquoise dome, reflecting the dying rays, turns
pure amethyst, and remain until the whole vast pile
stands silhouetted against the after-glow. Then—
when the roar from the distant bazaars dies down and
the air is heavy with a golden haze, when twilight falls
and ghosts of all Time come up out of Afrosiab to
walk with you—then you will have seen and felt the
work of Timur's hand and stood in awe.

But it will never be seen again as I saw it. In
my day, the dome, covered with those tens of
thousands of little brickets, 4 inches long, 2 inches
wide and 2 inches deep, covered on the one side with
a turquoise glaze, was more or less complete, sufficiently
so to give one a very good impression of what it must
have been like in its prime. During my visit, however, another earthquake dislodged the greater part
of it, and that is why this little turquoise bricket lies
on my table.

But choose high-noon on a hot summer's day to
wander through the courts and alleys of Shah Zindeh,
which is Samarkand's chief treasure. There you will
be struck dumb, if you have any feeling at all for
design and colour. No adequate description has yet
been given of the glories of those tombs of Timur's
faithful followers, perhaps because it is impossible to
do justice to the unrivalled wealth of coloured tile and
porcelain with which they are adorned. Curzon did
not attempt it, although he would gladly have
expatiated " upon the beauty of these Samarkandian
tiles—turquoise and sapphire and green and plum-
coloured and orange, crusted over with a rich
siliceous glaze, and inscribed with mighty Kufic
letters," he thought it more relevant to draw attention
to the deplorable state of repair into which the

IN SAMARKAND

monuments were falling. Schuyler's monumental work might have been expected to contain some appreciation of its glories—some detailed description of its special features, but one is disappointed ; and although he acknowledges that Shah Zindeh ranks, " with perhaps one exception, as the finest in Asia," he devotes only one page to it, and that is largely historic. Yet in these sepulchres the enamelled tile-work, for which Samarkand is chiefly famous, reaches the highest pitch of perfection. A more recent traveller, Rosita Forbes, comes nearer the mark by briefly stating " the court might have been steeped in sea-water. All the blues from turquoise to the deepest sapphire were reflected in the incomparable mosaics and this deep, quiet pool of colour contrasted or blended with the rich browns and golds of the earthen walls. Sea and sand with sunshine caught between them."

All these lovely things I had the free run of, unhampered, unhurried, uninterrupted. At peace and alone, I could wander in and out, unaccompanied and unaccosted. There were no guides, no custodians, no touts, no charges, no picture postcards. I saw them at all times of day and night, and at all seasons of the year, and came away with such a store of memories that I have not yet exhausted them.

> As when a scout
> Through dark and secret ways with peril gone
> All night, at last by break of cheerful dawn
> Obtains the brow of some high-climbing hill,
> Which to his eye discovers unawares
> The goodly prospect of some foreign land
> First seen, or some renowned metropolis.

But my real and ostensible reason for being in

Samarkand was to get out of it, and my eye was for ever on the far horizon beyond the city and its belt of cultivation. My minaret served me well, for from it I could survey a long stretch of the valley and get a fair idea of its physical features, and therefore of its possibilities from a natural history aspect.

The Zarafshan Valley has a run of roughly 450 miles, east and west. Samarkand is situated about midway, where the river leaves the mountains and debouches on the plain. On the one side, therefore, are two hundred-odd miles of mountainous country, running up to its glacier birthplace ; and on the other hand an open world of foothills, steppe and sandy desert ; the river and irrigated strip running like a green thread through it all.

This area was easily divided up, for my purpose, into winter, spring, and summer. Winter in the desert, spring in the oasis, summer in the hills. Moreover the Zarafshan runs conveniently due east and west, that is to say its 400 miles lie in the same latitude through the entire length, and it is therefore a more satisfactory zone to work than one extending north and south, with a consequent variance in climate.

What of the river itself, the fount of all this fertility, the founder of its cities ? The inhabitants and cultivators acknowledge their debt by calling it the " Strewer of Gold," the patron of their prosperity. The Zarafshan is a typical river of Central Asia, that is to say of a region where the land surfaces are so vast and the orography so complex that few rivers fulfil their normal function and reach the sea. Instead, they are doomed to wander to the lowest level attainable, and there to die an inglorious death by slow evaporation. Born with brilliant prospects, in magnificent mountain scenery, they either dissipate their waters in a network of irrigation canals, or flow, aimless, to their grave in the desert.

Three great self-contained basins mark the map of Middle Asia, Aral, Balkhash and the Lop, but there are scores of lesser ones, and the Zarafshan is one of them.

High up in the complex mountain mass which forms the northern bastion of the Pamirs, where the so-called Turkestan and Hissar ranges bifurcate from the Alai, is the glacier which gives birth to the trickle which is destined, with its tributaries, to create the Vale of Samarkand.

In its upper reaches the Zarafshan is shut in by high parallel mountain walls, conspicuous for their nakedness and for their apparent determination to prevent man from settling in the valley below. It is as if the desert has succeeded in creeping up into the mountains. One has to penetrate farther into the recesses of the mountains, under the highest summits, to find those alpine meadows and forests which are so delightful to the eye after the yellow plains below. Nakedness,. on a magnificent scale, might be the general verdict on the valley of the Zarafshan for its first hundred miles. Not ugly, as one might think, but rather appalling in its severity. Only where man has, by hard labour and with great skill, contrived to carry the water from the main river, or its tributaries, by irrigation canals to suitable spots, are there little paradises of orchards and fields. Small communities of hardy hill-men have thus made use of every available acre. But it is an everlasting battle between Man and Nature. Not until the hills recede and the valley floor widens can the great canals be led off; then the river assumes its character as the " Strewer of Gold," and casts its wealth into the lap of the dense population awaiting it. Now hamlets become villages, and villages grow to townships, and the view is over a broad expanse of tree and crop.

This cultivated area stretches for a couple of hundred miles, and is of extreme fertility, the soil being capable of producing three crops in a season. It begins a short distance above Samarkand, where, in fact, the water is first turned on the land, and it ends as abruptly as it starts, some forty miles below Bukhara, where the water fails. At the period of greatest need, and greatest heat, the river is at its maximum flow, owing to its glacier origin and reservoirs of melting snows, but this surfeit is all used up by irrigation ; it is only during the winter months that there is a surplus of water running to waste.

These great reservoirs, so common in Central Asia, which are fed by rivers which cannot escape to the sea, are capricious in character and irregular in their habits. Some are full in summer and more or less empty in winter, others are almost non-existent in summer but turn into lakes in winter, the deciding factor being Man, and the extent to which he has interfered with, and interrupted the natural flow of the rivers which form them. The Zarafshan lagoons are an extreme case of the latter type, namely, winter-born. So much of its water is used up for irrigation purposes in the summer months, when the river is at its maximum flow, that there is little or nothing left to form terminal lakes.

The Aral Sea, on the other hand, shows no appreciable annual variation, although it is the recipient of a vast catchment area.

In very ancient days the Zarafshan was a

tributary of the Oxus. But when man settled on its banks, and began to utilise its waters for irrigation, the flow was interrupted and the sand-dunes began to hamper what little was left of the river at its junction with the Oxus. Anon, as the population of cultivators increased, and more canals were engineered, and more water was led off for irrigation purposes, the sands encroached, until finally the Zarafshan had not enough surplus water to force its way to the Oxus, and found itself cut off. The sands then had their own way, and accumulated the barrier which now exists between the two rivers. In fact, all trace of the ancient course of the Zarafshan over those last fifteen miles is now obliterated. In historic times it meandered southwards and formed the lagoon of Kara Kul, but as cultivation extended this lake more or less disappeared. The residue, however, continued to flow on, until it reached a barrage of sand-dunes which forbade further exit, and there, almost within sight of the Oxus, it evaporated in a " low-ground," which at certain seasons became a morass.

" Foiled, circuitous wanderer " would apply more aptly to the Zarafshan than to the Oxus, for the latter river does eventually reach its destination in the Aral Sea, but the Zarafshan flows out into the desert, wandering hither and thither in vain attempts to reach the goal which it will never reach again.

CHAPTER II

"FAR AND FEW"

WINTER in Samarkand was as pleasant as any season of the year, and for the Englishman perhaps the best, for, not minding the cold, he appreciated the exhilarating dryness. Long periods of brilliant sun and a dead calm atmosphere were perhaps its chief features. Snow fell, but it lay dry as dust and added a new glory to the coloured tile-work of the mosques. It was the best moment, too, for the view from my minaret. No dust haze rose from the town below, no loess-laden atmosphere hid the far distance ; all was brilliantly lit and stereoscopic in its clearness.

From this vantage point I had seen one thing which caused me to ponder. In the surrounding panorama one special feature remained more fixed in my mind than any other, and that was the long rib of hills that ran out into the northern steppe until lost to view. It was like the last little ripple caused by a great wave, the ultimate effort of the gigantic mountain mass behind me. Away it stretched to the far horizon until it merged into the haze of the desert. Long, low and narrow, I had seen the same feature before in other countries, and been attracted by it. It was neither mountain nor desert. It could scarcely be inhabited, for there would be little, if any, rainfall and there was no possibility of irrigation. It was evidently a wild place, and I must go and investigate.

This outlying range is called Nura Tau, Nur

Ata Tau, or Nur Ata—The Father of Nur—which is a Bukharan oasis and frontier town near its western limits. But it also bears (on maps) the name of Kara Tau—the Black Mountains—a misnomer or rather no name at all, for it does not distinguish it from many another Kara Tau, whereas the hills of Nur fixes it at once. The nomad tribes are probably responsible for this loose naming of hills which they see in the distance, but do not frequent. Also, many low ranges are called Black, simply because they are not white with perpetual snow.

The Nur Ata are actually a continuation of the so-called Turkestan range which borders the upper Zarafshan on the north, and they have a run of roughly one hundred miles before expiring in the sands of the Kizil Kum. From Samarkand they appeared to be quite featureless, and without any character whatsoever ; nor did they give any indication of their height, for they rose in long, even, unbroken inclines. Their true nature is not displayed until seen from the northern desert.

Winter in the sheltered valley of the Zarafshan was severe enough, but it would be even more so out on the steppe, exposed to all winds and weather, where there was no protection between me and the Arctic seas two thousand miles away ; and this I found to my cost when I deposited myself and my servant one cold dawn in January at Jizak, the first town out on the fringe of the Hungry Steppe. But a little knowledge of the part it had played in Central Asian history took the edge off the bitter wind that swept in on me, and made the place less desolate than it appeared at first. I can recommend no surer antidote against the dull monotony of travel, when that inevitable stage is reached, than a knowledge, however slight, of the history of the regions immediately around one.

Jizak was notorious for its unhealthy climate and for the foulness of its water, resulting in a prevalence of that unwelcome parasite, the guinea-worm. But the town had other claims to fame. It was virtually the guardian of the Northern gate to the riches of the South. As its name implies, it was the "key" to Bukhara and Samarkand, and many a bloody conflict had taken place here when raiders tried to enter. It guards the narrow defile which leads from the steppes to the Vale below. Once a Bukharan fortress, it withstood, and turned back, the Russian advance into these regions, but was reduced to the insignificance of its present state by a second and more determined assault. The ancient fortifications are clearly seen, and they appeared to be formidable and of considerable extent. It may, or may not, be the *Zarmuk* of early geographers—Jenghis Khan's objective when he first crossed the Syr to fall upon the Moslems of the Zarafshan, but it must always have been a strategic position of paramount importance in this corner of Central Asia. It was a garrison-town and frontier outpost from earliest historical times until the Russians arrived before the walls in 1867-8.

The defile, or Gate, was the sort of place vainglorious conquerors choose for self-advertisement by scribbling on its rock walls pompous lines announcing their achievements, and thereby ensuring immortality. There were such writings here, but neither the authors nor their deeds were of any but local importance. It would have been otherwise had an earlier visitor, Alexander the Great, left us an inscription in

Greek recording that this was the limit of his conquests in Central Asia.

Jizak belonged to the nomad world and was a gathering place of the Kazaks from the steppes to the north and west. It was also a caravan town, if not now, certainly in days gone by, for it stands at the junction of four main routes leading north and south, east and west.

Through this town must have passed all communication between the formerly well-populated valley of the Syr and the Zarafshan, and beyond to Karshi and the Oxus, and beyond again to the cities of Bactria. This road ran due north and south. East and west the line of communication was equally distinct and important : westwards to Khiva, with bifurcations to Bukhara and Merv and Khurasan, for caravaneers hate cultivation, even as the cultivators hate them, and therefore they kept to the open steppes and avoided the Zarafshan Valley ; eastwards the route ran direct to the rich Farghana and its great centres Khokand, Margelan, and Andijan. Thence, by crossing the one and only feasible pass, it linked up with Kashgar, Yarkand and the Silk Route to Cathay. In fact, I can think of no other one place in Central Asia like Jizak as a meeting place for steppe-bound traffic from the four corners of the continent.

So, by setting forth westwards from Jizak, I was following an old, old road, " The Khan's Road," although little trace of it remained, and the map showed nothing to indicate that it was anything but a side track to the Nur Ata villages.

That it was a recognised route to Khiva I might have known, for had not the only other Englishman to come this way passed along it when travelling from

Khiva to Khokand ?   The traveller was no other than
Conolly of tragic and pathetic memory.*   Long before
Russia had extended her sphere of influence thus far
into Central Asia, when this region was still a cockpit
of warring factions, Captain A. Conolly was sent up
here " on a mission of diplomatic negotiations to the
Khanates of Central Asia, whose sympathies Great
Britain desired to enlist in consequence of her advance
into Afghanistan." Going first to Khiva, he failed to
obtain the support his mission required, so he would
try again at Khokand, and in order to get there he
took the direct route, the steppe route, between the
two cities—the road I was about to set out upon.
That was in 1841. Vámbéry was doubtless right in his
assertion that Conolly was probably the first European
to use this desert way ; he was certainly the first
Englishman—and the last.

In the bazaars of Jizak I bargained for transport.
Now if you have more than you can carry in saddle-
bags on horseback, the usual method of progress on
the plains is by cart.   The local cart is a high-wheeled
gig with a fixed hood, admirably suited to the locality,
for it rides easy and can pass streams and small

* Tragic, because, although he was the accredited emissary of
Great Britain, he was beheaded in Bukhara by the reigning Amir, and
the crime was unavenged. Pathetic, because he was neither suited to
the task, nor in any way fitted to undertake such a mission. Incidentally,
in the minds of many the name of Khiva is probably still linked with that
of Burnaby ; even as the name of Burton is inevitably attached to Mecca.
Burnaby's *Ride to Khiva* so struck the popular (Victorian) imagination,
that for long he enjoyed the reputation of being the first, and perhaps
the only, Englishman to reach that particularly uninteresting oasis. So
much so that the prior claims of Shakespear, Abbott, and Conolly were
overlooked ; yet they reached Khiva thirty-five years earlier, when it
was a really dangerous spot, and at a time when British and Russian
prestige in the Central Asian Khanates was at its very lowest.

rivers without difficulty. The driver rides, which is a. paradox reasonably explained :—since the vehicle is an invention of the plains no hill-work is expected, so the owner crams his cart to the maximum and himself rides the shaft-horse.

Transport facilities had evidently become as difficult as they were easy in the old days. Although the caravan trade was dead, the lust for gain survived, for the men of Jizak fleeced me unmercifully. When eventually a carter appeared who was willing to carry me, his demands were so extortionate that even his own. fraternity shamed him for such robbery. However, they had me in the hollow of their hands and the owner-driver of my particular cart got his fifteen shillings for a journey westwards as far as a cart could go—a.two days' drive over a mockery of a road. This was about three times as much as any native would pay, and yet it seemed cheap enough to me.

We were here on the fringes of the Hungry Steppe, which stretched without interruption to the Syr. It had terrors for early travellers, owing to its utter desolation, but it has a brighter future in that it could be brought under cultivation without much trouble. To illustrate the peculiar orography of the lands between the Oxus and the Syr, it is a fact that this Jizak desert was once watered from the Zarafshan by canals led off from that river above Samarkand. It is said that the whole of the Zarafshan could be diverted to irrigate this desert region. But if that was done it would seal the fate of Bukhara. However, this diversion of water so much needed by Bukhara is not necessary, for it would be sounder policy, and actually easier in practice, to utilise the waters of the Syr which are running to waste. In fact, it is only necessary to restore the old ruined canals dug by Timur nearly six hundred years ago to irrigate this very area. All this tends to show the actual fall of the land around Jizak, and the same was proved to me by a string of lakes, or low-ground morasses, which I could see away to the north of my route. Judging by the number of ducks on the move in that direction they were evidently not frozen over and therefore must be saline.

Two days later the cart deposited me at Bogdan, the first of a string of poor villages that exist under the northern slopes of the Nur Ata. Bogdan is the largest and seemingly most prosperous ; not without attraction, perched on its rocky hillside, with a fine view of mountain and of desert.

Beyond this the settlements diminish as one travels westwards, village becomes hamlet, hamlet becomes croft, until finally there is nothing but a few rock shelters used by shepherds in summer.

Here transport difficulties became acute. The few Russians who pass this way are of the official class and have their own independent transport. I was of no account, and was considered quite mad to want to go where I intended to go at such a season of the year. But a bribe of a few shillings secured the services of an ass to carry my belongings, and we set forth again on our flat feet.

A few other wayfarers were on the road, and amongst them a Russian in his " tarantass," drawn by three horses abreast, going " all out " for Jizak. As he passed me, noticing a somewhat unusual sight, he drew up and shouted the equivalent of " what the devil are you doing here ? " I explained that I was a hunter, and he immediately became most affable, ordered my men to take care of me, told me there were plenty of wild boars, and if I went as far as the village of Sintub I should find wild sheep! Then, saying "Farewell and good hunting," he buried himself beneath his furs, his driver shouted to the horses, and they were soon lost to view. This meeting put me in high spirits, and showed me that my suspicions about the Nur Ata hills were not far wrong, and that my journey need not be fruitless. Moreover, my previous knowledge of the wild sheep of Asia told me that no one, not even Russians, had recorded their existence in this region. What was their name? Where did they wander?

We proceeded slowly westwards, along the foothills of the Nur Ata. To the north lay the steppe, extending without interruption to the Syr Darya; in fact, I think I saw its waters once, gleaming in the sun. Although it was sixty miles away, yet, in the brilliantly clear atmosphere and from a slightly higher elevation it would not be impossible. The hills on my left I watched with interest, for as we moved westwards they looked more than ever like holding wild game. The smooth, rounded slopes of the southern side were here contradicted by steep declivities and rugged faces. There were cliffs, ravines, screes and scarps; it was all interesting, surprising, new.

From the south the Nur range had been uninspiring, almost unworthy of notice, but from the north it was definitely a feature, and this is probably the reason why the nomads of the desert below, eyeing its ruggedness, call it Kara—black. For it is a landmark for caravans and travellers far out in the Kizil Kum, and can be seen from a distance of many days' journey.

Moving on by easy stages, I either walked, rode the ass, or even, on occasion, got a lift from a passing stranger, and rode pillion with him. I lived " native " and in fair comfort, for their clay huts were warm and their food sufficient. It was all very easy-going, travel in Central Asia in those days ; there was no barrier between East and West and one felt quite at home. The days were spent in that delicious solitude where one is least alone, but the evenings were distinctly social, and after supper we slept where we lay, surrounded by my host's entire family.

And it all cost comparatively nothing—this wild sheep chase into the Kizil Kum. I eventually travelled about two hundred miles, lodged in at least ten different houses, employed two hunters, paid for cart, camel, donkey, and horse transport, gave away undreamt of wealth to my hosts at a cost to myself of less than ten pounds !

After four days I reached the hamlet called Sintub, said to be on the very edge of cultivation —the last inhabited place. This was not true, as I afterwards discovered, for there were what one might call granges or crofts still further out in the wilderness.

These tiny outposts on the edge of a desert world all showed signs of deterioration and of a departed prosperity, as is so often the case on the fringes of cultivation in Central Asia, but they bravely held their own against many adverse conditions. How they existed was a mystery. Baked in summer, and frozen in winter, with a scanty water supply during the critical months, and dependent solely upon the bounty of Allah for the success of their sown crops, they yet survived. The inhabitants seemed gay enough, and their hospitality was incredible considering how near they lived to the borderline of hunger. It was in one of these villages that I committed an unpardonable sin—I threw away a morsel of bread. It may have been soiled or perhaps, as is so often the case with native ground flour, gritty, it does not matter which, but I deliberately wasted what a bountiful Allah had bestowed. To me, fresh from the fat oases, it meant little, but to my hosts it was the last word in bad manners and ingratitude; it was almost sacrilege. They knew what that morsel meant in terms of hard work; they also knew that their labours depended upon the hazard of an uncertain rainfall to bring the crops to maturity and harvest. Their food was literally wrested from the earth by hard labour, aided by luck; to waste a crumb was a crime. The sad-eyed old " grey-beard " who got up to retrieve the scrap gave me a withering look of the utmost contempt, whilst the others in the circle muttered words that it would be as well not to repeat. But I learnt my lesson, and I have made many amends for that one discarded crumb! Incidentally, this little episode did a great deal to bridge the wide gulf between me and them. It gave me an insight into the lives of that particular fraternity who live so close to Nature, and it stood me in good stead throughout my travels. I always found a strong bond between myself and God's starvelings, whether wild men of the mountains, or the wilder men of the desert.

At Sintub, the Nur Ata range reached its maximum altitude, about 6000 ft.; from here onwards it began to drop until it disappeared in the sands of

Kizil Kum. But this did not mean necessarily that it was poorer game country ; on the contrary, it was better, for it assumed a more rugged nature.

Native report said there were plenty of wild sheep farther on, so I advanced with two men and a pony, and eventually found shelter in a tiny hamlet called Sauf. This was as poor a place as one could possibly imagine, its huts being built of stone, in amongst the rocks. But its inhabitants, in spite of their poverty, were generous in their hospitality and in their information on the wild sheep—" a little farther on " I would find plenty !

Up till now conditions had been tolerable, in so far as extremely low temperature and maximum exposure to the elements allowed them to be. The days had been mostly brilliant, the sun tempering the knife-like air. But now the weather suddenly worsened, it blew and rained and I was imprisoned in the narrow quarters of these rock-built hovels. Meanwhile, food was being consumed and my chances shortened ; also it was a warning that at any moment I might be storm-bound for an indefinite period, which was not a pleasant prospect in these particular surroundings. My hosts, of course, could not understand my impatience. " Haste is of the devil " to all Orientals. They wondered why I had come to such a place at that season of the year, when I could be keeping warm in my own village. " Had I no wives to cook for me ? " they asked. Ah, why ? I had no answer. Anyway, I thought it better than indulging in vice or religion, which someone said were the only amusements the English had. Emerson was surely nearer the mark when he described us as " the most voracious people of prey that ever existed. The more vigorous run out of the island to Europe, to America, to Asia, to Africa and Australia, to hunt with fury by gun, by trap, by harpoon, by lasso, with dog, with horse, with elephant or with dromedary, all the game that is in Nature."

So here I was at World's End as it were, in a half-starved condition, enjoying myself. Yet it made me think. What exactly was it that drove us to it? Why did we set so high a value on a pair of old and very gnarled horns—the older and more gnarled the more we prized them? What was it that made us leave home, comfort and safety, in order to wander and undergo unnecessary hardship? Most of us were of too serious a mind to be lured by the mere love of adventure, or to yield to the temptation to do what should not be done—just for the sake of doing it. It was not for notoriety, and certainly not for worldly gain. And yet we did it. "The lust to know what should not be known" was perhaps one reason; also there was that innate desire to attain the impossible which is so strongly developed in the make-up of the British race. But it was no good trying to explain all this to the cave-dwellers of Sauf.

Eventually the storm abated and a dawn broke blue and clear. The hills were under a fresh mantle of snow, and even the desert had a sprinkling of white. This would be beneficial to the local tillers of the soil for the snowfall on these mountains effects agriculture even in the well-watered Zarafshan valley. If there is not a heavy fall, the water carried from these hills, to supplement the main irrigation supply, fails at the critical moment; but a heavy fall is a good augury and is said to produce bumper crops. In old days it was customary for the bearer of good tidings that the snow was sufficient on the hills, to receive a silken robe from the reigning Amir of Bukhara.

But it was not so propitious for the hunt, although the mountains were so broken there was plenty of "black ground." The local hunter, Selim Hedin by name, was old, wise and silent, very like an old sheep in looks, in whose company I was always happy. He thought the wild weather might have driven the sheep farther away, but was ready to try a hunt. Passing up the gully, above the huts I saw more bird life than I had yet seen, probably owing to the snow having driven them down from the higher ground. There were plenty of partridges. There were rock nuthatches, larger than their English confrères, but otherwise alike even to the same jolly notes and same cheerful character. It was very noticeable how much better they harmonise with the rocks than do our own nuthatches with tree-trunks, their slate-blue and pink colouration making a most perfect camouflage. There were vultures and lammergiers sailing overhead, and so clear was the air that morning that I could plainly see the latter's beards at 1000 ft. There were some little finches singing on the snow—gold-finches—larger and more brilliantly coloured than those I was accustomed to, a veritable "charm" in these desolate surroundings. These are the little things that make "the toil of travel sweet."

A long day over the hills showed me the Nur Ata in its true character, and that it was a very likely region to hide some rare beast. It was very broken country, without permanent habitation, and although pastured over by shepherds in spring and summer, at this season of the year it was given over to the hunter and the hunted.

Moreover, I saw something else which was to prove an important factor in explaining the range, and indeed the very existence, of these Bukharan wild sheep, namely, that the Nur Ata had no definite ending. Beyond lay desert, it is true, but out of that desert arose little excrescences, pimples, ribs, and serrated ridges, and although none were of any great height, and would hardly appear on a map, yet they possessed all the characteristics of mountains in miniature, deep-cut, scoured, broken, clefted ramparts, which afforded protection and therefore might hold wild game. As for food, I have yet to see a desert, or desert hills, which cannot supply the necessary nourishment for wild life, at some seasons, if not all the year round. In the translucent light of the Central Asian climate, which makes the brightest day in England seem like a November fog in comparison, one can see an incredible distance. So, from my vantage point at about 1500 ft. above the plain I could command a very wide view, perhaps a hundred miles, into the Kizil Kum ; and all this wide region, as far as I could see, appeared to be possible sheep country. There was evidently nothing to prevent wild sheep ranging over most of the so-called Kizil Kum desert between the Nur Ata hills and the Sea of Aral.

So I tried again another day, going farther still ; so far, indeed, that I reached what one might well call the uttermost extremity of the true Nur Ata range. On a bluff, commanding an uninterrupted view westwards, I sat down and rested. I suppose to the many—the unimaginative—my view would have been the last word in God-forsaken desolation, but I confess I was thrilled by it. . . .

> " Full many a waste I've wandered o'er,
> Clomb many a crag, crossed many a shore,
> But, by my Halidom !
> A scene so rude, so wild as this,
> Yet so sublime in barrenness,
> Ne'er did my wandering footsteps pass,
> Where'er I chanced to roam."

This " hush'd Chorasmian waste " fired my imagination. There was nothing but distance between me and the Sea of Aral, three hundred miles away. There was nothing but sand and the Oxus between me and Khiva, that strange city which ranked with Lhasa and Mecca for mystery and the forbidden thing. I was definitely beyond the margin of the travelled world, and well away from the crowd. Only yesterday, as it were, to see Khiva meant either notoriety or a horrible death, but it had now become a mere backwater and was already one with Nineveh and Tyre. The days were when Khan succeeded Khan in ancient Khiva, and lorded it over wide areas of Western Asia. Only fifty years ago the desert capital still defied the West, and put up a good opposition to Russian encroachment. How are the mighty fallen ! Yet she may rise again, Phœnix-like, from the sands.

This reminded me that even these solitudes had not escaped the flood of war. In fact, this very spot where I, sat was historic ground ; it had lain in the direct path of one of the greatest upheavals which has ever shaken the world—the Mongol eruption of the thirteenth century. Had I been a lone hunter on these hills in March 1220, I might have noticed a great cloud of dust arising out of the desert to the north-east. From out of the whirlwind would have emerged horsemen—uncountable hosts of riders. They were the Mongol invaders, the vanguard of the human tidal wave which was to follow. They were led by Jenghis Khan himself, and they were out to conquer the world. Here, at this very spot, Jenghis and his men emerged from the desert, having made a forced march of a hundred miles across the intervening waste from the Syr Darya, in order to take Bukhara by surprise. They arrived literally " out of the blue," from the least expected quarter, and the result was a foregone conclusion. At Nur,* the township from which these hills take their name, he concentrated his troops before falling upon those rich prizes—Bukhara and Samarkand.

Six centuries pass by, and another military expedition, but of a very different nature, might have been witnessed from this same spot. This time the aggressor came from the West. Instead of a whirlwind of mobile Asiatic nomads, there came long, straggling, unwieldy columns of camel transport. By slow marches they moved along under the foothills, and out into the wilderness beyond, as strange a venture as any in military history. It was the Russian Expedition of 1873, led by General Kauffmann, for the final reduction of rebellious Khiva. The expedition attained its object, but not without undergoing incredible hardships, and barely escaping a major disaster from lack of water in the sands by the Oxus.

I awoke from my reverie into the past with a sudden jolt; I was desperately hungry, a gnawing that came from a prolonged period on short commons,

---

* Nowadays a desert outpost, but once a place of some importance and the focus of a pilgrimage.

an emptiness that would require much more than one square meal to put right. Insufficient native food of poor quality, hard work, discomfort, and intense cold were having their effects on me; I saw myself being beaten at the eleventh hour and forced to retreat empty-handed.

But Selim had not been wasting his time. A touch on my shoulder and a whispered " arkar " brought me to my senses. He had spied wild sheep far away below us in a confused jumble of rocky hillocks not far above the plain. Yes, there was no doubt about them, and a stalk seemed easy. Late that wintry afternoon I made contact with them, and although no big ram was in the herd, I killed two for meat. Here, anyway, was concrete proof of the existence and whereabouts of the Bukharan wild sheep, but I still lacked a specimen mature enough to show to which species it belonged.

It was a very, very long way home to Sauf that dark evening over frozen shale and snowdrift, carrying horns, hides and mutton, but it was well worth the effort for my reputation as a hunter was now established, and my popularity increased by reason of the free meal provided that night.

On a full stomach I reviewed the situation and planned a mobile expedition consisting of the old hunter, a donkey and myself, the idea being to be totally independent for several days, and so to be able to hunt as one wild animal hunts another—without impediments and without restrictions. In other words, I intended to search until I found the sheep, and to follow until I got 'em, and to sleep and eat where'er I found myself. So I ranged far and wide over those last declivities of the Nur Ata hills. I hunted over them until they deteriorated to mere ribbons of rock on the dusty desert. And there I found, as I had found before and have often found since, that wild hill game does not necessarily rely for its safety so much on height as on seclusion. Find the last native settlement and then advance several days' journey, and you may find your quarry. Get away from your fellow-men, find seclusion, and you may find your beast. This had always been my maxim, and it had proved a fairly reliable one.

And so it happened, one brilliant morning, in a temperature around zero, with my belt drawn in to its last hole, that is to say the one I had to make about two inches short of the last orthodox hole, I found what I am satisfied in thinking must have been the patriarch of all the Nur Ata flocks. He was very old and very lean, and his horns had that gnarled surface, which we fools admire so much, and one was broken at the tip—in proof of triumph over rivals. He was a perfect specimen, and fell to a single shot, and the snow froze onto his horns where he crashed. There was no stalk ; I just chanced to see him before he saw me, and he paid the penalty. He had had his day, and was now destined to be immortalised in some museum instead of being left for carrion.

The jackals and vultures got nothing off him ! After I had saved his complete skin intact, we cut up his carcase into suitable sizes and packed them on the ass. We then retreated on to Sauf. I shall never know how far I went on that last wild sheep hunt, but it must have been a very long way judging by the length of time it took me to get back. We slept one night in a rock shelter used by shepherds in summer, and reached Sauf the following day. Here the remains of the old ram were devoured by the inhabitants in one great and glorious feast.

I had now got my prize, but I had yet to get away with it. I decided to make a short-cut home, over the Nur Ata range, and down to the railway somewhere between Bukhara and Samarkand. The actual distance was not very great, but the pass over the hills might be difficult owing to the recent snow. With two donkeys and two men I started by starlight and worked my way up the valley leading to the summit. Before dawn we halted at a shepherd's hut, made tea, and refreshed ourselves. Passing on, we reached the higher slopes as it was getting light, and looked back at the sunrise. I had seen many dawns, but I had never seen one like this. It was yellow—yellow as sulphur. The whole sky and landscape was suffused with a jaundiced light. Great tawny wisps of cloud were flung out in advance, as if in warning of what was approaching ; long streamers and flankers heralded disaster. If I ever see a yellow dawn again I shall stay at home and not attempt a journey ; for I know now that it forecasts a *buran*,* which may be described as a blizzard and a typhoon combined.

Looking back, it appeared as if all the forces of Nature were gathering in violent conflict, and for our undoing. There followed a commotion in the heavens, like Judgment Day approaching. The air

---

* The Central Asian *buran* has to be experienced to be believed. I once witnessed the awe-inspiring spectacle of a stormy sea, whipped into violent commotion by a passing *buran*, freeze solid whilst in movement. This was Ebi Nor—the Wind Lake—situated at one entrance to the Dzungarian Gate, where doubtless all *burans* blow with concentrated fury. The picture it presented is indescribable, and although it left an indelible impression on me, I cannot expect it to be anything but a " traveller's tale " to others.

THE YELLOW DAWN

There followed the toughest struggle with the elements that I have ever had. My men said it could not be done and begged me to turn back. I was adamant, remembering " the difficult is that which can be done at once, the impossible that which takes a little longer." So we proceeded.

The wind, when it struck us, rolled us over like ninepins, and sent us sprawling and clawing at anything handy. The donkeys were merely blown over, and lay there in the snow anchored by their loads. Between the gusts, we managed to collect ourselves and the donkeys, and to advance at a slow pace by short stages. But this could only be accomplished by two of us ranging on the leeward side of each donkey, like buttresses, and holding them up.

The yellow dawn lived up to its evil reputation. For hours we struggled in our attempts to get ourselves and the wretched little beasts over that pass, and this with the *buran* on our flank ; had it been in our faces the *buran* would certainly have conquered. The snowdrifts sometimes supported *us*, but *not* the donkeys, and the loads had to be taken off them before they could be extricated from the drifts. All this in a wind which took one's breath away, and in an air so full of frozen snow that one could hardly see or hear. Twice we failed to make the ridge and were beaten back ; the third time we succeeded.

Once we were over the pass, the descent was comparatively easy, as the gradient was slight and we were protected from the full violence of the wind. But it was not until late in the afternoon that we came to the first habitation and finally found shelter, food and warmth in the little hamlet of Sowrak. Here we lay a few days recuperating, until the *buran* blew itself out, and my men could return whence they came. Before leaving, I rewarded my hardy hunters with such a feast of good things in recompense for our little adventure together, that I feel sure if any other wandering Englishman should penetrate to this out-of-the-way corner he will be sure of a welcome.

Three days later, riding at the tail-end of a camel caravan, I reached the railway, and eventually returned to Samarkand.

That was the end of my hunt, but not of my story, for, although the Bukharan wild sheep was mine, his getting came near to being the end of me. As a result of this mid-winter's journey I developed acute rheumatic fever. My lodging, consisting of a mud-built one-storied house, was not exactly suited to the occasion, and as I had no fuel for heating, and rubber hot-water bottles were not invented, I was in a sorry plight. For a whole week I lay in agonies, unable to move ; I could not even turn over in bed. Every single joint in my body, from my toes to my fingers, was affected. What food was brought to me I could not lift to my lips ; I had to eat it, as a dog would, out of the bowl. For this period I lay unattended and without medical aid : whilst the skull of that old ram, lying in the corner of my room, grinned at me as if to say, " I'll get home on you yet." But he didn't—I triumphed. I had been through this sort of thing before, having grim recollections of the grave dug for me in an African swamp, but which I had left— empty ! Eventually a Russian Army doctor heard of me and swiftly rendered the relief which saved my life.

We became good friends, and I often used to go to his home in the military cantonment, but he never believed in my ostensible reason for being in

Turkestan, and always winked when I talked of birds
and beasts. Years afterwards, in London, a certain
Russian military attaché used to poke fun at me in
the same way about wild sheep chasing in Bukhara,
—I don't know why.

" Far and Few " I have entitled the foregoing
account of my hunt for a rare animal, for few I found
them, and far had they retreated from the haunts of
man. Although this wild sheep was already known
(to Russians), it had not yet been classified, and did
actually belong to a new sub-species. My forerunners had been three, namely,—Rychkov, who first
reported their existence in the northern Kizil Kum
in 1772 ; Khoroshkhin, who made contact with them
in the central desert exactly one hundred years later ;
and Bogdanov, who also recorded them in 1882.
Khoroshkhin must have been one of the earliest to
travel intelligently in these regions. He came in the
wake of the Russian occupation of Bukhara, and was
evidently attached to one of the parties which
reconnoitred the Kizil Kum in advance of the armies
converging onto Khiva. Ak Kunduk, where he first
saw these wild sheep, was nearby the desert rendezvous
chosen for the two columns which were to set forth the
following year from Tashkent and Kazalinsk respect-
ively. But these early discoveries of the wild sheep
received no recognition for many a long year ; in fact
it was not until some time *after* I had brought home
these first specimens to reach museums outside Russia
that they received attention—and a name.
    Yet its isolation was a sufficient guarantee that it
should be something out of the ordinary. Away to
the west, across the Oxus, was the nearest known

habitat of any other race of wild sheep—the Urials of Northern Persia and of the Ust Urt plateau. Away to the east, beyond the Syr, was the nearest habitat of any other form of wild sheep—the *Ovis ammon* of Middle Asia. Here, midway between the two, but cut off by some hundreds of miles from either, was this urial or *ammon*, or some link between them, and although on first acquaintance it suggested affinities with the smaller urial, it very soon became established that it really belonged to the *ammon* family.

With the limited material at our disposal, it was naturally linked, in the first place, to its nearest neighbour, *Ovis ammon nigrimontana*, which inhabited somewhat similar country on the Kara Tau, a westerly extension of the Alexandrovski range, running out into the Kirghiz steppes, parallel with the Syr. These sheep were discovered by Dr N. Severtzov in 1873, and were named by him after their environment —the Kara Tau, or Black Mountains. For a period, therefore, my Bukharan* sheep shared the name, but when the Russians collected more material, and comparison became possible, it soon became evident that they were easily separable from those of the Kara Tau. Nasonov, therefore, renamed them after that greatest of all Russian naturalists, and they are known to this day as *Ovis ammon severtzovi*.

Its distinctive characteristics are these : it is the smallest, least specialised, and most westerly member of the *ammon* species. It lives at a lower altitude, and under more desert conditions than any of the others.

---

* I call it, familiarly, Bukharan, because this name fixes its habitat precisely, there being no other wild sheep in the vicinity of Bukhara. Perhaps Kizil Kum would be better, since there is the Bukharan Urial in the eastern provinces of the old Khanate.

It probably approaches closer to the domestic breeds than does any other form of wild sheep, and it may prove to be the connecting link between wild and domestic breeds ; Sushkin calls it " a wild parent form of domestic sheep," and puts its origin as pre-glacial. Since it is a desert form, its habitat is less likely to be encroached upon by man, and it may therefore survive the longer. Severtzov's sheep is confined to the desert area between the Oxus and the Syr, broadly known as the Kizil Kum. Almost every little hill, escarpment or excrescence—and there are many of them—arising a few hundred feet out of that sterile region may hold, or did hold at some time or other, small herds of them. They have been recorded from the miniature mountains of Sultan Uweis to the north of Khiva. They survive on the succession of ridges that crop up at intervals out of the Kizil Kum, whose names vary with the dates of the maps on which they appear, such as Arslan Tau, Kuliuk or Kuljuk, Kazak, Kusiz Kara, Kukurtli, Urekti, Altyn, and Tamdi Tau. They certainly extend deep into the desert, going as far north as Bukan Tau, eastwards to the Nur Ata, and southwards to Ak Tau, a low ridge which lies between the mountains of Nur and the Zarafshan.

A point of special interest is their geographical distribution in relation to the rest of the *ammon* and to the *vignei* group. The Oxus had always been considered, and virtually is, the hard and fast dividing-line between the respective zones of these two sections of the genus—the Mouflon and the Argali.* Both extend, in various forms, up to the Oxus, but neither

* A synopsis of the various classifications of the genus *Ovis* appears in the Appendices.

OVIS AMMON SEVERTZOVI
Adult

cross it, nor do they overlap, with the single exception of *Ovis vignei*, extending across the Oxus into Eastern Bukhara, but even here there is no overlapping with any form of *ammon*. Further east the Himalayas take on the duty of being the frontier line, and here again there is, in one locality, an overlap, namely, on the Tibetan-Ladak borderland, where the true *Ovis vignei* actually encroach on the range of the Tibetan *O. ammon*.

Severtzov's sheep is the first of the Argali group to be met with on crossing the Caspian, the intervening region, which embraces the mountains of north-eastern Persia and of the Ust Urt plateau,* being occupied by members of the Mouflon group, here at the limit of their range northwards. Whether or not there is any intergradation between the two remains to be proved. The head which the late Major Maydon picked up in the Eastern Elburz (actually at Nardin, half-way between Asterabad and Bujnurd), which has officially been pronounced to be *severtzovi*, seems to suggest that there is. If so, it is a very interesting discovery, for it is a case of two species overlapping, and one assumes that if there is infiltration, in the case of sheep, there is likelihood of

---

* The term Ust Urt needs explanation. The locality thus named occupies roughly the whole area directly between the Sea of Aral and the Caspian. It is, as the name implies, a table-land, of about 600 to 700 ft. in height, clearly defined in most places by a steep cliff where it rises from the lower steppes. This scarp demarcates the limits of the Ust Urt. It is a land feature of some consequence, for it is impassable in some sections by reason of its steepness. It is called by the local Kirghiz the " Chink." The plateau itself is featureless and lifeless, now that the wild ass has gone and the saiga is very rare. The wild sheep of the region, the true *Ovis vignei arkar*, are to be found on the bluffs and declivities of the " Chink," as well as on certain little ridges on the Mankishlak peninsula and around the shores of Mertvi Bay.

interbreeding. But personally I am not satisfied about the classification of this controversial head. It seems improbable that a species would skip a wide area like the Kara Kum desert, and yet another (mountain) area already occupied by another species, and turn up again beyond them both. Yet the local inhabitants told Maydon that these so-called Bukharan rams " came in rarely from the north-east." As for the horns, although they are unlike all others we know of from the Nardin area, and, indeed, all other recorded specimens of *orientalis* and *vignei*, they bear little resemblance to my *severtzovi* from the Kizil Kum, or to those figured by Nasonov in his Monograph. I suggest that they belong to the Mufloniformes, *not* to the Argaliformes, and that, for the time being, we can safely relegate *severtzovi* to Trans-Oxiana.

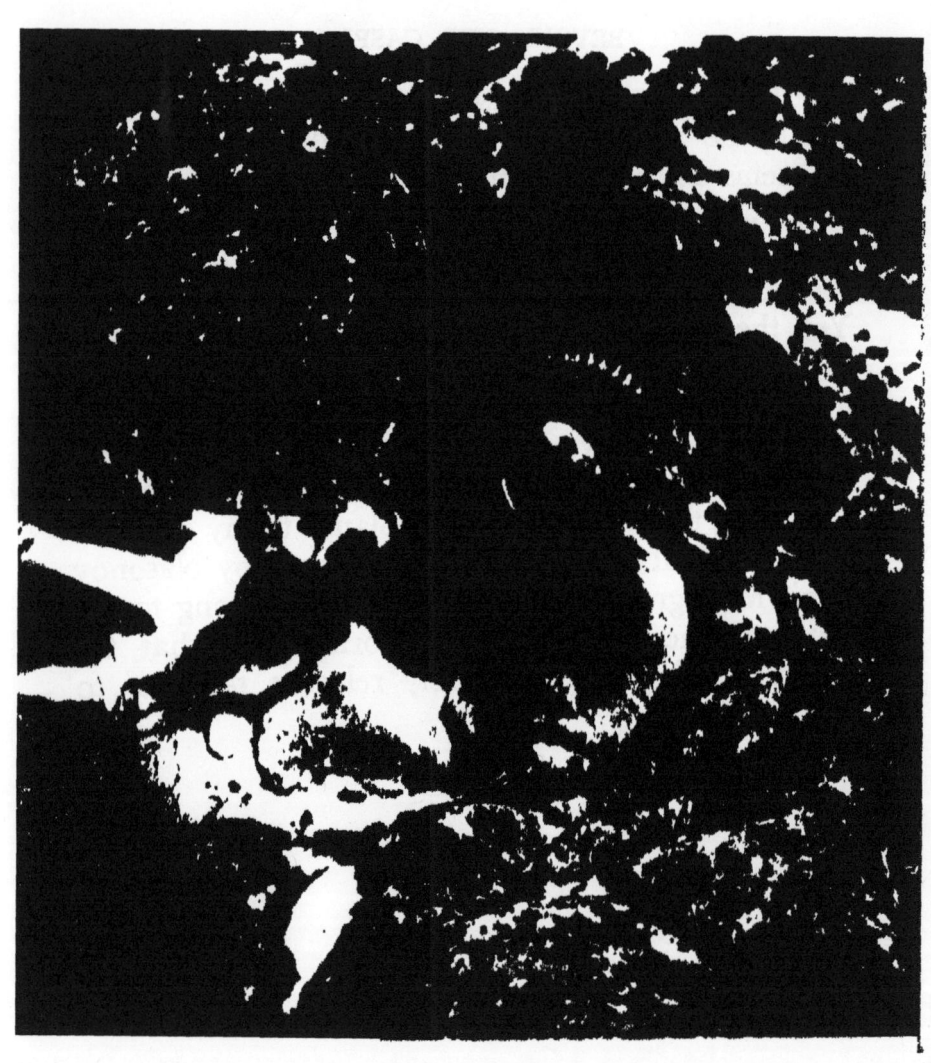

OVIS AMMON SEVERTZOVI
3-4 YEARS OLD

CHAPTER III

DESERT DAYS

THE ambition to see the locality where the waters of the Zarafshan run to waste in the sand-dunes was born in me when reading in an early history that "Bukhara was in old times a hollow, which was covered with swamps and marshes, with woods and reeds. The rivers and brooks were swollen by the snow of the eastern mountain range in the neighbourhood of the present Samarkand, and inundated every year the low-lying country, which, unsuitable for agriculture, was all the more profitable for hunters and fishers." Vámbéry adds that this was a favourite place for killing swans, and that Jenghis Khan was in the habit of having supplies of wild fowl sent up from here—fifty camel loads at a time while the Emperor Timur had a tiger-shoot in the same locality.

This may be true, and judging by what we know of Mongolian appetites, and of Tamerlane's great banquets, swans were probably a most suitable dish. Smaller game would have been considered insufficient at such a feast as described by Clavijo, when "horses and sheep roasted whole" were an item of the menu, and the various courses were served by the cart-load or on camels!

Swamps and marshes that could supply such an abundance of wild game should be worth a visit, and what better hunting ground could be imagined than hundreds of square miles of freshly flooded desert, in complete and undisturbed solitude, situated, moreover, in the very fairway of migrating bird hosts.

45

Taking a general view of the position of this particular locality, in relation to its immediate surroundings, what does it show? Two thousand miles from the Arctic Ocean, but only two hundred feet above it, the Aral basin lies like a trough between the Caucasus and the Central Asian highlands, and up it comes the main spring flood of bird-life from India, Persia, Arabia, and far Africa ; and back again down it flows the autumn migration from the western half of Siberia. Half Siberia : the largest contiguous area enjoying conditions most favourable to breeding birds, and giving them the three essentials—ample space, unlimited food, and last, but not least, prolonged daylight. Half Siberia : an area almost as large as Europe, of complete uniformity in character, vegetation, altitude and climate, the greatest of all breeding grounds and comparatively immune to disturbance.

The almost unimaginable bird population of this region moves south-westwards towards the Caspian-Aral gap when the urge comes to them. This, then, must surely be a major migration route. For even if some birds, such as geese and ducks, take the Himalayas in their southward flight, smaller birds in the main do not ; and in order to avoid this mountain barrier, well over perpetual snow-line, which stands like a wall across two thousand miles of Middle Asia, the stream of migrants from Western Siberia circles round it, and is therefore concentrated into the gap between the central massif and the Caspian Sea. Perhaps this factor accounts for the south-westerly trend of migration which is known to be the principal autumn movement across the western half of the Asiatic continent. As Colonel Meinertzhagen has recently observed : " There is evidence to show that some species pass north from India, keeping west of the main Himalayan massif, and it is quite possible that the bulk of migrants from Turkestan and Siberia, after wintering in India, pass round the Himalayas either east or west (mainly west) in order to reach their breeding grounds. No great migratory movement has been observed to my knowledge via any of the big Himalayan valleys between Kashmir and Sikkim." On the other hand, " the Himalayan extension from Kashmir to Quetta offers no obstacle to this migration. It is known that migrants pour through the Kurram and Bolan Passes in incredible numbers, and it is likely that the passage moves on a broad front from Gilgit to the sea "—and this is the flood that passes up into the Aralean gap, where, joined by another stream from Africa, the two fan out to spread over all Western and Central Siberia.

With regard to bird-life at high altitudes, Marco Polo recorded that the Pamir " region is so lofty and cold that you do not see any birds flying." It was doubtless a popular belief of the time that if you went high enough you would reach a birdless atmosphere. But of course there are no such places. We now know that birds go as high as man on earth, and higher still than him in the heavens, unless he, too, takes to his wings. " The absence of birds," comments Yule, " reported by Marco Polo probably shows that he passed very late or very early in the season." But this is no evidence, for I passed a higher plateau, with the last caravan of the season (and that a late one) and my observations show that in mid-October on the Karakorum route, patridges were seen up to 14,000 ft., rock pigeons and a wagtail at 15,000 ft., and at the same height a woodcock, a winchat, a plover and a dove. Larks went up to 18,000 ft., while a quail was observed near the summit of the pass, which is just over 18,600 ft. Marco Polo himself could not have been higher than 16,000 ft., and the time of his crossing would not have been at a worse moment for seeing birds than was mine at a greater height. From the end of October to early April he might have found the passage birdless.

My Russian friends had tried to direct me to the Oxus as a suitable locality for my purpose. At Charjui, where the one and only bridge spanned the historic river, they said I would find hospitality, good company, and plenty of bird-life. But the Oxus I knew to be a river of little interest at this particular crossing, a mile-wide current in a many-channelled bed, between banks of no particular character ; whereas my aim and object was pure desert, supplying true desert forms, alternating with zones of temporarily flooded land which would be frequented by migrant hosts from far countries : and as for company, I preferred my own.

So I picked on the oasis of Kara Kul, a remote backwater but world famous, its name familiar in London and Paris, for it is the home of a certain little grey sheep, which produces coal-black lambs with such closely-curled, silky fleeces that the fashionable world pays anything to possess them. Kara Kul is the last oasis to be irrigated by the Zarafshan, surviving as best it can on the residue left to it by the cultivators upstream, but the land is not really suitable for cultivation for it is intensely saline. Hence the particular pasturage which is the secret of the curly lamb-skin business, " Black, glossy, curl'd, the fleece of Kara Kul," can only be produced where the pasture is of an exceptional quality; it must be very good and, more important still, of an exceeding dryness. Now, these two essentials occur so rarely that the area which does fulfil the required conditions is a very small one, namely, Afghan Turkestan and Western Bukhara —the desert, in fact, on both banks of the middle Oxus, limited on the north by the lower Zarafshan and on the south by the string of settlements, Mazar-i-Sharif, Akcha, Andkhui.

In spite of assertions to the contrary, the Kara-kuli lamb-skins *have* an association with Kara Kul, even if they are also an important product of North-western Afghanistan. " Persian-lamb " belongs to another variety, and " Astrakhan " is merely a trade-name for lamb-skin of any type and quality. But Kara Kul, by Bukhara, is, and always has been, their homeland. Whilst there I went into the question of their range, distribution and breeding, in so far as stubborn suspicion allowed, for I had been commissioned to try and purchase ewes for export, with a view to experimenting their acclima-tisation on saline pastures in Europe, but the opposi-tion which I encountered made me defer the attempt until I had better support. Rams, and a few ewes, had already been exported from here, and introduced with fair success into North America; while others had been given a trial in certain chosen localities in Southern Europe. No other environment, how-ever, but their own original one, seems to suit them, for the lamb-skins lose their special characteristic. Even in their homeland it has been found that the interbreeding of rams and ewes selected solely on

D

the merits of the fleeces of their progeny is not successful, without occasional cross-breeding with the fat-*rumped* sheep—not the fat-*tailed* variety from which the Kara Kuli is derived. This keeps up the stamina, and is a method of rejuvenation fully believed in by Central Asian shepherds. The Kirghiz are in the habit of leaving their ewes out on the mountains in the hopes of getting a male lamb by a wild ram. I have seen examples of such crosses kept for stud purposes.

The Black Lagoon from which the township takes its name has more or less dried out. In olden days the whole area was swamp and marsh and lake, and supplied the Mongol Princes with their loads of game and duck, but as cultivation extended, irrigation canals drained the land, and so now the name applies to the busy little bazaar which grew up as the oasis increased. But decline has already set in. For it would appear that these terminal oases often suffer from an accumulation of mineral salts, a surfeit of which is disastrous to agriculture. In this case, Kara Kul is the sufferer. There are, however, other lagoons formed by the Zarafshan, when there is water to spare. One, called Makhan Kul, lies to the north in the desert of Khalata,* and thither I intended to wander.

Whilst held up in Kara Kul for lack of transport, I turned my attention to collecting sparrows.

Now, although the House-Sparrow of Turkestan

* Khala Ata, the Father of the Fortress, is actually a " mound," marking an ancient site and watering, about one hundred miles to the north-west. Without doubt it was a stage on the old desert route between Khiva and Bukhara, at the point where it bifurcated to the Khanates on the Upper Syr and the Farghana. Its name has become attached to a wide area of the Kizil Kum owing to the prominence it obtained during the Russian campaign against Khiva, General Kauffmann using it as his base before his final advance to the Oxus.

THE ZARAFSHAN EXPIRES IN THE DESERT

KARAKULI SHEEP IN KARA KUL

is as unattractive a bird as his European counterpart, he is in some ways more interesting, for he is a migrant, not a resident. The resident sparrow of the towns and villages is, or was, the Tree-Sparrow (*Passer domesticus dilutus* Richmond), a dear little bird with nice manners ; but I think he is being rapidly pushed out by the aggressive non-resident House-Sparrows (*Passer domesticus bactrianus* Zarudny and Kudaschew, or *Passer domesticus griseigularis* Sharpe). These birds spend their time between Turkestan and India, going south for warmth and returning north to breed. They are large sparrows, and know it, and consequently have little consideration for the rightful local inhabitants. At Kara Kul in mid-March the Tree-Sparrows were already nesting in the native house in which I lodged ; when I returned in May they had been evicted by a noisy crowd of House-Sparrows, which were already well ahead with their domestic affairs. They behaved very much as our European sparrows do, in that they showed the same tendency to vulgarity and bad taste, but they were not so particular as to their billets, for here they frequented town and country alike, and were just as much at home high up in the mountains as in the bazaars. They nested anywhere, in houses, trees, old storks' nests, or in holes in the rocks.

But the main interest in these Indo-Bactrians* lies

* It appears to me that the Russians of Turkestan called *their* summer migrants from India *bactrianus*, whilst we call *our* winter visitors to India from Turkestan *griseigularis*. Zarudny says *bactrianus* is a resident of Turkestan, but " in the cold season of the year only comparatively few numbers of its representatives remain, the rest migrating to the southern and south-eastern countries ; " while Whistler says of *griseigularis* " this name must stand for the large migrating House Sparrow so common in Turkestan, Tibet, Afghanistan, Kashmir, etc., which winters in parts of India."

in their migration route, for the line they take is exactly what you or I would choose if we wanted to go from India to Tashkent ; that is to say, if there was no international boundary. They swarm up through the passes of the Hindu Kush, avoiding the Pamir Massif and all its off-shoots, and flood the plains to the north of the Oxus. They have never been seen to the *east* of the Pamirs, in Chinese Turkestan. The movement, therefore, is curved like a waning moon. But the sparrow problem in Turkestan does not end here. It is complicated by the fact that there is an ever-threatening invasion by European House-Sparrows (*Passer domesticus domesticus* Linn.) from the north and west, and when this takes place it will mean permanent occupation, not summer tourism. As is well known, the recent expansion of the European sparrow into Northern Asia has been spectacular. It would appear that the sparrow increases and therefore demands more living-space, in direct relation to increased grain production, which, in turn, is the result of an increase in the human population. Man breaks new ground, sows his crops, and the sparrow arrives. In Russian Central Asia the recent swift change-over from wilderness to cultivation, from waste to production, has been phenomenal, if not without parallel. Towns have sprung up like mushrooms, these built-up areas being as popular with House-Sparrows as are the wheat fields. Deserts have become granaries, and the sparrows follow the grain. Therefore the invasion is imminent, if indeed it has not already started, and there will be " trouble on the waters o' the Oxus " as to who will be the dominant sparrow !

Beyond the oasis, in the reed-beds beside the river,

the Spanish variety (*Passer hispaniolensis transcaspicus* Tschusi) ruled the roost, and amongst them I chanced to see and secure a solitary specimen of yet another species—the Saxaul-Sparrow (*Passer ammodendri ammodendri* Severtzov)—a peculiar bird and a local one, taking its name from that strange flora, the saxaul, for it is seldom to be found far from it.

The saxaul tree or bush, it assumes the character of both, is a desert form of very specialised type, growing only in the deep sand areas of Middle Asia from the Caspian to the Gobi. Its chief characteristic is its ability not only to grow, but to make a considerable timber-content in pure sand. Of infinitely slow growth, the saxaul makes comparatively little show above ground, but it extends its roots for an immense distance below the surface, running for twenty to thirty feet in search of moisture. Its slow growth means, of course, very hard wood, but on the other hand it is brittle ; it is difficult to saw, but it can be broken by hand. Gnarled, knotty and primitive, its presence in Transcaspia has been as coal to the " Midlands," for it has provided the railways and the home fires with cheap, local, and very excellent fuel where no other is available.

The fact that the desert can grow such a crop is of some interest, especially as saxaul can be coppiced. If felled at about fifty years' growth it will shoot again from the stub, which means that vast areas of unproductive sand-dunes might become a green-wood of great economic value, and give a good return for the labour of afforestation. Moving sands would thus become stabilised and fuel supply assured.

Wherever the saxaul flourishes, its parasite, the

sparrow named after it, flourishes too. I have collected specimens of it at points fifteen hundred miles apart across Middle Asia, but the saxaul was ever present, or very nearby.

A curious genus the sparrows, some of them being firmly established residents, others inveterate migrants. Some members of the race are common cosmopolitans, indifferent to climate and environment, wide-ranging, adaptable and populous : others are rare, forming small secluded communities and very fastidious as to their surroundings. A good example of the latter type exists not far away across the Oxus, in the Helmand delta—Yate's Sparrow (*Passer moabiticus yatei* Sharpe)—which does not occur anywhere else. Yet another, Tristram's *moabiticus*, closely allied to the latter, is only found in two separate localities, five hundred miles apart, namely, in Iraq and Palestine, where they seem to enjoy the peculiar climate of the Dead Sea basin, at 1300 ft. below ocean-level.

To move out of Kara Kul presented some problems. There was neither trade nor traffic except that which went along the railway ; there was no caravan route but the one leading on to the Oxus or back to Bukhara. Only the shepherds went out into the deserts with their flocks, and, at the moment, they were all to the south-east in the Karshi steppes where the pasture was more forward. They would come north later. So for independence I went alone but for one servant, and for transport I took two donkeys.

By far the most practical and peaceful means of progress for the field-naturalist is the ass. This may sound strange, especially in Central Asia, which is unquestionably the domain of the horse. But after trying every conceivable means of transport, from human-beings to yaks and reindeer, I would choose the donkey every time for leisurely wandering. He is cheap to buy or hire, easy to load and unload, and you can shoot off his back. He seldom lets you down, either by failing in poor country or falling on rough ground. He can climb where no horse could stand, and survive where a pony would starve ; he can do on little water, will carry almost any load, and not one has ever died on me. I have walked thousands of miles with donkeys, and although I have never been able to entertain any affection for them, I can yet sing their praises. They thrive in heat, dust and drought, hating cold and damp ; yet, for a comparatively northern latitude, and at times a very cold region, the Turkestan ass is a very good utility type. This may be partly due to the fact that the region is very far from the sea, an element which donkeys particularly dislike. One does not see many of the showy, thoroughbred, white breeds familiar in Baghdad and Damascus, but for stamina and endurance those of Bukhara would be hard to beat. In build they compare with their southern cousins as the Asiatic " Dun " horse compares with the Arab. I know of no proper donkey inhabiting a colder climate, and, of course, those to be found in this cold damp island are, to say the best for them, a mockery of what a moke should be.

At Kara Kul, where on any bazaar day the ass seems to be more numerous than man, I invested in a couple. They would suffice my small needs, one to carry my belongings and the other to mount myself or my man. Little baggage means few worries ; those whose needs are numerous, who cannot dispense with this and that, carry loads of trouble as well. But to travel light is to travel with freedom.

I reduced my needs to a minimum, although collecting in the field does actually demand a good deal of impedimenta. Tent, traps, guns, ammunition, collecting boxes, are incidental to the necessities such as clothes and food. I have moved, lived and worked for months without a tent, but it was only at considerable inconvenience, for the preparation of natural history specimens is an exacting operation if properly carried out. I have skinned birds under appalling conditions, in emergency, but it is unpleasant work, and very unsatisfactory if the standard aimed at is a high one. The reputation my specimens earned for me at the British Museum recompensed me a hundred times over for that extra half-load—a small Whymper tent.

It was the middle of March when I moved out of the oasis. Others were on the move too,—the duck and the wild geese were passing northwards. Although the swamps had been reclaimed and cultivated, wild-fowl still frequented the locality in vast numbers. At this season of the year the fields were mostly under water, the hamlets and farms standing up like little islands in the broad flood. The water was only a few inches deep and therefore all this inundated land was most attractive to ducks. Every evening I flighted them, even close under the walls of Kara Kul itself. They were mostly mallard, teal, pochard and wigeon, and they were there in myriads.

Other birds were moving south—the Sand-grouse—for, like the shepherds, they knew that the spring grass would flush earliest on the banks of the

Oxus, and thither they hurried in countless thousands for a quick feed before going north to their breeding grounds. They did not stay long, for within a week (23rd March), they almost darkened the sky with their legions as they passed over me heading in the opposite direction. They were mostly Pin-tailed (*Pterocles alchata* Linn.), with a few Black-bellied (*Pterocles orientalis* Linn.) amongst them, and they moved as only sand-grouse can, with direct, arrow-like flight, accelerated to sixty miles per hour. Curiously enough, there were no members of that capricious species, Pallas' Sand-grouse (*Syrrhaptes paradoxus* Pallas), whose strange and unreliable habits are so well commemorated in its name—*paradoxus*. This is its true home, but I came across it only once during my year's work in Russian Turkestan. However, I was treated to a rare sight some years later, when I found myself underneath its main mass-migration from Central Siberia to its winter quarters. On that memorable occasion, in October, for two whole days, from dawn to dusk, the sky was full of moving hosts of Pallas' Sand-grouse. As far as eye could see, and in every direction, there were large packs and small parties passing south, and as the country was the open Dzungarian plain, and the weather very clear, and we were on the move, the numbers necessary to make up the whole kaleidoscope, and to keep it running for that period of time, must have been very great indeed.

Immediately after crossing the Zarafshan to the north, one meets the desert ; in fact, in some places the sand-dunes appear to be encroaching upon and actually altering the course of the river. It would appear that the Zarafshan, like the Oxus and the Syr, and for that matter the Volga, *presses* upon its right bank and consequently the alluvial cultivated strip is on the left bank. This is certainly true of the Zarafshan on this lower reach between Yakatut and Kara Kul.

But the so-called desert is of a very varied type. There are sand-dunes it is true, but they mostly grow a phenomenal amount of herbage. There is hard steppe, but it is covered with tamarisk, and at certain seasons with good grazing. The vast region, called vaguely, Kizil Kum, which fills the void between the Oxus and the Syr, is of much greater variety than is indicated by the map. It is neither a Rub al Khali nor a Sahara of virulent type. We know of at least one early Russian expedition which made light of crossing it, at its widest extent, with a cumbersome caravan of 500 camels, 230 Cossacks, and as many infantrymen, plus two cannons ! It is not all sand-dune and steppe by any means ; there are outcrops of hills, and many " lows " growing dense reed-beds and poplar thickets. For it must be remembered that this land has seen many changes. The Oxus and the Syr have not always flowed as they do now, and there are many indications of old river beds which once carried water and supported cultivation, but are now jungles. All the way from the Oxus to the Syr and to the Aral Sea this type of country holds. It is about as big as England and Scotland combined, and it is without permanent habitation.

We—the expedition consisting of myself, my servant Juma, and two donkeys—were rather overcome by its greatness and its solitude. But there was a certain friendliness about it ; it had none of the austerity of the Arabian waste ; there was not the

UZBEG SHEPHERDS

ever-present risk of a death by drought, nor the likelihood of meeting an enemy. On the other hand, the exhilarating atmosphere of those high deserts was absent. Here there was a silence, a sadness, and a deadness about the " feel " of the land, which may have been due to its low altitude, and possibly to its remoteness from the ocean.

So we wandered where we willed, following the northern bank of the Zarafshan, keeping its waters within view as a guide. I usually shot my way over the sands, while Juma drove the asses along the river bank, and we would meet at evening in some delightful hollow in the great dunes, where a roaring fire of aromatic desert herbs was cooking a savoury mess of rice and game.

The river—the Strewer of Gold—now shorn of its wealth, flowed beside us, a sluggish stream, sixty yards wide, aimlessly wandering to its end in the desert, and I looked forward to the summer days when I hoped to explore those Alpine meadows where it had its birth.

Beyond, on the opposite bank, loomed up a single weeping-willow tree, which I thought was the most beautiful thing I had ever seen. So it struck me at the time, and as I have never forgotten it, it must have been very lovely. For out of the yellow dust-laden murk, in that vast, meaningless, dead world of monotony, there stood this one solitary emblem of awakening life—a willow tree just bursting into leaf. A small thing in itself, but one of those trifles which creates an indelible impression and is remembered all the days of one's life ; and how few there are that produce such a sensation. Yet it is the seemingly little things which have the capacity for giving great pleasure. That willow tree in those particular surroundings fulfilled all desire ; it was perfect ; and I have carried the memory of it with me ever since.

Now I settled down to my real work. Not that I had neglected any opportunity of collecting, for I had long since learnt that one was just as likely to make a new discovery at, say, the railway station as in the depth of the desert or on the top of a mountain. Mr Oldfield Thomas had instilled in me the necessity of trapping always and everywhere ; had I not already seen him roused to enthusiasm over a mouse I had caught in a local bar in Beirut ?

But here was a veritable harvest to be gathered from virgin soil. One never knew what one was going to meet, or see, or hear. Night cries told me that there were some strange birds—and beasts— about. Tracks in the sand showed me that the small animal population of the dunes was great and varied. I would make my friend, Oldfield Thomas, skip round the Mammal Room of the British Museum in ecstasy, when my boxes of specimens from the Kizil Kum were opened up ! For the enlightenment of the uninitiated, I might say, here and now, that the collecting of small animals, even if only rats, mice, moles, voles, shrews and the like, becomes as exciting as big-game hunting. And indeed many of them are as hard to come by as are some famous trophies of the chase.

There were the Susliks, for instance, the desert counterpart of the Marmot of the mountains, which were as wary a quarry and as difficult a target as any I have come across. These ground-squirrels, as they are sometimes called, combine the wisdom of a Solomon with the aloofness of a Buddha. They must have many enemies, for they are never off their guard.

But if you are good to eat, and your neighbours are foxes, wild-cats, caracal and cheetah,* not to mention an " umbrella " of birds of prey during the migration season, you doubtless become painfully aware of the fact, and learn to take every precaution. They are jolly little fellows, independent and impertinent. They sit up and laugh at you, cocksure of their position on a sand-dune, eighty yards away, and they never let you diminish the distance. They say, " Catch us if you can," knowing perfectly well that you can't. They have no usual " runs," so gins and snares are useless. They despise all forms of bait, so your traps are left empty. They are too small to pick off with a rifle at a distance, and your only chance is to happen on them unawares far away from their holes. But even then they move with such rapidity that escape is often successful, for their hind-legs, being well splayed out like a lizard's, make a wide track over the soft sand, and are thus especially adapted to the terrain.

As time went by I became more efficient at Suslik hunting. Those I obtained here were subsequently named the Yellow Oxus Suslik, *Citellus fulvus oxianus* Thomas. But some years later I collected such a fine series of skins of another variety, which I came across in Dzungaria, a thousand miles farther east, that Mr Oldfield Thomas was able to mark it down as something quite new, and actually named it for the finder. So the Susliks, which gave me so much trouble, now have one branch of their family saddled for ever with the impressive name—*Citellus carruthersi* !

The Susliks, like myself, enjoy the wide open spaces of the earth, being found from the Russian

* These two last-named wide-ranging species reach their extreme northernmost limit in the Kizil Kum.

Steppes to the Great Wall of China, and in some cases even to the Pacific. The drier the climate the happier they are, for they are great diggers. Living in deep burrows, they prefer sand as a medium, but all the loess country is friendly to them, and they thrive in it. Here there are two sorts, the true Susliks—*Citellus*, and the *Spermophilopsis*, the difference between them being greater than their outward appearance would suggest, for the latter belong to a different genus. The *Spermophilopsis* are typical of the saxaul sand-dunes and the loess zone, and they occupy a narrow strip across Central Asia, from the Caspian Sea to Lake Balkhash, spreading southwards to Afghanistan. They do not vary much, in fact it may be said that the genus is represented by the one species—*leptodactylus*, although local forms from Kushk and North Afghanistan have been separated under the names of *schumakovi* and *bactrianus*. The *Citellus*, on the other hand, are legion, and their range Holarctic. *Spermophilopsis* live either solitary in simple temporary dwellings, with bolt holes, or united in communities which construct complicated and well-thought-out burrows. In this locality they do not always hibernate in winter, but in summer they retire below ground in order to avoid the heat, and there they take a long siesta till the autumn. Their coats conform to this habit, being very short in summer and long enough in winter to supply a cheap but serviceable fur. Chiefly vegetarian, they climb and dig in order to obtain what is in season, enjoying the young shoots of certain shrubs as much as tulip bulbs and wild onions.

The best example of a highly specialised type of desert fauna is to be seen in the Jerboa family.

Endowed by nature with coloration perfectly adapted to their environment, with incredible powers of speed, silent movement, of hearing, as well as of sight by night, they are admirably fitted to survive the many perils that surround them. Their make-up for this purpose is one of extremes ; they have tails in some cases twice the length of their bodies, hind legs

several times longer than their front legs, ears like bats' and eyes like owls'. They live and thrive in these very arid regions, under extremely rigorous climatic conditions, there being few, if any, places on this planet where the fluctuations in temperature, both diurnal and seasonable, are as great as they are in the Kizil Kum. Yet these delicately built " aery creatures . . . of pitiful beauty "* seem to have solved for themselves the problem of life in a land of

* C. M. Doughty

excessive heat and intense cold, and of very sudden change from the one to the other. By digging deep they avoid both extremes, for at a depth of even three feet anywhere in this sandy waste, the soil is cool and moist. Their burrow is usually, but not always, a one-way affair, except for a bolt-hole, which is not opened except in extreme emergency, and by closing up the main entrance they seek to evade detection and do obtain more equable conditions. In winter they hibernate, and it does not take a great drop in temperature to render them dormant.

They are edible, and their flesh is said to have the peculiarity of being cool, even when freshly killed ; therefore falconers like to use them as a special diet for hawks in moult.

They are nocturnal in habits, and biped in action, using their front paws only to feed with and to dig. Their long wiry tails with a terminal " brush " serve a treble purpose—a balance in movement, a rudder in turning, and in repose they use them as we use a shooting-stick. Their silky fur and large eyes show that they are night prowlers. Although their front legs are not especially developed for digging, some races, such as the *Allactaga*, seem to prefer the hardest steppe, rather than soft sand in which to make their burrows ; but there may be a good reason for this—holes easily dug are easily opened up, and their most attentive enemies are the little desert foxes. Others, such as the ordinary *Dipus*, like sandy soil, while the *Paradipus* burrow in the softest dunes. They are not easy to collect unless there are Arab urchins, or their counterpart, at your disposal to grub them out ; and they are brutes to " make up " into nice skins, but a good series is a joy to behold.

How to deal with a six-inch Jerboa's tail is one of the tests I should set a prospective candidate for the job of taxidermist to my next expedition !

There are several members of the family, *Jaculidae* or *Dipodidae*, here in the Kizil Kum, both of the large five-toed *Allactaga* and the smaller three-toed *Dipus*. But the luck of the collector is proverbial, for in spite of a long stay and careful work I missed several interesting new species which Russian naturalists have brought to light more recently. On the other hand, when travelling fast and only scratching the surface of Dzungaria, I stumbled on a new sub-species, because I chanced to pitch my tent over its bolt-hole. A dog digging at the main entrance sent *Allactaga elater dzungariae* straight into the bag, thence to the British Museum where Thomas described it.

But work still remains to be done, and many problems await solution. There is an elusive race of miniature Jerboas—*Salpingotus*, for instance, tiny little fellows two inches in length, with tails nearly five inches long, which are of such rarity (or perhaps cunning) that only four specimens have ever been procured, and this in spite of the fact that they have a wide range over Middle Asia. These four known examples represent three different species, and come from such widely separated localities as the Altai, the central Gobi desert, and the frontier of India. It is unlikely that they do not occur in the intervening regions. Here is a chance for someone wishing to see Asia, but who is not afraid of hunting for a needle in a Continent. There are few clues to help in the search, either as to the distribution or the environment of the quarry. Sharasume, where the single specimen of *Salpingotus crassicauda* was discovered, lies in the cultivated area of the middle Kran valley, on the south-western slopes of the Mongolian Altai. In its upper course the Kran river runs through forests of spruce, larch, birch and poplar, but around Sharasume the valley widens and allows cultivation by irrigation at an altitude of 2900 ft. Beyond the cultivated zone are barren hills growing steppe vegetation, and it is probably there that *crassicauda* originated, for the locality given to the type is *near* Sharasume. I trapped the length of the Kran valley, getting nothing but marmots and mole-rats, and certainly never expected anything in the nature of a Jerboa. Kara-khoto, near which the specimens of the species *kozlovi* were collected, has entirely different surroundings, namely high sand-dunes encroaching onto a ribbon of dead and dying vegetation bordering the delta of the Edsin Gol, with some gravelly steppes in the vicinity. The altitude is 2854 ft. If I were to go in search of either, I would strike a mean between the two localities, and try the Barkul-Karlik Tagh area, where there is a strong infiltration of Altai and Gobi elements into Tian Shan fauna. No exact locality is known for the third species—*thomasi*—other than Afghanistan or Tibet; but it is almost certainly the former, and most probably the northern part of it, since in Afghan Turkestan one might reasonably expect to meet a Mongolian form, such as *Salpingotus* presumably is.

The story of the finding of these three new species reads like fiction. Vinogradov, the Russian zoologist, who recognised a new genus in the first two specimens brought back by Kozlov from the central Gobi, discovered the second species in the local museum of a small Siberian town. This success doubtless encouraged him to continue the search, and he eventually unearthed the third species in a certain world-famous museum, where it had reposed unappreciated and unrecognised for many a year. *Salpingotus thomasi* did not receive its name until nearly ninety years after its demise.

This digression is made in order to show that there is some romance attached even to such small-game hunting as this, and also to emphasise the extreme importance of recording the exact locality of, and the nature of the country inhabited by, each specimen collected. A skin, or a skull, without the locality attached to it, loses half its value, and one without a label is quite useless. *Near* Sharasume, for instance, might refer to pine-forest, melon-patch, wheat stubble, or rocky hill-side, and we should like to know exactly just where these intriguing pygmies make their home.

For colony-builders the Gerbil desert rats would be hard to beat. The ground, in the hollows between the dunes, or on the harder steppe, often gave way beneath our weight, and we sank to the knees, so honey-combed was it with holes and subterranean passages. There were several different sorts and sizes, some more nocturnal in their habits than others, and consequently more easy to trap. One big fellow—*Rhombomys opimus*—which preferred the daylight and laughed at my traps, had the habit of whistling to his friends on the approach of danger. The whistle was so like that of a wigeon that I was constantly taken in. Of the others, which were not so wary, I soon got all I needed.

Then there were the mole-rats, *Ellobius*, which I

had been urged to look out for, and to collect at all costs. These rodents are in no way related to the moles, although they are more or less blind, live entirely underground, throw up the orthodox mole-hills, and are in fact highly specialised for a subterranean existence. But they burrow with their claws and teeth, not with their hands, and are vegetarian not insectivorous. The genus is confined to this part of the world, that is to say they are found from Southern Russia to Mongolia, spreading south through Central Asia to Persia, Anatolia and Baluchistan; an area large enough to produce some seventeen local races, to which number I eventually contributed four, namely those from Samarkand, Dzungaria, the central Tian Shan, and the remote Hami mountains. They are difficult to collect owing to the very nature of the concrete-like steppes in which they usually find a living, but if you can catch them on soft ground they are easy prey. I once chanced to notice mole-hills being thrown up around me while pitching my tent one evening on a grassy flat beside a river, and by midnight I had trapped and skinned half a dozen.

But at this job the actual trapping is only the start; when that is successfully accomplished the real work begins, namely, the skinning and making-up of a good specimen, fit for the best museum. This is a long, laborious and exacting performance, necessitating skill, care and imagination—in fact, fine craftsmanship. You cannot hurry over it if each skin is to be perfect and uniform with the others, which should be the aim of every collector. All this has to be done under difficult, and sometimes exasperating, conditions. The work is usually done at night, since daylight is too precious to waste, and this means either by the light of a flickering candle or at the best an oil lamp. Cold, tired, and in a poor light, the collector tries to preserve his specimens before they go bad, or he falls asleep over them. Yet, on my return to civilisation, I was frequently asked, " What on earth did you do with yourself in the evenings ? "

I have often been forced to work at preparing my specimens the whole night through and to snatch only a couple of hours sleep before starting on another day. And the day often meant twelve hours in the saddle, or on foot, to be followed inevitably by another long night's work—if the day's hunting had proved successful. My record was fifteen consecutive days hard travel, with an average of two hours sleep out of the twenty-four. In spite of the express rate of our journey I collected many birds and animals, and preserved the lot ; after which I slept solidly for two days and nights. My aim was high, and it is a fact that if a hundred skins are laid out on a table I can recognise at a glance those made up by myself twenty years ago, without looking at the labels.

Collecting specimens of the permanent mammal population occupied me until the first main spring rush of migrant birds arrived. I listened to the last wild-geese leaving for the far north ; the duck population grew less and less as days went by ; the sand-grouse had all gone by 23rd March. Then, as if by magic, the first trickle of birds from the south began to appear. The earliest to come were, as in England, the Wheatears or Chats. On the 14th of March the Isabelline (*Œnanthe isabellina* Temm.) and

Indian Pied Chats (*Œnanthe capistrata* Gould) * suddenly arrived, being followed on the 21st by the Desert
Wheatear (*Œnanthe deserti atrogularis* Blyth). Two of
these—the Isabelline and the Desert—might have
come either from India or Africa, for these summer
visitors to Transcaspia have a wide winter range,
some going south-east to India and some south-west
to Arabia and Africa. Others, we shall see, go *only*
to Africa, others again *only* to India, but they all
converge here ; this is the junction for Siberia.

The Zarafshan Valley may be said to be the area
where the two migration streams meet ; for it has
been shown by Kashkarov and Kurbatov that the
summer migrants coming into, and passing over
Transcaspia are, like its resident avifauna, almost
entirely of Mediterranean origin. If this is so, it
offers a good example of a migration route developing
with the spread of species, in this case the expansion
of all bird-life from the Mediterranean region into
Transcaspia, as, by slow degrees, conditions there
became suitable for bird-life.

The Chats started to think about breeding
immediately on arrival, if their aerial displays meant
anything. The Indian Pied Chats, for example, had
a remarkable habit of taking long flights high in the
air, going through curious and beautiful evolutions
before suddenly dropping onto the identical bush
or sand-hill from which they had started : obviously

* Most likely *capistrata*, for Whistler considers this to be the breeding
Indian Pied Chat north of the Oxus, where it replaces *picata* of
Afghanistan. This is confirmed by Buturlin and Dementiev, who
say that *capistrata* belongs to the region north and west of that occupied
by *picata*. However, they consider the one to be merely a phase of the
other, or possibly a geographical race, while Meinertzhagen thinks that
the two may well prove to be conspecific.

a sexual display. They had a fine loud song, which was uttered on the wing as well as at rest, and, for Chats, a remarkable variety of notes. They could also mimic, and I repeatedly heard one copying to perfection the Quail's " Wet-my-lips."

The first Warbler to come was the Desert Warbler (*Sylvia nana nana* Hemp. and Ehr.). It doubtless came from Africa or, anyway, from the south-west, for its seasonal movements are always south-west to north-east and vice versa. The tamarisk thickets resounded with its pleasant Whitethroat-like chatter, which was most welcome after the long months of silence. Every day brought new interest. A page from my diary reads :—" I got four gerbils and one other rodent in my traps, and so remained at this camp. Worked all day long with two short outings on the sand-hills, where I shot two sand-grouse, a hare and four Desert Chats. The latter arrived in great numbers to-day. The weather suddenly became warmer, even a fly buzzed into my tent to-day, and the willows by the river showed a film of green. It was a lovely spot. The Zarafshan flowed close by, bordered by a belt of thick tamarisk and some grass, and beyond that the dunes. The contrast was remarkable. The edge of the sands was inhabited by a great variety of small animals—two kinds of susliks, numerous sorts of gerbils and mice. The susliks presented a ridiculous appearance as they ran for shelter with their hind-legs very wide apart, and their tails carried perfectly straight up in the air, at right angles to their backs. They can travel very fast like this, even on loose shifting sand.

" Putting down more traps at dusk, I had caught nine more small mammals by the morning. On my round of the traps I shot another couple of much-needed ground-squirrels, so I had enough to occupy me all day."

Spring, which had not been in evidence at all in mid-March, came with a sudden rush. One day there appeared a flush on the desert grass, the next day the hollows in the sand-dunes were tinged with green, and the tamarisk showed red, where tiny shoots were budding. The air became less keen, in fact it was almost balmy. I could work outside, skinning my specimens in the open, which was a wonderful relief after the cramped quarters of a six-foot tent.

With the grass came the sheep, tended by rough-looking Uzbeg shepherds, in long pelt coats and tall black " busby " hats. The flocks were guarded by even tougher-looking dogs, which were the biggest-boned, most massive and thick-coated breed I have ever seen. Their ears were cut short, and their tails were docked, to give them a better chance when in combat with intruders.

On reaching the point where the Zarafshan divided I followed the branch leading off to the north-west, and after a long tramp came to the indeterminate shores of Makhan Kul.

I had first seen the waters of this inconstant lake from the crest of a sand-dune, while pheasant shooting in the locality, a sight as unexpected as it was welcome. That was during the first days of November, when the weather was so hot that I discarded coat and waistcoat while shooting. Pheasants abounded, and were fairly easy to get, as the native falconers had not been after them. In December, in brilliant but very cold weather, a more thorough investigation was made of this northern outlet of the Zarafshan and its terminal lake. At this time of year the surplus water was sufficient to form a very large expanse of open water, with innumerable bays, gulfs and inlets. Narrow straits led off to further lagoons, and these again connected with others even more remote and secluded. Doubtless the flooded area varied in shape and size every season, so that no map of it would hold good for very long. The summer's sand-storms, for instance, would alter the configuration of the dunes and the levels of the hollows, therefore the water would run in new channels the following winter. Another year it might be gone altogether, to reappear again elsewhere. As I saw it, it presented a novel combination of wilderness and wandering waters, attracting a profusion of wild-life. Vast congregations of birds frequented the newly-flooded desert. I have seen fowl in strength from Canada to Kashmir, but for numbers, variety and sublime surroundings, I would go to Makhan Kul. Geese,* swans, flamingos, ducks and pelicans filled air and water ; bustards, pheasants and wild boar swarmed. Now, on my third visit, in April, all seemed to be much as it had been in mid-winter, except that the wild-fowl had departed, and instead of a frozen rim along the margin of the water a fringe of grass showed fresh and green. No doubt as the waters subside good grazing comes up, and this was the ultimate destination of the shepherds and the flocks I recently encountered. For the time being it was given over to wild-boars, which were constantly in view, working along the shores of the lake, plashing through the shallows, and generally behaving as if the whole place belonged to them—

* Principally Grey-Lag, but there were White-fronted, Bar-headed and Red-breasted as well.

which, indeed, it did, except for that inevitable hanger-on of the pig tribe—the tiger. That night the silence was broken by the unmistakable " woof-woof" and the heart-rending squeals of his victim. Juma called it *yulbars*, which is Uzbegi.

All of this was obviously good tiger country, but not as good as it used to be ; tigers had not been seen in the vicinity of Bukhara for the last fifty years. However, they still wander across from the Oxus, and hunt for pig to their heart's content on the terminal marshes, at those seasons when pig are plentiful and man is not. They belong to the Hyrcan, Persian, Caspian race, *Panthera tigris virgata*, but having a much wider range than those names imply would be better called the " Central Asian." A line drawn from the south of the Caspian Sea straight across Middle Asia to Lop Nor in Chinese Turkestan, up north-west to Balkhash, and back again to Aral and the Caspian, would enclose all the existing haunts of this species, and its subspecies *lecoqi* and *trabata*, if you care to separate those of Chinese Turkestan and Balkhash. His habitats within this zone are necessarily isolated and far apart, but whenever jungles, large enough and wild enough, occur he is still to be found. In type he stands midway between the Indian and Manchurian races, as shown by his slightly warmer coat ; in size there is little, if any, difference between him and the average Bengalee.* As regards character this (mainly)

* Kennion's, killed in the Elburz, compares favourably with the largest Indian tiger, but the measurements were taken of the (freshly killed) pelt stretched out to dry. The only record that I know of, of one measured in the flesh, was the old tigress killed on the Upper Murghab, and acquired by the Afghan Boundary Commission, in 1886, and this again matches in size the average for an Indian tigress.

Soviet tiger seems to be of a milder disposition than either his Indian or Manchurian relatives, if Russian naturalists are right in their judgment of him. For they say that their tigers keep themselves to themselves, and are not aggressive, and that this particular trait in their character constitutes the main difference between them and their cousins. Being well provided for—by an abundance of easily-killed wild animals— they do not prey on domesticated herds or attack human beings ; therefore they should not be considered a pest. But still they are not protected and are in danger of becoming extinct. Around Balkhash they are now very scarce ; on the Syr they are gone for ever—except as a rare visitor from the Oxus delta (Russian officers used to hunt them from Tashkent) ; their Dzungarian haunts were never very extensive, but, on the other hand, they are more remote and as yet undeveloped, so tigers may still survive there ; the Hyrcanian forests on the northern slopes of Elburz, the Atrek region and the Murghab still hide a few ; but the basin of the Oxus probably holds a larger population of Central Asian tigers than any other area at the present day. Chiefly relegated to the reed-beds around its many-mouthed delta, they occur spasmodically over the whole length of the Oxus valley as far as the frontiers of Darwaz, right under the Pamirs. A line drawn across the river from Chubek to Chayab would mark their eastern limit.

Hares swarmed, too, around Makhan Kul— *Lepus tolai*—the hare of Middle Asia from the Caspian to the Amur, split into innumerable local races (here *desertorum* Ognev for choice), but always a light-bodied hare, as unlike a Norfolk eight-pounder as a kitten is to a cat.

By the end of March it became obvious that the main spring migration was in progress, so I hastened back to the cultivated zone to meet it, spending the month of April collecting in the neighbourhood of Samarkand. The vale was now at its best. The tawny-brown, clay-tinted landscape of winter was splashed with colour, even the uncultivated land was carpeted with flowers, and gay with iris and tulips.

I went back to the Registan and climbed to the summit of my minaret, where I found that the Alpine Swifts (*Micropus melba tuneti* Tschusi) had already returned to their nesting holes. This was on 2nd April, yet some winter birds such as Grey Crows (*Corvus cornix sharpei* Oates) and Black-throated Thrushes (*Turdus ruficollis atrogularis* Temm.), which should have gone north, were still here. But they had all gone by the 10th of the month, their places being quickly filled by new arrivals from the south.

A few days more and the miracle happened. All the gardens of Samarkand burst into blossom ; apricot, apple, peach and plum seemed to reach perfection simultaneously, and the summer birds flooded into them—Bee-eaters, Rollers, Cuckoos, Hoopoes, Orioles, Nightingales and Doves. The whole aspect and atmosphere of the country changed in a few days ; indeed it was hard to believe that it was the same place where I had endured the winter. But to appreciate fully the coming of spring in this particular clime, one must go through the preceding period, for the one is as gentle as the other is severe.

The three principal life-zones of the Zarafshan were the high mountain, the cultivated area, and the low-lying desert. But the cultivated area also included the foothills, which were neither true mountain nor true desert, although they might be called desert-hills. These also were within reach of Samarkand. I used to ride out at daybreak, across the intervening ten miles of steppe, shoot for eight or ten hours over the hills, and return at dusk. These bare, treeless, uncultivated hills produced a wealth of bird-life. My collection was swelled by the addition of some hundreds of specimens of many varieties. All were summer visitors, come to breed in the locality, or on passage to a higher altitude, and a few—such as the Scarlet Finch (*Carpodacus erythrinus roseatus* Blyth)— on passage to a higher latitude. Typical birds on these foothills of the great mountain mass behind them were—Wheatears of many varieties, Buntings in several, Larks of five sorts, six kinds of Shrikes, the Rock Thrush and the Blue Thrush, Rock Nuthatches and a Desert Bullfinch. The Chukor Partridge swarmed, and so did a great variety of birds of prey— Eagles, Buzzards, the Saker Falcon, the Shikra Hawk, the Hobby, Lesser Kestrels, Kites and Vultures— both Griffon and Egyptian. On the highest ground there were Choughs, and to my astonishment, a colony of Black Storks (*Ciconia nigra* Linn.), breeding in solitary state on the cliffs, scornful of their social cousins nesting on the minarets in the towns below.

These hills I have called foothills but as a matter of fact they attain a height of 7000 ft. Yet compared with the mountain world beyond they are as the first rungs of a ladder. From their summit one is treated to a ravishing vision of the Hissar range to the east, although its 20,000 ft. peaks, not more than eighty miles away as the vulture flies, were hidden from view. The call of the mountains became very strong as the days lengthened, but there was yet just time to go again to see Makhan Kul under summer conditions. So I hurried back to Kara Kul, where Juma and the donkeys awaited me.

We wandered as before, but under very altered conditions. The Zarafshan had already dwindled to an insignificant creek. The old ferry-boat was stranded high and dry, its winter's work accomplished, for it was used principally by shepherds needing to pasture their flocks on the northern bank, when the river was too deep to ford. It was an immense flat-bottomed ark of a boat, unwieldy but suitable for the purpose. Its appearance suggested that it might have been in use in the days of Timur, so antiquated and weather-worn was its hulk. As a figure-head, it bore a large goose's head roughly hewn out of wood, and its owner was as crabbed as his craft. I had used. it of necessity in the winter, but now the donkeys paddled across without wetting their loads. Yet I gave the old ferryman his fee, although I waded his river, for he was out of a job until the autumn.

As I approached Makhan Kul I became aware that it was no longer the solitary place that it had been. Large flocks of sheep were grazing around its dwindling pools, for the water-logged sand grew a catch-crop of succulent grass, and a magic green-sward of vivid colour sprang up as the waters subsided. But all would be gone in a week or two, and the desert would return to its own.

Air and earth vibrated with sound and song. The tamarisk, which used to give out a thin whistle as the icy wind passed through the bare stems, now uttered the softest whisper, as breeze makes through barley, only far more seductive. Individually, the tamarisk

is noiseless, but in their millions their little green
shoots tell you a lot and their story now was that the
winter was over and gone. The general aspect of the
landscape had changed, too, from clay-brown and
grey-green to a pink—exactly the tone of Sea-pink
on a salting—for the tamarisk was already in flower.

The scrub, which grew only about four to five feet
high, swarmed with small birds. Perhaps the
commonest was one called Syke's Warbler (*Hippolais
caligata rama* Sykes), which comes here from India to
breed. This little slip of olive-brown used to frequent
the guy-ropes of my tent, singing its short, but to me
very sweet song. Bird-song in desert regions is apt to
be rated above its real merit, because of its rarity and
its cheerless surroundings. Thus the wandering poet
Doughty wrote : " I heard then a silver descant of
some little bird, that flitting over the desert bushes
warbled a musical note which ascended on the
gamut ! and this so sweetly, that I could not have
dreamed the like."

Syke's Warbler belongs to a small group
(*Hippolais*), some of which have pleasing names—
Icterine, Melodious, Olive-Tree. It is one of the four
species of the group which find their way up here
for the summer, two coming from Africa and two from
India, and in this particular locality Syke's was the
most numerous. Its cousin, the Booted Warbler
(*Hippolais caligata caligata* Licht.), was here too, but
it sang all night as well as all day, a non-stop chatter
like a Sedge Warbler, to the strange accompaniment
of Jackals howling and Eagle-Owls booming.

Of a very different nature was the Grey-backed
Warbler (*Agrobates galactotes familiaris* Ménétries), shy,
elusive, and with an abrupt melancholy song. He

flew low amongst the tamarisk, and even ran along the ground when chased ; yet he was not a rarity, nor persecuted by man. The Whitethroats were represented by eastern forms of the Common (*Sylvia communis rubicola* Stresemann) and of the Lesser (*Sylvia curruca affinis* Blyth), and the smaller *minula*. More surprising was the presence in this desert of innumerable Cuckoos and Doves. The former, no doubt, found easy dupes amongst the Larks and Wagtails, on whom to play their tricks. The Doves were the Persian form of our common Turtle Dove (*Streptopelia turtur arenicola* Hartert), and very pleasant to the ear were their everlasting love-songs in the wilderness.

The Doves rank high in my estimation, and are well up in my list of bird favourites ; I was therefore pleased to find that the natives here appreciated them, for their callous Oriental mentality is reflected in their insensibility to bird-life in general, and their utter disregard of it. But they appear to have a soft spot for the Doves, for they welcome them into their houses and feed them lavishly.

The Wagtails, being victimised by the Cuckoos, were nearly all the Black-headed variety (*Motacilla feldegg melanogriseus*, or *aralensis* Homeyer), smart-looking and very busy following the flocks of sheep, where food was evidently plentiful. They were nesting beside my tent and were already feeding their young on the 18th of May. There were still a few waders round the rapidly diminishing pools, and Terns—Caspian, Common and Little, were having a good time amongst the fish which were trapped in the shallows, and which would soon be left high and dry if not eaten beforehand.

The chatter of some Oyster-catchers sounded out

of place, but they served to remind me that all this region had been under salt-water once upon a time and that the birds themselves were probably "Relicts" of that bygone age, having adapted themselves to the new conditions, and survived. There are many such relict-survivals in Central Asia. It is not easy for us to visualise the heart of this Continent as a part of a vast extension of the present-day Mediterranean, stretching over the Black Sea, and the Caspian, covering all western Middle Asia, and connecting with the Indian Ocean, but certain birds and mammals tell the secret. The seals of the Caspian, for instance, and such marine shore-birds as the Turnstone, the Kentish Plover, the Avocet, the Sheldrake, and certain gulls, all resident breeders in this region which can scarcely be regarded as their *natural* habitat.

The most remarkable instance of " Relics "—that is to say, of " remnants of a fauna which do not succumb, but remain, perhaps even thrive, under conditions which originally were strange to them, widely separated geographically from their own relatives and other members of the fauna to which they once belonged " *—which I have come across—in literature—is the crocodile, which lingered on in the Syrian Desert up till the last quarter of the seventeenth century. The Abbé Carré, who slew " un crocodile épouventable " in a saline, reedy swamp in the neighbourhood of Taiyibe, is unlikely to have been mistaken as to its identity, for he had already become well acquainted with them in Madagascar and in India. His encounter with the last relict crocodile in that particular region at

_____
* Professor Einar Lönnberg

that date, 1672, may seem fanciful, but it is *not* impossible.

The now shrunken lagoons were becoming almost tropical in appearance; they hummed with insect-life and glittered with gorgeous dragon-flies. Dense reed-beds were growing up around them, where the wild-pig wallowed and the pheasants nested. Here lay one of my most difficult problems, namely, how to get the pheasants in their spring plumage. Luckily I had already procured a good few in November and December, when they were comparatively easy to flush, but now in high, rank vegetation, and without a dog, it was a very different matter. All pheasants are skulkers until they become runners, but this particular variety had so much territory to run over that pursuit was out of the question. Early in the season it was possible to put them up, but now nothing would induce them to take to their wings, and it became a case of taking a running shot or none at all. I got pretty good at it, but inwardly longed for a dog.

As is well known, the so-called Common or English Pheasant originated in the Caucasus region, although it has been much hybridised by the introduction of other varieties in more recent years. This pheasant of the Caucasus is known as *Phasianus colchicus colchicus*, and has been accepted as the type of which all the other continental forms are subspecies, there being no less than twenty-three " good " ones, to which many perhaps less " good " forms have been recently added, bringing the grand total up to over forty, according to the most recent estimation. Considering that every suitable locality from the Caspian Sea to the Pacific is inhabited by

some form or variety of this Colchic Pheasant, it is
not surprising that there are so many. Some of these
forms are well defined, others not so well. The
deciding factor would appear to be the amount of
segregation enjoyed by the variety in question, or,
conversely, the amount of inter-breeding that can
take place between it and some other variety. In the
5000-miles-wide desert zone which belts Middle Asia
it can well be imagined that there are many such
localities in varying degrees of proximity or seclusion.

For instance, the local pheasants of the Murghab
and Tedjen river systems probably enjoy complete
seclusion, as there is little or no chance of them
interbreeding with their neighbours on the Oxus or
the Caspian—a segregation, by the way, which is
already a thing of the past, for modern irrigation
schemes have joined up what was asunder. Even as
I write, the sands which Nature has piled up are
being removed by Man, and Oxus water flows once
more towards the Caspian Sea. On the other hand the
pheasants of the Oxus and the Syr, although belonging
to two separate forms—*turkestanicus* and *chrysomelas*—
certainly do overlap and interbreed.

The pheasant of the Zarafshan is one of those
which has a very small range—a range, in fact, which
is more restricted than that of any other. It extends
only over the lower half of the river valley ; that is
to say from its terminal marshes up to Samarkand, a
distance of under two hundred miles, its lateral range
being decided not by the altitude—2000 ft.—but by
the fact that no suitable ground is to be found in the
valley *above* this point. I used to think that the
pheasants of the Zarafshan valley were entirely and
completely segregated, and that the desert zone

dividing it from the Oxus was a sufficient barrier in itself to enforce this. But I am not at all certain that this is so. The dividing march is only fifteen miles wide in some places, and as I have shot pheasants in desert scrub at a considerable distance from water, I see no particular reason to suppose that they could not cross that intervening desert barrier if they wished. After all, wild sheep and ibex will link up with other sheep and ibex, although cut off from each other by wide desert tracts.

Therefore I sought a good series of skins of *Phasianus colchicus zarafshanicus*, for the museums of London, Tring, New York and Berlin. In early winter, as I have already said, they were fairly easy to obtain. I found them numerous along the edge of cultivation, on the river banks, and even right out on the tamarisk-covered desert well away from water, and was able to flush them without a dog, for they had never been hunted or harried. But later on the local falconers came along, took their toll and scared the birds to such an extent that after they had passed by I could not find a pheasant. But it was a goodly sight—the cavalcade of gaily-clad Bukharans, well-mounted, and flying perfectly-trained hawks—ranging along the river bank. It was as if a Persian miniature had suddenly come to life. They worked the best ground, wasted no time, and killed a lot, for they were evidently adepts at the game. This is not surprising considering the length of time they have practised it, for their ancestors must have been masters of the art thousands of years before ours had tried their hand at it. They flew Goshawks mostly. But, as I have said, when they had gone by, it was almost impossible to find a pheasant.

The reed-beds, and rank vegetation were to their advantage, not mine, and had it not been for their habit of wandering out onto the sand-dunes I should have been unsuccessful in obtaining my quota.

Had I been shooting for sport, I would have stopped after filling the pot. I was only too ready to do so when I had got the necessary number of specimens, especially as I felt it my bounden duty to skin every bird I killed, which incidentally saved me the trouble of plucking my dinner. These pheasants were fat and in wonderful condition, although there were no Berberis thickets, such as there are in the mountain valleys, to supply an unlimited quantity of nourishing berries; on the other hand, at this season, there was prolific insect life, which I believe can form as much as 35 per cent. of the pheasant's diet.

Perhaps one of the most curious inhabitants of the Transcaspian deserts is the bird called, for want of a better name, the Ground-Chough (*Podoces*). They were difficult birds to classify, for although they bore certain superficial resemblances to the jays, magpies, crows and choughs, they were obviously none of their ilk. Called at first Thrush-Chough, the name was happily altered to the more befitting and far more euphonious Ground-Chough. But, whereas Choughs in general suggest sea-cliffs or high Alps, and some members of the genus are fond of sailing over the heads of mountaineers already 27,000 ft. above sea-level, this particular bird is relegated to a terrestrial existence. It is practically ground-tied, scarcely ever flies, and then only laboriously, as if under compulsion. Moreover, the Ground-Choughs are confined to the veritable deserts of the heart of a continent. From Eastern Persia to the Gobi, in the most sandy and waterless wastes, or in the zones of even more waterless gravel, they thrive : but they are not to be found elsewhere. Seek out the abomination of desolation and you will come across the Ground-Chough, a most interesting character, and one very fastidious as to its habitat. This is confined to desert, but by no means all deserts. It must be exactly the right sort of waste place, and though it may all look the same to you, the Ground-Chough will select one special region as his abode, while leaving another, which appears to be equally suitable, untenanted. For instance, some keep to the sand-dunes and others confine themselves to hard, stony but equally waterless steppe. As Ludlow has already pointed out, of the two varieties found in Chinese Turkestan, one—Biddulph's—is purely a sand bird, while the other—Henderson's—keeps to the gravel fringe between the sands and the mountains, and they never encroach upon each other's preserve. This is surely a very fine distinction for any bird to make, but the terrestrial habits of the Ground-Chough may cause them to be abnormally sensitive to the terrain. Ground-Choughs seem to be a product of those dead-ends, where land-locked rivers find their graves—the Aral-Caspian basin, Balkhash, Lop Nor and the Persian Lut. Regardless of temperature they exist from below sea-level up to 4000 or 5000 ft., while one doubtful relative frequents the Tibetan plateau at no less than 14,000 ft. above the ocean. Like their habitats they are melancholy cheerless fowl, and in keeping with their lifeless surroundings they are very silent ; some make an unmusical rattle, and others a few plaintive whistles ; they have no song. Lonesome to a degree, they are seldom seen in company, preferring complete freedom from their fellows, and even from the opposite sex—a most unsociable bird.

In Russian Central Asia there are three varieties, one to each of its three major self-contained basins, namely, Aral-Caspian, Balkhash and Zaysan. Here, just beyond the Caspian, is the home of Pander's * Chough (and of its paler form, *transcaspius*) ; the small isolated sandy patch to the south-east of Balkhash supports a shrunken colony of another closely-allied form—*ilensis*—while the gravelly margin of Lake Zaysan is the most northerly limit of Henderson's.

Where Pander's Chough is found it is resident, enduring the great heat and intense cold of the locality with complete indifference, except that it breeds very early in the year in order to avoid the hottest period. Like Biddulph's it keeps to the sand area, but it is " local," even in a region which for hundreds of miles on end appears to be exactly the same all over. For a bird which is not especially adapted by nature—that is to say, it is encumbered with a long hind-toe and claw—it moves with extraordinary rapidity over the ground (" Swiftfoot " has been suggested as a suitable familiar name for it), and when forced into flight it is a weak, floppy effort of short duration. However, the bird usually has the intelligence to build its nest above the ground, or else well below it in a hole, or under a protecting rock. Its choice of habitat is the type of desert which grows bushes, such

---

* Dr Pander accompanied one of those early Russian Embassies to Bukhara, which prefaced her entry into the Central Asian Khanates. He was attached as naturalist to the Embassy of 1820, and hereabouts first reported the Ground-Chough which bears his name.

as saxaul and tamarisk, and these usually form its nesting sites above ground. To give some idea of what this drollish bird looks like, I reproduce a Russian artist's vision of the variety *ilensis* in its natural surroundings.

My camp had been in a lovely spot by the water's edge, where all life congregated, and I was loath to leave it. The weather was so perfect that I now lived and worked in the open air, only using the tent for storage and shelter from sun or wind. Lying out here at nights, under the stars, in dead silence, one felt— and now I am going to make a bold assertion—one *felt* the Oxus. I cannot explain exactly what I felt, but it was the same sensation that one experiences when coming within a certain distance of the sea, before seeing it or knowing that it is near—a premonition, as it were. I remember once reacting to the same emotion the day before emerging from the forest and finding myself without warning on the banks of the great Congo river. In that case travel was slow, and the distance may have been only fifteen to twenty miles. In this case the Oxus was a bit farther away, but instead of forest there was nothing betwixt us but sand. It seems to me that it is not improbable that so great a waterway might distil an atmosphere which could have reached me across the droughty desert. Anyway, I felt the presence of something to the west of me which was *not* sand.

Of all the great rivers of Asia, and some of them have impressive names, perhaps the Oxus inspires the imaginative more than any other. It may be its remote seclusion, which has been successfully retained well into the twentieth century, or may be its great historical associations, or perchance its more recent but much less creditable connection with the petty jealousies of two great Empires, but the fact remains —the Oxus implies romance.

The Mighty Oxus it has been called throughout the ages. But as a waterway it is not to be compared with the other giants of the Asiatic continent. It cannot compete with the Indus, the Brahmaputra or the Mekong, while the Yangtze, the Hwang Ho, the Yenisei, and other Siberian rivers, all beat it by hundreds of miles, and exceed it in volume. Yet the adjective is applicable ; the Oxus *is* mighty. The Greeks—Alexander's rank and file—were more impressed by the Oxus than they were by the Euphrates. Nor were they alone in their regard. " Superior in volume, in depth, and in breadth to all the rivers of the earth " was the reputation it held in the eyes of an early Moslem geographer. " No river, not even the Nile, can claim a nobler tradition, or a more illustrious history," re-echoes Curzon.

Rivers, like mountains, have their own individual characteristics. Some of them stir the imagination and call forth emotions quite out of proportion to their actual size. One of the best examples of this is Mount Hermon, which, in spite of its modest altitude of 9000 ft., possesses such great character and engenders such enchantment that the memory of it lingers for ever ; whereas there are mountains of three times its height which fail to impress one at all. And so with rivers : there are some vast floods which you may cross without comment, and there are others that arrest your attention on sight. Come with me by camel-caravan out of old Bukhara and arrive on the banks of the Oxus by moonlight, and you will hold your breath. You will know then why the ancients considered it one of the Four Rivers of Paradise : why the Greeks stood in awe : and why it is the river *par excellence* of Middle Asia. You may be influenced by the knowledge that it is born on the high Pamirs, and wanders to its death in forlorn, sand-bound Aral, and that a profound mystery seems to hang over the whole course of its existence from cradle to grave : but, on the other hand, you have to remember that this so-called historic river cannot claim greatness on account of its services to Mankind. The Oxus does not give a livelihood to millions, nor create a granary ; nor, curiously enough, has it ever done so, even in days long gone by. In spite of its long journey through desert country it does not bring into being an Egypt, nor a Mesopotamia, but flows on unblushingly through hundreds of miles of waste land and does nothing about it, yet the two together in collaboration could work wonders. It has no famous cities on its banks, except Khiva, where it doles out for Man's use a mere residue of all that swollen flood which goes to feed a useless sea.

Yet, in spite of all this, the fact remains that the Oxus presents one of the most impressive spectacles in all Nature. Standing on its banks I was lost in contemplation and wonderment. The imagination travelled upstream to the lofty regions where it rises—where three Empires meet—and downstream to the lone Aralean waste where it expires ; and then I wandered back to my little tent in the sand-dunes still puzzled by the riddle of this giant dissipating his strength—the Mighty Oxus running to waste.

But perhaps the Oxus has not yet come into its own, perhaps its grandiose title is prophetic, it may be destined to a *tremendous* future. Already irrigation schemes on a vast scale, conceived long ago, are being put into active operation; while others of an even more ambitious nature are being considered. Oxus may, in fact, once again be united to Caspian, and all the intervening deserts brought to a fertility that they have never known. Merv and its oasis may be rendered independent of Afghan water; the Black Sands may become a green-belt hundreds of miles long. Then the Oxus will have achieved its destiny, and have acquired greatness.

Towards the end of May the temperature rose by leaps and bounds, giving me some idea of what this low country would be like in mid-summer. For this desert is not like others which come within the influence of the ocean. Its so-called " desert " climate—that is to say, its dryness, heat, humidity, evaporation, etc.—is aggravated and intensified by its mid-continental position. All its various climatic factors are exaggerated. Extreme seasonal and diurnal changes occur. Mid-summer heat may be 110° in the shade, but the rivers will be frozen solid in winter. Frost at night may be followed by a sweltering day. I have had my tent frozen so stiff that it stood upright for long after the tent-pegs had been knocked out, but by mid-day I was searching for shade from the sun. The evaporation was excessive. I found that my bird-skins dried in a few hours instead of taking a week; sodden clothes dried on one almost immediately. As for myself, I felt so desiccated that, seeking a place where the sand-hills were steep and the river cut into them, I found a pool and bathed. The water was deep enough for me to dive in, swim and return without touching the bottom. I could feel my parched body absorbing the water, a glorious sensation that must be experienced to be appreciated. My bathe in the tepid silted waters of the expiring Zarafshan sent my thoughts upstream to those crystal-clear, icy torrents that were their origin. Visions of alpine meadows passed before me. Desire hastened my steps, and I turned eastwards to the mountains.

CHAPTER IV

TO THE MOUNTAINS

THE entry into any mountain fastness is always impressive and sometimes inspiring. My first introduction to the Central Asian highlands was definitely both. The fastness, if we include all its ramifications, covers an area half as large as Europe, the Hissar Range, into which I was walking, being the extreme western end of that mountain-world which reaches without interruption to the plains of India and China and the deserts of Mongolia. The Hissar,* springing suddenly out of the Transcaspian waste, grows into the Great Alai, links up with the Tian Shan, and runs as such for fifteen hundred miles before dying out in the Gobi desert. I was to see the whole spread of this glorious uplift at various times during the next five years, from the extreme west to the uttermost east, nearly three thousand miles of such magnificence, such beauty, and such aloofness, as is not to be found elsewhere on this planet.

Asia, all Asia that matters, lies at the foot of these divine altars ; India, China and Siberia lift up their eyes to these hills, which have been throughout all time a dominating factor in their destinies. Small wonder, then, that I thrilled to the occasion as I crossed the threshold.

The Voru or Kishtut valley is a veritable gateway to paradise. As you pass in, the door closes behind you, shutting out the whole vast, naked, realistic

---

* Or Hazrat-Sultan, as the western portion of the range is sometimes called.

world of steppe and desert, and you enter upon a realm of romanticism, of gloomy gorge, and happy valley, of sacred groves, of fountains, forests and flowers. I chose this particular valley as it was a quick route to high altitude. And to show the abruptness of the hills, it is a fact that I shot sand-grouse—a typical steppe bird—one day, and heard snow-cock calling close under the snout of a glacier the following evening. There were no interminable foothills to take the edge off your appetite for height. You plunged in and climbed straight from the floor of the Zarafshan valley up to the eternal snows in twenty-five miles, or in two days on your legs.

The track up this valley actually constituted a main route, if one can call it by such a name ; but in this country almost any passage through a mountain range is a highway, for the passes are few and far between. For instance, anyone needing to travel swiftly from Samarkand to the eastern provinces of Bukhara, to the upper Oxus, or even to Badakshan beyond, would come this way. Or, in days gone by, a passenger wishing to join a caravan to China would have taken this short cut in order to do so. For there are two easy passes leading from here over to that tributary of the Oxus up whose valley the caravans used to go, and which is called in its various portions Vakhsh, Surkh Ab, Kizil Su, and Alai.

This, naturally, raised in my mind the problem of the Silk Route over this stage of its long journey—the only stage on which it encountered a formidable mountain barrier of this category. For the first few thousand miles across China the caravans had little choice of route, except to by-pass the Takla Makan to north or south, according to exigencies of the moment, or the drift of war. The bulk of land-borne traffic between Cathay and the West converged on Kashgar or Khotan, coming to rest at one of these great termini under the eastern ramparts of the Pamirs. But from this point westwards there was a choice of three alternate routes, namely, to skirt the Pamirs on the south by Wakhan, to by-pass them on the north by the Alai valley, or to cross over into the Farghana. The ultimate destination of the goods was probably the deciding factor as to which route was chosen ; those intended for the Black Sea were unlikely to go by the southern Wakhan route, even as those booked for India would not go via the Farghana. Probably the two first-named were used as alternative routes (in difficult times) to Balkh, where the traffic turned south to Indian ports, or continued onwards across Persia to the Mediterranean. The last-named served the cities of the Farghana and Tashkent, passing on to Bukhara, Khiva, and finally to the Caspian and southern Russia.

Whatever the respective claims of these alternative routes, the Alai must always have been a principal highway of commerce. For the Silk Route was not a disjointed affair, built up in sections, linking likely markets. It was as if one laid down an imaginary pipe-line between Kashgar and the markets that demanded its oil, in this case and at that period Rome and Byzantium, and the line led straight through Bactria, and Persia, to Baghdad and Aleppo, and so to Antioch on the Mediterranean seaboard.

The question therefore arose in my mind as to whether Samarkand and Bukhara were not served by a branch off this Alai route, rather than by the most northern artery which fed the Farghana and the cities of the Syr. I have never seen an opinion on this point, except for Herrmann, who definitely includes Sogdiana amongst the countries served by the Farghana route. But the Terek Pass between Kashgar and the Farghana is, for a comparatively low pass, a notoriously bad one and would have been avoided as much as possible; whereas caravans forking at some place such as Baisun or Termez would reach the Zarafshan without encountering any such natural obstacles. But to all students of the subject, I should say, follow Stein's advice and study (if possible) " on the spot." There the difficult passage may perhaps be made plain, or, on the other hand, the apparently simple explanation may be upset by some impassable barrier. But the great thing is to see for yourself the lie of the land and to follow in the footsteps of your mediæval monk or merchant-caravan. Living here, in the vicinity of these old ways, one acquired a certain insight as to their nature, even if one did not follow over them.

In the case of the Alai—Wakhan argument, and as to which should be considered the most important, of one thing I am certain, and that is—when prosperity returns and communications are opened up, one particular route will regain its old popularity, and that is the old way up the Alai valley. All goods traffic, which is not airborne, will go this way. Hence perhaps the far-sighted policy of Russia in creating the township of Stalinabad out of an insignificant Oriental village on this particular line.

Therefore I give prior place to the Alai, for it seems probable that the major weight of the trade must have been carried along its comparatively easy gradient, rather than by the more direct but far more laborious Wakhan track, which may have been an express route for passengers rather than for goods in bulk. And I think east-bound merchants from the Zarafshan would certainly have chosen the Alai route and come up this Voru valley to join it.

As such it was of interest, although in little use when I was there. I had the whole place to myself except for a few shepherds and occasional visitors from the far beyond.

On entering the mountains I met with such a luxuriance of birds, flowers, and other beauties of Nature that I was absorbed in work. Compared to the niggardly but peculiar fauna and flora of the desert, this was as a tropical jungle. At the lower altitudes it was a case of quantity rather than quality. There was nothing of outstanding importance until 7000 to 8000 ft. was reached, then both flora and fauna became exciting, and from that height upwards to the limit of all life it was intensely interesting. For it must be remembered that this was no island of mountains, but the fringe of a whole world of them, comprising the highest summits on earth and possessing a wonderful and unique fauna.

Where Nature allowed Man a footing, he made use of every parcel of land granted to him. This did not happen frequently in the Kishtut valley ; in fact there were only three villages of any note—Kishtut itself on its lower course, Gazza and Voru on the middle reaches, with several groups of farmsteads which could hardly be ranked as hamlets. But their picturesqueness was unquestionable, situated as they were on the banks of the mountain torrent, half-hidden in orchards of fruit trees or embedded in groves of giant walnuts.

Thickets of rose-bushes surrounded the terraced fields, where nightingales sang all day and all night. These, by the way, were the birds I had seen come and go at Samarkand towards the end of April, and which had caused me to wonder whither they were going. Here they were, in full song and breeding.

The roses were mostly deep yellow briars (probably *lutea* or *foetida*), but there were others which the rose catalogues would describe as " vigorous climbers," and they grew here as roses should be allowed to grow—untamed and unpruned, ramping over the rocks, rambling up trees or straggling the thickets. The enormous trusses of blossom were white with dark yellow stamens and deliciously scented, for they were the Musk. There were honeysuckles, mostly of the bush type, but very fragrant ; one a lilac colour, another old-rose, and the sweetest of all a white, which, I think must have been *myrtillus*. Another, with a somewhat insignificant flower, grew into an immense bush twelve to fifteen feet high. But the best of all was a climber, which, if not our very own Wood-bine, was just as lovely and very welcome, for to meet such a precious friend unexpectedly in the wilds was a pleasure indeed.

I wished I had had training in plant-lore, and time to observe and collect, for I am sure these valleys held many surprises. Eremurus, for example, looking far more in place here than in an English garden, were in a variety of colours. I recognised a Clematis, not yet in bloom, which gave me the impression of being something out of the ordinary by the size of its flower-buds. Perhaps it was *tanguticus*, and, if so, a prize well worth coming a long way to see, when festooned with its gigantic deep-yellow flowers. There was one little village Mosque, timber-built and very time-worn, which was literally smothered with these old climbers, and looked so inviting that I was compelled to halt and camp for the night on its veranda. Apparently this was quite in order, although I did it with some diffidence—having respect for the stiff-necked, bigoted religion it represented. Yet the village elders came to pay their respects and to offer hospitality. They had never met an Englishman before, but they knew of Hindustan and heard well of our government.

I was agreeably surprised to find the inhabitants as attractive as their country, for it is only too true that there are many places " where every prospect pleases, and only Man is vile." However, that was not the case here. They appeared to be pleasantly behaved people of the Persian type, Aryan, not Turanian; men of the mountains—not of the plains—men who had remained stationary for a very long time and who had succeeded in retaining their own individuality and type and customs by the natural seclusion of their mountain homes—not men who had roamed and mixed and acquired characteristics other than their own.

These hill Tadjiks were, in fact, a people to whom I at once felt akin—not foreign—which is surely an acid test of mutual understanding. Here were communities of men of character, living normal healthy lives, hard-working and clean-living. Indeed, they shone out like a bright light against the dark background of sordid life in the cities of the plain—Sodom and Gomorrah, Bukhara and Samarkand. The unhealthy, unclean, lethargic atmosphere of the bazaars was absent. For the first time in Central Asia I became conscious of the fact that family life existed—almost like that in the West; men had wives whom they treated as equals, not as cattle; and there were happy homes. Secrecy, suspicion and deceit were absent. They had nothing to hide : they were proud people and, consequently, approached one on terms of equality and friendship.

These highlanders were obviously a very pure race, and probably freer than any other from contamination by the outside world. For they had lived on in these deep-cut valleys for ages and ages, untouched by the human floods which at various periods in history had inundated the plains below, and washed up against the ramparts of their fortress. If any outside influence had ever reached them it was probably Macedonian Greek, for the magic of Alexander the Great still lingers in local beauty spots named after him ; and indeed it was not far from here that he—" the most signal example in history of the subjection of the flesh to inordinate pride "—fell to the charms of Roxana.

The narrow, confined valley eventually opened out, the rock walls receded, and I emerged onto an open flat—a Maidan, defined as Archa Maidan—the open place of the Junipers. If ever there was an abode of Pan, it was here. An immense amphitheatre was formed by the surrounding snow summits, the arena was an alpine meadow, gently swelling to grassy slopes sparsely covered with an open forest of magnificent and aged junipers. Nature may be a bad forester, but she is a wonderfully good landscape gardener. Here she had arranged park-like scenery of perfectly spaced trees, each one fully developed and exhibiting to the best advantage its gnarled and twisted trunk and rugged limbs. The background was composed of snow-fields running down to flowers, and hanging glaciers poised for their final fall under summer suns.

Such was the beauty of Archa Maidan, where I pitched my little tent and worked for a week collecting birds and beasts. The altitude was 9500 ft. ; snow-line was then about 11,500 ft. This life-zone in the Central Asian highlands is comparatively short-lived—that is to say, it has but a brief summer season.* The permanent inhabitants are few, the visitors many. Now, in June, the season was at its height. Around my tent the commonest birds were the little Gold-fronted Serin Finches (*Serinus pusillus* Pallas), which were remarkably tame and confiding, until I attempted to take their eggs—then they attacked me fearlessly. They bred in the junipers, making their nests entirely of shreds of fibrous bark. A gay little bird for these parts, with its flaming forehead and orange rump, its only competitor being the Goldfinch.

Bird-song was not much in evidence, for the majority of these high-altitude birds are singularly voiceless, except for their call-notes. It befits them, for they are mostly dour, hardy species, battling with the elements, and hard put to it for food. It cannot be an easy life up here on the verge of where all life ceases—on the threshold of perpetual snow and ice. Neither is there an abundance nor variety of life, but

* There are, of course, much higher plateaux and " Pamirs " situated above the average Central Asian snow-line of 12,000 ft., which, being kept clear of snow by wind, are frequented by birds in summer and by mammals all the year round.

what there is excels in quality. Although plant life
becomes smaller, the birds become larger. The
Rock Patridge becomes the big Snow Partridge, for
example—a fine bird, living in magnificent surroundings. "In height and cold, the splendour of the
hills," might be his motto. Mountain ranges of only
the first rank befit him. The Taurus, the Caucasus,
the Tian Shan, Himalayas, the Altai, and Tibet, each
possess and preserve their own species of Snow
Partridge. I have seen them all. Contrary to
general belief, this bird is by no means peculiar to
very high altitudes. They are found as low as
5000 ft. Nor are they scarce, for at certain seasons
and in the right locality they can only be described
as very numerous. They are caught up by the natives,
tamed, and trained for cock-fighting in the same way
as Chukor and Quail are used. Their capture is
rendered comparatively easy under certain conditions.
Snow Partridges are wont to " pack " like grouse in
the autumn—a habit the local falcons make good use
of, and for a brief season they thrive on fat young
birds. The natives, knowing that terrorised Snow
Partridges can be picked up for nothing, wait on the
falcons and gather up by hand those that are too ·
frightened to risk taking to the air.*

Another method of catching them in the winter,
when they are forced to lower altitudes in search of
food, is by sinking large earthenware jars up to their
necks in the ground and feeding the jars with grain.
The hungry Snow-cock cannot resist such a temptation ; they drop in to get the corn, but cannot get
out. For a very shy, wary mountain bird difficult to
stalk or to procure, they seem at times to become

* *Lahore to Yarkand*, p. 282.

complete fools ! Their call-note, a weird wild whistle, is unforgettable. The local (Turki) name for them is *Ular*, or *Ullargh* in the not far distant Caucasus. The Hissar bird (*Tetraogallus himalayensis* Gray) is the same which spreads over the whole mountain systems of Himalaya, Hindu Kush, Pamir and Tian Shan.

The finches, which frequent the same inhospitable region just below the snow-fields, were also of the large robust type, wild in their habits and strong in flight, preferring the air of 10,000 ft., well able to cope with rough weather and hard times, and to find a living on rock and shale. Rose Finches, Snow Finches, Red-mantled Finches, Crimson-winged Finches*—lovely birds all of them, birds that I would go across half a world to see—birds that I used to lie in wait for, " belly down on frozen drift " just as if they were some giant trophy on which I had set my heart. Dawn was the time to enjoy them. I used to leave my tent at the first glimmer of light and make the stiff climb to the snow before the sun touched the topmost peaks. Then, from some sheltering rock, I could watch the pageant unfold and the birds arrive. The very edge of the melting snow-fields seemed to be a favourite feeding-place, ground which had only recently been exposed by yesterday's sun, the soil still sodden, and as yet not showing any growth of alpine plants. Immediately the sun touched it the birds came. Birds such as Snow Finches, which merged into their surroundings so as to be almost invisible ; Rose Finches that looked like drops of blood when caught by the rays of the

* *Carpodacus erythrinus roseatus* Blyth, *Montifringilla nivalis alpicola* Pallas, *Carpodacus rhodochlamys grandis* Blyth, *Rhodopechys sanguinea sanguinea* Gould.

sun ; Horned Larks (*Eremophila alpestris albigula* Hartert), smart in their buff, black and white. A few forest birds came up for a change of diet, Grosbeaks (*Mycerobas carnipes speculigera* Brandt), swift on the wing, with a curious undulating flight like that of a Hawfinch ; silent, shy birds, difficult to approach, and when frightened apt to leave the locality altogether. Snow Partridges whistled around me, and on one occasion a cock bird presumably, for the hens should have been otherwise engaged, lit on the snow patch by which I lay. He then proceeded to cross it at a run, with head bent low and his tail cocked up, every now and then stopping and uttering the loud wild whistle so typical of these highlands. He was coming to feed on the same oozy patch where the other birds were, but the sudden appearance of a hawk, probably a Hobby, of which the only evidence to me was a shadow passing over the sunlit snow, broke up the breakfast party. The Snow-cock went, like a bullet, straight across to the opposite side of the valley, a mile away ; the small birds scattered like leaves in an autumn gale.

Then silence, except for marmots whistling and the thunder of a snow-slide. Down in the valley below the day had not yet begun.

This upper region, between perpetual snow and tree-line, was one of extreme austerity but great fascination. The weather was wild, even in June, and on the tops I suffered much from cold, wet, and exposure. In spite of this I kept a " string " (a score) of traps going just below snow-line, 2000 ft. above my camp, and I used to run up there twice a day to go round them. There were a lot of small mammals but they were not easy to trap, and if caught they often disappeared, trap and victim too. I suspected birds of prey until I caught the real culprit—a marmot ! Troubles of the trapper are many and varied, and this one was certainly a poser, for a trap anchored by anything less than a chain was at the mercy of a marmot. In Africa we had the same trouble, only the thieves were of a very different type, and even more difficult to outwit, namely, ants. These most destructive and rapacious robbers would devour piecemeal any trapped small animal in a few hours. In fact we suffered so much from their depredations that we were forced to devise a spring, whereby the trap, on being sprung, was hoisted aloft by a cord on a stick. But even then the indomitable insects would climb up the stick, descend the string, and devour the precious specimen.

But my labours were worth the hard climbing, for at 10,000 ft., on the spongy ground just below the melting snows, I caught another *carruthersi*. This time it was a little Vole. He may not be an *Ovis poli*, but he was an interesting discovery, being the type of a new species-group of the genus *Neodon* (*Phaiomys*), and he still remains the sole representative of the group. Although my locality for the type has been enlarged somewhat by more recent collectors, the group has a very limited range around here at the extreme western end of the Central Asian uplift. The genus is presumably one of Chinese origin, having extended its range to Sikkim and along the Himalayas to the Pamirs and here.

Below the snows, flower-spangled grassy slopes swept down to the first juniper trees. The great contrast between the frowning mountain-mass above, and the gay carpet below renders this particular zone

one of the most impressive and lovely in all Nature. The composition is simple but the effect is overpowering. One wonders how these tiny flowers can ever reach such perfection—Harebells, Anemones, Rock Jasmin, Erinus, Gentians, Ranunculus, Sedums, Silene, Iberis, Dianthus, Arenaria, Achillea—all in their own special way gems of colour and form, all thriving in exposed positions, under inclement weather conditions, and in close proximity to a forbidding background of crag and ice.

The slope is so steep, but the " going " so easy, that you drop a thousand feet without realising it, and behold ! you enter a completely new zone of life. A wood-pigeon coos, a flash of colour denotes a Redstart, and a familiar Mistle Thrush scolds as you approach her nest in the junipers. This juniper forest supplied several necessities, otherwise lacking, for the bird-life of the valley, namely, shelter, nesting-sites and coniferous food supplies ; it also gave us mortals two things we sadly miss, if absent for long— song and scent. Being mid-June, all the birds were either nesting or had their broods fully fledged and flying. Birds that come up from India for the purpose, such as Severtzov's Tit-Warbler (*Leptopœcile sophiæ sophiæ* Severtzov) from Kashmir, and Hume's Willow-Warbler (*Phylloscopus inornatus humei* Brooks), whose little domed nest of woven grass I found as high as 9500 ft. There was the Blue-headed Redstart (*Phœnicurus cœruleocephala* Vigors), remarkable for its clear blue head, and its lack of red where most Redstarts have it—on their tails ; and Eversmann's Redstart (*Phœnicurus erythronotus* Eversmann). Of residents, a Crested Tit (*Lophophanes rufonuchalis rufonuchalis* Blyth), belonging to the highlands of

Turkestan, Afghanistan and the Himalayas, was one of the commonest ; there were Rock Nuthatches up to 9000 ft., but much rarer was a Tree-Creeper, nesting in the cracks in the juniper trunks (*Certhia himalayana tæniura* Severtzov), a Turkestan form of this circum-globar little bird.

In addition, a few Wheatears were breeding on the slopes between the forest and the snows, the Isabelline (*Œnanthe isabellina* Temm.) and the Common (*Œnanthe œnanthe œnanthe* Linn.). In fact, up here and at this height was the only occasion I came across the Common Wheatear in Turkestan, but the Isabelline was everywhere from the lowest levels up to 10,000 ft.

All those Meadow Buntings (*Emberiza cia par* Hartert), too, which I had seen passing through Samarkand in mid-April were up here, nesting at 9000 ft., and very numerous ; but the other migrant Buntings—the Ortolan (*Emberiza hortulana* Linn.), White-capped (*Emberiza stewarti* Blyth), and Grey-necked (*Emberiza buchanani* Blyth) did not extend their breeding-quarters above 7000 ft.

Magpies were here, a few of them, right up to the snows, and of course Choughs, the latter being mostly Yellow-billed Alpines (*Pyrrhocorax graculus forsythi* Stoliczka), not Himalayan Red-bills (*P.p. himalayanus* Gould), but there were some of them as well. The common Turtle Dove of the plains was here replaced by the larger Indian Rufous Dove (*Streptopelia orientalis meena* Sykes), which frequented a zone between 8000 and 10,000 ft. I did not come across the local " Bird of Paradise," which the Russians told me to look out for, but the Indian Paradise Fly-catcher (*Tchitrea paradisi leucogaster* Swainson, synonym *turkestanica*) is to be found in the neighbouring valley, the Fan, where Iskander Kul would be a likely spot, the altitude of 7500 ft. being correct for breeding birds. They go farther north still, to the Farghana and Western Tian Shan, and are one of a crowd that move between their summer and winter quarters keeping to the *west* and never passing to the *east*, of the Pamirs. The Paradise Flycatcher seems to be another example of a migrant wintering in India under one name, and summering in Turkestan under another.

The only mammals in and around the forest were hares and marmots, and small fry such as voles and field mice, all of interest and some of them in great demand. Perhaps the marmots rated first in order of merit, for although marmots are common enough in their habitats they are not often collected and brought home, therefore museums were in need of them. Also, these far-ranging genera (Manchuria to the Alps in this case) demand careful study in order to obtain a true classification ; and in order to do so a good series of skins from many different localities is essential. So I had to get a few of the Hissar marmots, much as I disliked killing the friendly little fellows, and still more hated skinning them, for they were as fat as butter and very difficult to clean. But Juma informed me that the fat was a wonderful cure for the rheumatics ! So I bottled what I could, and traded it for curdled milk. My labours were rewarded when my Hissar skins proved to be a new form of the marmot which the late St George Littledale brought back from the Alai in 1888-9. It is *Marmota aurea flavinus* of Ellerman's encyclopædic work, *M. caudata aurea* of Ognev's.

The marmots were not much disturbed here, but further east they are the quarry of every Kirghiz and Mongol fur-hunter. " Pigs " the natives call them, and it is true there is a certain superficial resemblance, but they err when, as good Moslems, they forbid them as food. In spite of their appearance they are clean feeders and good to eat.

As an example of harmonisation the marmot is a puzzle and upsets most theories. On the high tawny plateaux he is a fair example of protective coloration, but here on these green grassy slopes and amongst the junipers he shows up like a fox in young corn.

As the summer advanced the traffic increased. Shepherds came up from below, driving enormous flocks of sheep, making for the pastures around the head waters of the Fan river, the next left affluent of the Zarafshan. They proceeded by easy stages, some of them spending the night near my camp. This helped to solve the problem of my food supply, which was rapidly running out, for an ample supply of *kaimuk*—fermented ewe's milk—was available. This junket forms an almost complete diet in itself; augmented by barley-meal bread and tea, I existed on it until my return to the plains.

I joined up with one of these convoys and went up with them to have a look at the Dukdan Pass at the head of the valley, four miles above my camp. The juniper forests ascended to about 10,000 ft., and the snow lay deep on the pass itself; I estimated that there was about a mile of it. But the sheep had trodden a hard track through and I went over without mishap. Great snow peaks and hanging glaciers walled it in on the west, but the eastern side was composed almost entirely of steep precipices and shale slopes. I took a long climb up this side in the hope of seeing Ibex (which do exist here), and looked beyond with hankering impatience, for at this point the Hissar range swings round and sends off a long extension southwards—the Baisun Tau and the Kuh-i-Tang—the Mountains of the Defile, the defile being the famous Iron Gates which have been for all time the main approach to the wealth of the Zarafshan for conquerors and caravans from the south ; in those far distant hills dwelt an unnamed race of Markhor. All I got was a couple of marmots, a Snow-cock and my first specimens of the Hill Rock-Pigeon (*Columba rupestris turkestanica* Buturlin), a high-altitude bird which starts life at 9000 ft., where it replaces the common Rock-Pigeon, and continues upwards to almost any height. This gave me a long day's work in camp, which I did not mind after an eighteen-hour tramp.

The Ibex on these hills would belong to one of the many local races of *Capra sibirica sakeen* Blyth (probably *alaiana* Noack), hereabouts at the extreme western limits of their range. Across the Oxus, Ibex of the *sakeen* group (see p. 176) extend a little farther westwards, up to the Afghan-Persian frontier, which appears to be also the line of demarcation between the habitats of the two species *Capra sibirica* and *Capra hircus*. A line drawn from Quetta to Seistan, and thence northwards to the Russian frontier on the Tedjen, would mark their limits precisely. These two wild-goats do *not* overlap, although they can certainly view each other's territory. The one, *sibirica*, seldom descends below an altitude of 5000 ft., and never comes south of latitude 30° N. The other, *hircus*, is indifferent to low altitudes and southern latitudes. I have found them at 2000 ft. in the Syrian desert, and they can endure the heat of Sind.

All the main traffic was one-way, up the valley, southwards, and it was only very rarely that anyone came down from the regions beyond the snows. When they did come they were foot-passengers, men and women, carrying their belongings on their backs, having come by secret tracks from their remote mountain homes. These hardy mountaineers were a joy to behold ; the men were like gods, lithe and limber, and the women, suitable companions for such a splendid type, were fair to look upon, feline in movement, and fearless in eye. " In stormy freedom bred," they showed a dignity, a charm of manner, and a virility that made me feel *parvenu*.

Whatever the exact ethnographical affinities of these Galcha hillmen may be—and there seems to be some doubt still as to where exactly they should be placed—it was a pleasure and a surprise to come across them here in a country where society as a whole was very much the reverse of what *they* were. Also to see women free, not imprisoned ; and dressed to give comfort to themselves and pleasure to others, rather than to avert jealousy. These people came to my tent in passing, and partook of the customary cup of green-tea, leaving me with an intense desire to know them better, and in their own homeland.

I had now collected some hundred or more birds and beasts, so leaving the peaceful solitudes of Archa Maidan, I explored the Saramat tributary. For the Voru valley has two heads, the Archa Maidan and the Saramat, the importance of the former resting only on the fact that it carries the " way through " to the pass over to other lands. The Saramat, on the other hand, leads nowhere, but its waters are as many as, if not more than, its brother's. There was the usual cavernous, walled-in lower course, through which the river swirled and foamed, and through which foot-passengers could only pass with difficulty, alternating with delightful open flats where juniper, birch and maple grew, and rose-bushes laden with blossom hung over swards of green grass.

There was more vegetation of all sorts here, wherever space allowed, and consequently a few more birds were added to the collection. Amongst them the Himalayan Whistling Thrush (*Myiophoneus cœruleus turkestanicus* Zarudny), an amusing starling or rather grackle-like bird, with an unexpected song. To me it resembled the warble of a Blackcap, very soft and very sweet, and indescribably beautiful in these particular surroundings, for it seemed to love to frequent some gloomy gorge where the river was a cataract and the sound of falling water almost drowned its efforts. They were nesting in the rocks above. On these high streams the Brown Central Asian Dipper (*Cinclus pallasii tenuirostris* Bonaparte) abounded, the White-bellied species (*Cinclus cinclus leucogaster* Bonaparte) having been left behind at 5000 ft.*

* In the Hindu Kush, it appears, the White-bellied Dipper keeps to high altitudes, 8000 to 11,000 ft., and the Brown Dipper takes its place at lower altitudes, the two just overlapping at about 8000 ft. In the Hissar mountains my experience was that the Brown Dipper lived *above* the White-bellied. In the Tian Shan the White-bellied certainly inhabits lower altitudes than it does in the Hindu Kush. Further north still, in Dzungaria, I found them as low as 3000 ft. Severtzov also noted the irregular distribution of these birds in the Tian Shan, for he found that on the same range of mountains the north side might be inhabited by the White-bellied, while the southern flanks would be occupied by the Brown Dipper.

Eventually the valley opened out, and against a superb panorama of snow peaks there was spread a broad and pleasant meadow, with rolling hills covered with excellent grazing. Here I found that I was not alone, for it was tenanted by the summer camps of the shepherds from the village of Voru. There were three or four groups of tents pitched right up under the snows at about 9500 ft. I camped nearby in a little glen, under a group of junipers. These annual migrations of the villagers to the alpine pastures assume the character of a summer's outing. There is little or no work to be done, the livestock eat their heads off on the wonderful pastures, milk in every form flows—fresh, sour, curdled or cheesed ; it is a general *tamasha* and the girls get married. The holiday spirit was infectious. I took a day off, lay out on the grass, and did nothing but enjoy the pleasures of solitude and sunshine. I could watch the quick cloud-shadows passing over the lovely grass; and even see the rainbows ending on the glistening snow-fields. Overhead wheeled the ubiquitous Lammergier, and Snow-cock whistled to each other from their impregnable fortresses. All was at peace, except for the thunder and crash of avalanches, which, at this season, were incessant.

The next day—back to work. Opposite my tent the hillside was composed of that peculiar rock formation called conglomerate. I was particularly interested in it because I knew that not very far away to the south-east, around the great bend of the Oxus, there existed what is probably the most extensive area in the world of this fantastic configuration, and it was one of the places I had a mind to visit. The geological phenomenon, amazing as it is, did not concern me, until it presented me with a new animal. For the conjurer suddenly produced guinea-pigs out of his hat ! From the numerous cracks and crannies which honey-combed the conglomerate, scampered innumerable Pikas, which, perhaps, are best described as little guinea-pigs (South American Cavy) or miniature

conies (*Hyrax*). As in the case of the latter, the " stony rocks are his refuge." Being diurnal in habits, the whole colony was at work, for this was their harvest-time, and they are great hoarders. They were, literally, making hay while the sun shone, running out onto the hillside, collecting up loads of grass, and racing home with bundles as big as themselves. Whether this was . for winter storage or bedding, or both, I cannot say, but they do lay up provisions against the winter, and their period of hibernation at this altitude must be a long one, probably six months. They move with extreme agility over the most precipitous places, in spite of the fact that they are not provided by Nature with those crêpe-rubber soles, such as the *Hyrax* wear. Yet they vie with the lizards in their contempt for vertical rock walls, and are also swift on the flat.

They are very energetic and always busy; in fact I have never seen a Pika loafing. They whistle while at work, and have another warning note if danger threatens.

Having small round ears, and rudimentary tails which are not visible, their superficial resemblance to a guinea-pig is evident. The similarity holds good for colour, too, for they have a very distinct winter and summer pelage, which varies considerably, so that when changing their coats in June they are pied, and therefore more guinea-pig like than ever. I collected some from one colony, of which no two specimens were alike in colour. Some observers hold that Pikas are a good example of protective coloration, while others disagree. All I can say is that I have never seen a Pika in the flesh that was not either buff, grey, cinnamon or russet, nor any locality frequented by them which was not of the same range of nondescript colours. These, here, were parti-coloured—grey and tan; but when they have lost all their grey hairs and are in full summer coat, they must look like little red marmots. Severtzov says that they attain their summer pelage between mid-June and mid-July, but these were only just starting to change over on the 23rd of June. For safety's sake they must disguise themselves in neutral tints, and at the period of transition from winter to summer pelage, when they are most busy outside their burrows, and therefore more exposed to danger, their camouflage is at its best. There must be some good reason for this: their enemies may be many, and although never persecuted by man, I found them unaccountably shy. Consequently they were not easy to collect, and in addition, the terrain on which they lived made it difficult to retrieve even a dead one.

The English names—Tailless-Hare or Mouse-Hare—are both fatuous and inappropriate. A Pika is a Pika, and is far too great a personality to be linked, or likened, to anything else. Apart from belonging to the same sub-order of rodents, there is no relationship between Pikas and Hares, whilst in outward appearance and in habits there is no resemblance whatsoever. Pikas live in burrows or in holes in the rocks, they have short round ears, and sub-equal limbs ; hares live above ground (mostly), and are characterised by the great length of their ears and their elongated hind-legs. Here, in the Hissar mountains, the dominant race is *Ochotona rutila*—the Red Pika—but *macrotis* (also a true species) of Tibet and the Pamirs, trespasses on to its territory so that the ranges of the two just overlap in this area. For the *Ochotona* form a large family widely distributed over the highlands and lowlands of Asia, extending from Persia to Manchuria, and from the Himalaya to Siberia. They are a very ancient group, and have had to adapt themselves to the various drastic climatic changes which have taken place in their country. But they have succeeded well in doing this, for they can accommodate themselves to hot arid steppes, wet forests, and cold mountain-tops. Consequently, they are subject to considerable variation ; the species are ill-defined, the local varieties and the true species being still undetermined. They usually, but not always, prefer high altitudes. I have collected seven or eight varieties, including two new sub-species, many thousands of miles apart, and at altitudes varying from 5000 ft. to 15,000 ft. Up in Mongolia, where a higher latitude compensates for a lower altitude,* they live on the open steppe and excavate burrows in the ground instead of utilising skrees and rock-falls. This difference in their environments causes their periods of hibernation to be erratic ; some go to sleep for long periods, others do not hibernate at all. In the same way their habit of laying-by surplus stores for emergency is not always for the same purpose ; some garner up for winter's use, others for famine during summer's drought. In dry climates, like Persia, they are adepts at acquiring anhydrous food-stuffs, which they carry home and pile into miniature haycocks before the entrances to their burrows.

I said the Saramat valley had no outlet, but I was wrong. There *is* a way out, but it is only feasible at the tail end of the summer, when the snows are at their minimum, and it leads over to Kara Kul, at the head waters of the Saratagh tributary of the Fan. There is also a goat track over into the next valley westwards—the Margian or Shink—and this I faced one day at dawn. It was a stiff climb, but I was rewarded by arriving at the top of the ridge before the clouds gathered, and I got a clear view of the summits of the Hissar range, peaks that I had heard of but never seen. There were three good ones, which suggested a height of not much under 20,000 ft. They had beauty of shape, too, they were not ordinary

---

* Other similar cases of high latitude compensating for low altitude, and of high altitude neutralising low latitude, that have come to my notice, relate to reindeer and yaks. The reindeer which inhabit the northern tundras, at little above sea level, can survive at the extreme southern limit of their range, around the head waters of the Yenisei, only on the highest mountain tops. While yaks, which the traveller from India does not expect to meet until well up into Ladak or Tibet, thrive at a comparatively low altitude in the Altai.

mountains. One was a sugar-loaf of rock and ice, another an enormous hump and therefore not looking so imposing, and a third, to the south, which I thought the highest of the lot. All of them would have fired the imagination of any climber. They provoked desire in me, too, for although I am no mountaineer, I have the urge to stand aloft to see what lies around ; and the view from any one of those summits would have been inspiring. They were some way off, ten or twelve miles, and unapproachable from this valley. Mountaineering and bird-collecting, however, do not harmonise ; in fact they are almost impossible to combine, from the fact that where one begins the other very naturally ends. But there are occasions when the two may overlap, and then comes the chance of a life-time. It happened to me once, and I had the unique opportunity of securing a double honour, namely, that of climbing a virgin mountain and at the same time collecting a new bird. This took place on the Ruwenzori Mountains, in the early days of its exploration. The bird was an outstanding discovery—a Sun-bird of great beauty (*Nectarinia dartmouthi* Ogilvie-Grant), inhabiting the uppermost regions of those mist-enshrouded mountains. At an altitude of between 12,000 and 14,000 ft., in semi-twilight and drifting fog, dwelt this delicate-looking splash of iridescent green, with scarlet wing-tufts—reminiscent of tropical jungle rather than of alpine scenery. Incidentally, this was the only occasion during many years' bird-hunting in wild places, on which I found that the fear of Man was not upon every fowl of the air. These little sun-birds would sometimes alight innocently on the barrel of my gun.

And the mountain ? Well, in those days anyone

who reached the snows of Ruwenzori was a pioneer ; and in the course of a day's work I would cross many a virgin snow-field, whilst my companion, the late Captain R. B. Woosnam, disregarding all the laws of mountaineering, and without any sort of alpine equipment, actually climbed as high as any man had ever climbed—with his collecting gun on his back ! Ruwenzori was untrodden ground, every peak was new, and many birds were, too, but these peaks I was looking at in the Hissar range were not in the same category ; for although they had never been climbed, it was unlikely that they hid any zoological secret.

The clouds surged up and hid them from view, and I dropped down into a new valley. The descent was the worst I had encountered. Loose skree slopes made me anxious for my donkeys and their now precious loads of specimens. At the beginning I thanked Allah that I had donkeys and not horses, but later on I would have given anything for human bearers in place of asses, such was the hazardous nature of the descent. At times I implored my men to unload, and portage my belongings across the places where one slip meant disaster. I could well believe that the inhabitants of these valleys were completely cut off from each other all the year round, except for a few months in summer, for I do not think that even a hare could make the passage in winter. I pictured my donkeys and their loads slithering down into the valley bottom, whither I would have to follow to gather up the remnants. But on turning a shoulder I saw with horror that the valley had no firm bottom —it was water ! Below me was a long narrow fiord-like lake, into which the mountains shelved at a sickening slant. The only way to proceed was to

crawl, spider-like, along the precipices that over-
hung it, and which tilted at such an angle that I
calculated I could spit into the water a thousand
feet below.

But alarm was quickly changed to wonder by the
amazing and unexpected colour of the water. The
lake must have been very deep for it appeared to be
pure turquoise, and it lay so still that it looked opaque.
There wasn't a ripple, nor an eddy ; there was no
reflection ; in fact it resembled coloured mud or a
newly opened tin of paint. Seldom have I seen such
savage scenery associated with such placid beauty :
it was terrible and yet sublime. The general
uniformity of tone, the lack of gradations of colour
and its curious consistency were the things that struck
me most. There appeared to be no local colour.
The water was the same in the centre as it was under
the steep rock walls, where it should have been
ultramarine or indigo. It was, as I have said, just
as if some giant had dammed the valley at its
narrowest, and then filled it up with millions of
gallons of turquoise paint (see Frontispiece).

I now realised that the slightest accident meant—
not picking up the pieces—but a swift and certain
death in fifty fathoms. So, advancing slowly, I
endured the anxiety of seeing my collections poised
on the edge of the abyss. Where the track was as
Nature made it, it was just passable, but where Man
had been forced to come to its aid, I took the precaution of unloading, and carrying, my belongings
across the most dangerous passages, since I had no
intention of losing the results of my labours. For the
natives' efforts at road-making up here were decidedly
primitive, indeed Primitive Man would probably

have made a better job of it. Yet I could but admire the ingenuity and the labour expended on these efforts to keep open some sort of communication with the outside world, for it must be tiresome to live in a valley which has no exit. Hence these so-called " balconettes," built by driving stakes into any odd hole or crack in the rocks, and thus setting up a scaffolding on which to lay a rickety platform. Only these balconies have no hand-rail.

It can be well imagined that these tracks are built for single-file, one-way, unladen traffic, for there is no room to spare. The native carries his load on his back. Man and donkey require but a few inches hold for his feet, and perhaps a two-foot clearance for his body; but anything in the nature of a load, except perhaps a saddle-bag, is asking for trouble, for one touch on a protruding rock—and the donkey is spun into space.

When we came to a section that actually hung out over the lake, I accomplished my spit into the water below, but it proved nothing. Then I hurled a stone, and counted ten before I saw a tiny circle form, but I heard not a sound. It must be oil, I said to myself. But it wasn't, for when we came to the barrier which Nature had flung across the valley to dam it, I could see a silver cascade of water running out to form the next tarn. There were seven altogether.

In places the track descended to the water's edge, in order to take advantage of some narrow shelf, which would facilitate the passage of an otherwise impassable cliff-face. And at times it was actually built out over the lake on piles driven in below the surface. But we never had to resort to the water itself as the only means of progress, as one has to do in some of the other narrower and even more inaccessible gorges.

Juma said he wished he was home again, but the water had a long, long way to go before it reached his home in Kara Kul. I could see how helpless his Uzbeg (plainsman's) legs were up here on these cornices ; compared with the cat-like native, he was a cripple.

I have been criticised for saying that this region contains some of the roughest country in the world. But if the valley of the Shink is not bad going I do not know what the term means. My companions told me that there were far more difficult paths farther east, which I can well believe, for this is only the fringe of a mountain uplift which increases in ruggedness as it climbs to the Roof of the World. The next valley, the Fan, is notorious, even amongst people who are as accustomed to " balconettes " as we are to pavements.

At last the perilous way descended to firm ground and I came to a village. But the village was deserted ; it was as empty and as silent as Pompeii or Petra ; there was neither dog nor fowl, nor any sign of human life. The houses stood empty ; the doors stood ajar. So complete was the summer exodus of the inhabitants to their alpine pastures, and so few were their household belongings, that they could go away and leave their front doors open.

I rested awhile on a grassy bank by the water's edge, for although the day's journey had not been really bad, it had been an over-anxious one—because of my collections. As a matter of fact, in the course of all my journeys, I have never lost one single specimen by accident, damage or theft. Once, indeed, a night-prowling jackal stole a skin off my tent-ropes, but even that was recovered, and the robber's also added to the bag.

The lower course of this valley was, like so many others in these parts, an almost impassable ravine. Foot passengers could traverse it, but beasts of burden had to skirt over the hills, and make their way *down* to the plain by stiff climbs *up* and over successive shoulders. I reckoned that, at times, I did not cover more than one mile per hour on my descent to the Zarafshan. However, this barrier forms an obstacle sufficient to embarrass anyone who might contemplate driving a motor-road up to the lovely lakes above. So the valley may retain its sublime seclusion, and preserve for ever its dual-character—of Beauty and Terror.

CHAPTER V

HIGH TARTARY

ONE of my objectives in the lands beyond the Caspian was a certain secluded tract of country situated under the western declivities of the Pamirs. The Pamirs themselves were of course fairly well known, even by Englishmen—the least likely, because the most suspect. But no matter how remote and forbidden the region, wherever big-game exists the hunter will, somehow or other, by hook or by crook, succeed in reaching it, even if the place be such a bone of contention as the wind-swept, good-for-little " Roof of the World."* But at that time Anglo-Russian jealousies were rampant ; no Englishman had been on the Pamirs for many a long year, and none were to be allowed. Anyway the Pamirs held no particular interest for me, but their western declivities—where the high valleys drop in precipitous decline to the Oxus, where the Oxus itself, escaping from its gorges, debouches on the plain, and forested islands replace the narrow canyons—that was the sort of place where there ought to be what we naturalists call " new stuff." We usually know where to look for it. Our knowledge is founded on innumerable scraps of information collected in a variety of ways. A stray feather, an old skin, a single horn has often provided a clue, which, when followed up, has resulted in the discovery of a new bird or beast, or information of equal value. A native name, a place-name on the map, a scrap of

* Of those who had been on the Pamirs with the express purpose of hunting *Ovis poli*, 95 per cent. appear to have been of British nationality.

bazaar gossip, may give away the secret. A knowledge of geography, climate, and vegetation contributes its quota. But there is also that subtle ray of imagination, granted to certain individuals but withheld from the many, which is worth more than all else combined.

The Darwaz region of Eastern Bukhara, where the Oxus makes its great bend round Badakshan, I considered to be well worth a visit. My speculations were strengthened by a certain amount of information which I collected locally, principally from an old Russian gold prospector, who had lived for years in that particular region. He told me of a small wild-sheep, not *Ovis poli*, which inhabited the rugged conglomerates of Yakhsu, whereas the nearest sheep of this type that I knew of were in Afghanistan. Hitherto the Oxus had been considered the hard and fast boundary between the respective ranges of the great *ammon* tribe of Middle Asia, and the small *vignei* races of South-western Asia.

He also described to me an animal which must have been a Markhor, but, except for Burnes' reference to Markhor being found on the hills south of Kunduz about a century ago, there was no reliable news of them north of the Hindu Kush—one hundred and fifty miles away. There was no apparent reason, it is true, why they should not extend their range north-wards into, and all over, Badakshan, but one *north* of the Oxus was a point of great interest, and should be investigated; for as a race the Markhor are not wide-ranging, and in their narrow domain they vary considerably in type.

Then there was the so-called Bactrian deer, a species represented in our National Museum by one solitary head of doubtful origin. The jungles of Urta

Tugai were certainly one of its principal refuges. They were very numerous thereabouts, so were wild-pig and tigers. Altogether it appeared as if the region would repay investigation. It held out a promise of useful work, and although I had speculated rather heavily, there were reasonable hopes of a good return. But it was not vouchsafed to me. International jealousy survived in spite of the fact that long-disputed frontiers had been finally fixed. An Englishman loose in Russian Turkestan was bad enough, but one on the Oxus was out of the question.

So, considering myself lucky in having been left undisturbed for so long, I did not risk the chance of incurring further suspicion by urging my case. After waiting eight months in hopes, I found myself baulked of my enterprise and had to turn to fields farther removed from the centre of the storm.

Star-eyed science, not being internationalised, suffered accordingly, but only temporarily. The Russians subsequently described my wild sheep, thus proving the old gold-digger to have been correct. For there *is* a wild sheep of the Urial type, the only representative of the group—*north* of the Oxus.

This Bukharan Urial was first described by Nasonov as a new sub-species, *Ovis vignei bochariensis*, closely allied to *Ovis vignei vignei*, but differing from it by reason of its slightly smaller size, and correspondingly lighter horns. Later on, Russian scientists, C. C. Flerov for instance, in 1935, came to the conclusion that all the various geographical races of Urial, as we know them, were really indistinguishable, that they all intergraded, and that they were but an Eastern form of the Persian *Ovis orientalis*. Accordingly, this Urial became, to them, *Ovis vignei* Blyth, or

Ovis orientalis vignei. Still more recently, however, its position has been clarified, and it is now re-established as *Ovis vignei bochariensis* Nasonov. Doubtless those unexplored mountains just across the Oxus, in northernmost Badakshan, are full of Urial, which we would expect to be *Ovis vignei cycloceros.*

In habits and type of habitat these sheep do not seem to differ much from their cousins. They prefer hill country of a type that grants protection by its rugged nature, even if this necessitates living at a low altitude. They seem to prefer steppe vegetation to alpine. In Eastern Bukhara, which has a background of mountains running up to 20,000 ft., the Urial choose for preference the outlying spurs which have an altitude of under 10,000 ft. They like the forested hills where pistachio groves flourish on northern slopes. It will be remembered that Marco Polo reported the Urial as being especially numerous hereabouts, actually referring to Badakshan—" In the mountains are vast numbers of sheep—400, 500, or 600 in a single flock, and all of them wild ; and though many of them are taken, they never seem to get aught the scarcer." That was some years ago, but the Urial are a prolific race and in remote regions such as these they can still muster flocks of a hundred or more during the winter period.

Apparently all the country that I intended to traverse, between the Hissar mountains and the Oxus, was the home of this Urial. Its principal present-day refuges are the Yakhsu conglomerates, the Kara Tau— which lie to the east of the Vakhsh in its lower course, and all those lesser ranges which run down to the Oxus from the north, even as far west as Kelif. They do not, apparently, range eastwards beyond Darwaz, nor has their occurrence north of the Vakhsh on the Zarafshan divide been confirmed since Fedchenko and Severtzov recorded them from there more than seventy years ago.

The Markhor, too, extend northwards from Afghanistan, into Eastern Bukhara, where, depending on low rugged hill-country rather than on height, they find ample ground, exactly to their liking, in the conglomerates of Yakhsu. Their range is not very wide, and their type seems to be confusing. By rights, they should be allied to their neighbours across the Oxus, the Afghan or Kabul sub-species, *Capra falconeri megacerus*, but some Russian zoologists (Trubetskoy and Flerov) are insistent that here in their country the Markhor show such a diversity of form in their horn structure that our classification of them into six sub-species should be reconsidered and revised. They claim that the Markhor of Eastern Bukhara, a comparatively small area, exhibit every conceivable type of horn, from the wide-spreading spiral such as *Capra falconeri falconeri* of Astor, to the straight screw pattern, such as *Capra falconeri jerdoni* of the Sulaiman mountains. They say that even one herd may contain more than one type—a peculiarity by no means exclusive to Russian Markhor, for those south of the Hindu Kush exhibit the same tendency to variation. The zoological museums in Moscow and Leningrad provide an abundance of proof of this statement regarding specimens from *within* their own territory, but it is questionable whether they have sufficient material for comparison, from regions *beyond* their frontiers, to enable them to form a sound judgment on the classification of the genus as a whole,

One of the main difficulties in attempting to classify the various races of Markhor is due to the lack of reliable " localities " for existing material. Without these essential facts at our disposal the comparison of specimens is unprofitable. On the other hand, any attempt to distinguish the various forms by their geographical status alone would be equally futile. According to Burrard, examples of, or akin to, the five races of Markhor belonging to British India and Afghanistan have been recorded from one and the same area, namely, that between Northern Baluchistan and Chitral, the Kabul, Sulaiman, Astor, Pir Panjal and Chialtan races (or types akin to them) all overlapping here, and, what is more important, apparently without intergradation, unless the head of dual nature, carrying horns of two types, can be said to be of this category. If, indeed, types as distinct as those from the Kashmir district can turn up so far away from their true habitat as Northern Baluchistan, and if the Afghan *megaceros* extends also to Quetta and Chitral,* there must, indeed, be a considerable mixture of types within a small area. And this is exactly what Flerov says of the Markhor of Eastern Bukhara.

* Stockley says " it is hard to define the borderline, for heads from Chitral, and even from Baluchistan, are sometimes of the ' Pir Panjal ' type, while there is great variation in Afghanistan heads." Of the ten examples of the Kabul *megaceros* listed in the British Museum Catalogue of Ungulates, two only are labelled " Afghanistan," the remainder are alleged to have come from Quetta or Chitral. But " localities," as given on the labels of museum specimens are often unreliable. This applies especially to those which have been " acquired " or picked up in native bazaars, and even to those seen hanging on tombs and mosques. Horns travel far and endure for ages. For instance, those roe-buck horns, already green with age, and the favourite perch of the Flycatchers, hung to the walls of my farm-house home in Norfolk, may confuse some enthusiastic enquirer into East Anglian roe-deer in years to come; they actually came from Siberia !

• Recently, however, Russian zoologists have gone to the opposite extreme. Zalkin (1945), after an exhaustive examination of all available specimens from Russian territory (sixty in all), contradicts the conclusions arrived at by his forerunners. He declares that he finds a distinct uniformity of type, instead of pronounced variation, and notes such marked differences between the Markhor of Bukhara and *all* other races, that he feels justified in creating two new sub-species. Accordingly, those of the Yakhsu region are now known as *Capra falconeri heptneri*, and those of the isolated Kuh-i-Tang hills as *Capra falconeri ognevi*. The former appear to conform to the Kashmir type, the latter to the Kabul.

We have neither photographs nor horn measurements of these Russian specimens, but Zalkin's outline drawings of his two new sub-species are not distinguishable from many a Kashmir and Afghan head. The only other illustration we have of a Bukharan Markhor, namely, that in *Wild Animals of Tadjikistan*, under the section on the Ungulates by C. C. Flerov, depicts a typical straight-horned, screw-pattern head of the Sulaiman race.

If Zalkin's observations are correct, then Bukhara is the *only* locality wherein Markhor conform to type ; if Flerov is right then Markhor show the same tendency to abnormality all their world over.

The localities given on the Moscow specimens show that the Markhor used to extend over all those outlying ranges which lie between the Oxus and the Hissar mountains, from Darwaz in the east to the Baisun district, north of Termez, in the west. The Baba Dagh and the Kuh-i-Tang both held Markhor, and a few still survive on the latter range, for although of no great height—it reaches 10,000 ft. at one point only—the Kuh-i-Tang is of a peculiarly rough limestone formation. But their present-day habitat is concentrated within the area bounded by Baljuan, Kuliab, Kala Khum and Garm, which suggests that their main refuge is, virtually speaking, the Yakhsu conglomerates, from where they were first reported to me. And I cannot imagine a safer retreat, or a more perfect preserve for a goat, than that labyrinth of crags running up to 13,000 ft., carved and cut by a network of deep canyons, forming one great impregnable fortress for any wild thing that took to it for safety. The Yakhsu might hold any mystery, and could keep any secret ; the Markhor was one of them.

Since Markhor extend thus far north of the Oxus, one wonders how far they may range westwards across Afghanistan. It would not be surprising to find them over the whole of its mountain area, even to the uttermost outlying spurs of the Paropanisus system ; but we do know that there is no record of them ever crossing the frontier into Persia.

The Bactrian or Bukharan Deer (*Cervus bactrianus*) still exist in that region, but in reduced numbers, and, happily, are now " protected." This rare and little-known species is a small red-deer, usually with a four-tined head of no great size, allied to the Kashmir Hangul, but with the habits of the Yarkand deer. They frequent the riverine belt of vegetation and never go up into the hills, relying for safety on the protection afforded by swampy ground and jungles of reeds, tamarisk, and berberis. One would have thought their chances of survival slight, sharing as they do so small and confined an area with tigers, but the Russians say that they more than hold their own.

Elsewhere they survive only around the mouths of the Oxus and the Syr, and possibly in the region connecting the two deltas, as well as the lower course of the Sary Su. Their supposed existence on the Tedjen, in the Transcaspian Kara Kum, seems doubtful. But on the Upper Oxus from the mouth of the Kafirnahan up to Chubek, and in the jungles bordering the lower courses of its tributaries, the Kafirnahan, Vakhsh, Kunduz, Kokcha, and Kizil Su, they are probably more numerous—or rather less rare—than elsewhere. The island of Urta Tugai, formed by a branching of the Oxus, and covering an area of about two hundred square miles, is doubtless their main refuge.

This is also the last resort of the tiger on the Upper Oxus; its range coinciding almost exactly with the area frequented by the deer.

Geography, climate and vegetation, I remarked, are often a clue to a discovery of biological interest. In Central Asia there is one particular land feature of outstanding character, namely, the Pamir, a phenomenon more fully developed here than anywhere else in the world. Typified by the group of seven or eight Pamirs, composing the so-called Roof of the World, there are several others, less well known, but of exactly the same formation, with more or less the same climatic conditions and the same vegetation. These are mostly situated around the central Massif, or in the neighbouring western Tian Shan. The distinctive characteristics of these Pamirs are very high altitude, very slight erosion, phenomenal dryness, and consequently steppe-like vegetation. To enlarge on these peculiarities : high altitude means from 12,000 to 14,000 ft. above sea-level ; slight

AK SAI "PAMIR" PASTURES

TIAN SHAN FOREST BELT

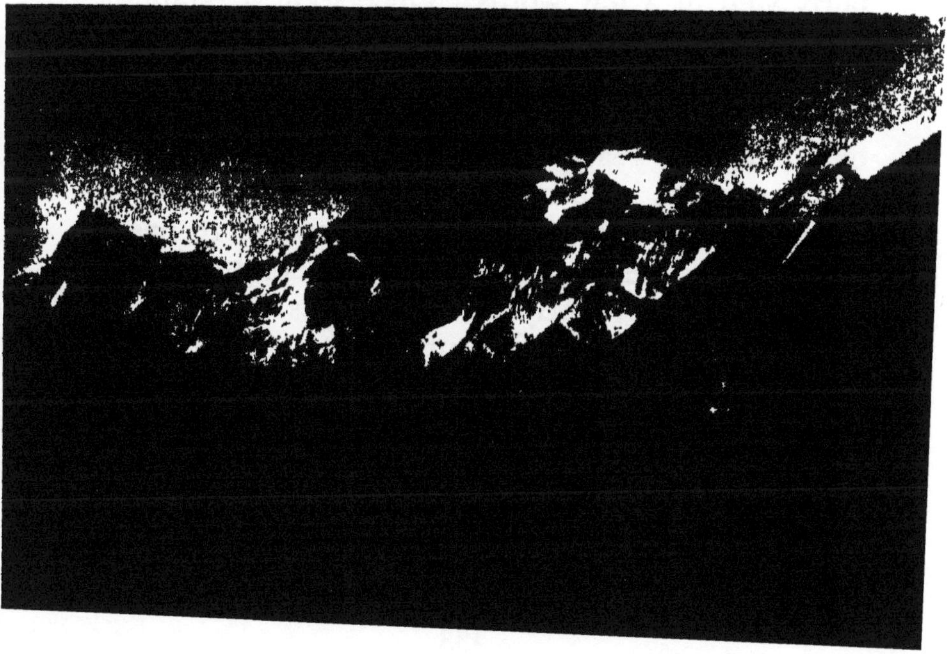

erosion, resulting in wide open valleys, means that the rivers have not been able to carve out deep valleys for themselves, owing to the third factor, unusual dryness. And this last is perhaps the most significant of all, for altitudes such as these rarely escape a heavy snowfall. But here, in the heart of Asia, certain elevated areas do escape, owing principally to their being situated within a surrounding wall of even greater height which, catching the rainfall, robs the inner area of its due. The result is that these high valleys have a precipitation which scarcely equals that of the most arid desert. In consequence, they can only support a desert type of vegetation, a scanty though very nourishing grazing, and there is a complete absence of trees.

A Pamir is notoriously difficult to describe concisely. A series of high, wide, sheltered depressions in a surrounding world of shale and snow—covers it fairly well in a few words. Once seen, it establishes itself as a distinctive type of scenery, a land feature all to itself, as for instance a Scotch moor does. In the same way a glacial moraine, whether of recent origin or millions of years old, is recognisable at a glance, and cannot be mistaken for anything else. So with a Pamir; it is difficult to define because it has no counterpart, there is nothing exactly like it elsewhere, and, as Curzon aptly remarks, it is " among the deliberate paradoxes of Nature."

It is easy to see, therefore, that such a phenomenon should have an interesting fauna. In the case of the Great Pamirs, it is principally the giant mountain-sheep, named after Marco Polo, who first reported their existence in 1274. But there are other Pamirs which, although of lesser historic interest, might also furnish study for the naturalist. The nearest approach to the prototype, in size and construction, and at no great distance from it, is the Ak Sai.

This Pamir lies to the east of the Farghana, where the Tian Shan mountain system is linked to the true Pamir massif, by the connecting ridge of the Alai.* Although lying wholly within the Russian frontier, the Ak Sai actually drains to China, for it is situated around the headwaters of the Ak Sai source of the Taushkan branch of the Tarim River, which ultimately ends in Lop Nor. Adjoining the Ak Sai, but separated from it by the self-contained basin of Chatir Kul (corresponding to the Kara Kul basin on the Great Pamirs) is another, but smaller, Pamir, the Arpa. The two together cover an area about as large as Wales. They were famous grazings in Timur's day, and still are. The more I examined this particular region, the more I realised its possibilities, for the Tian Shan was a distinctive faunistic and floristic zone, and in no way connected with those lands beyond the Caspian wherein I had so far travelled and worked.

The way to the Ak Sai and Arpa Pamirs led up through that great cul-de-sac of Central Asia, the Farghana, which entices the traveller hopefully

---

* This hundred-mile long range running from the true Alai to the true Tian Shan is called the Tian Shan by some authorities, the Alai by others. I think it is without doubt an extension of the Alai system and should be so called. There are no recognised routes across it east of the well-known Terek Pass, but there are hypothetical passes, probably of the same category as the one I attempted to cross (see p. 147), but which are, like it, impracticable three years out of four. The effective character of this—Nature's Great Wall of China—is clearly shown by the fact that the best route which can be found by a brisk trade between Kashgar and the Farghana is by this indirect and arduous Terek Pass, and the present day motor-road follows the same line.

eastwards, only to bar his further passage by a formidable mountain wall. There is no easy exit from the Farghana. Perhaps this accounts for its peculiar atmosphere, which I found to contrast strangely with other parts of Central Asia. If I wished to feel the pulse of Asia, I should go to the Farghana and sit in the bazaars of Khokand, being certain that if anything of importance happened in Khiva or Kumul, Kabul or Kuldja, I should know of it sooner here than I should elsewhere. Although the Farghana might be called the Kashmir of Central Asia, in so far as climate, scenery, fruit and flowers are concerned, there is a very marked difference in their respective inhabitants. The men of the Farghana are men of action, and have thrown up such comets as Baber and Yakub Beg. Under any but Russian rule, the green flag of fanaticism would have been unfurled more often. The Khokandis are of a particularly explosive temperament, and are certainly more full of guts and energy than the dwellers in more southerly oases. As fiery as the horses, for which they were famous, they have more than once provided the spark that set alight a local rising or some more serious conflagration.

That indefinable line of demarcation between what have been called northern and southern temperaments, which runs across southern Europe, the Black Sea and the Caucasus, seems to extend across Central Asia on about this latitude. The Farghana I should place on the borderline. To the north are hardier and more virile races than to the south.

The Farghana is chiefly famous for Baber's brilliant, if somewhat ephemeral, little kingdom. And you have only to read his *Memoirs* to understand what a delectable region it is. Even to Baber, who loved life and all the good things of life, and enjoyed to the full everything that life had to give, the Farghana seemed the last word in excellence. Whether it was food, hunting, or horses, those of the Farghana were, to him, the best. Its pheasants were the fattest, its waters the purest, its melons surpassed the finest Bukharan, its horses were " celestials " and the envy of all Asia. He extols its climate ; I do not think he exaggerated. For the climate of the Farghana, being ameliorated by the surrounding protective mountain-walls, is more mellow than that of any other part of the Duab of Turkistan. It does not suffer from those extremes of temperature for which the region is remarkable. It is unusual for the Syr to freeze up here, although it freezes at a *lower* altitude. Hence the wealth of fruit of all sorts : the wild varieties, such as strawberries and raspberries, grow in such profusion that there is unlimited jam for all who care to go and pick, while even the tender Pistachio produces nuts. Such was the Farghana in Baber's day and so it is now, for of all Middle Asia it is the least changed, tucked away between the ranges, and cut off on all sides but one from the outside world.

The whole of this region drains by one great river system, the Syr—the Jaxartes of the Greeks, the Saihun of the Arabs—to the sea of Aral. The Oxus, as we have seen, is a river of great renown, with brilliant prospects, but the Syr, with less notoriety, may be its competitor. Although the Syr is the longer by more than two hundred miles, its catchment area is slightly less, and its volume—after watering the Farghana, considerably less than that of its historic brother ; yet it creates at the present time a larger area of cultivation, and flows through a land whose potential wealth may well prove to be as great as, if not greater than that of the Oxus basin. In ancient days the Syr watered even larger areas, which, although they have slipped back temporarily to desert, must some day return again to the use of man.

On entering the Farghana valley from the west we are immediately upon historic ground. It was here, in the narrow entrance gap, that Alexander the Great founded the farthest of his cities—a veritable outpost of Greek civilisation in the barbarous wilderness. The position was well chosen, on the southern bank of the river Syr, with the main trans-continental trade-route between East and West, the northernmost Silk Route —the most northerly indeed of any established way across Asia—passing close by. The Syr in those days marked the uttermost limit of settled life and government in this direction, for beyond it was Nomad's Land, where nothing was established, and nothing remained fixed. It was the frontier of Iran and Turan ; many centuries were to elapse before the Turanian flood flowed southwards to the Hindu Kush. All that vastness of Asia north of the Syr—" eternal motherland of vigorous migrants "—had been for all time the home of those innumerable, fluid, roaming peoples, against whom not even the Greeks could make any headway, and into which void the Persian Empire at its zenith never expanded one yard.

This bottle-neck leading to the Farghana is about twenty miles wide, and through it flows the Syr Darya, the third of our great rivers " beyond the Caspian." It has flowed through the heart of the Farghana without dissipating much of its waters, for it is a significant fact that all the great areas of cultivation but one, live by tributary water originating in the Alai mountains, and *not* by the Syr. There remains, therefore, a great opportunity here for irrigation works on a colossal scale, an opportunity the Russians have not failed to make good use of, for the Syr carries a very great deal of water, and is snow fed. One wonders what the conditions were in the centuries B.C., when, according to reliable Chinese sources, the Farghana boasted seventy walled cities. To-day there are only half-a-dozen towns of notable size. All these, except Namangan, lie close under the southern wall—the Alai, so close, indeed, that one can obtain no real idea of its true height and grandeur. In order to appreciate this one should ride out into the middle of the basin, to the banks of the Syr, from where the Alai and its subsidiaries stand up in their full beauty—a two hundred-mile-long snow-capped ridge, averaging 14,000 ft. in height, unbroken by any visible pass or divide. The range rises sheer from the floor of the valley, behind the settlements of Khokand and Margelan, and continues to the east, north-east and finally to the north in one great glorious unbroken half-circle.

Cross-sections, especially from unusual angles, are always instructive. With the eye of a vulture soaring high over the Syr, I let my imagination take a short cut direct to India. Below me the black frowning flanks of the Alai stood like the guardian of the South; and close under it I could just discern the track that the old caravans used when passing from Kashgar to Sogdiana. Beyond the Alai lay a broad, flat, transverse valley, like a green trough, dotted with innumerable Kirghiz encampments, and along it ran the second great arterial trade route between

East and West. Beyond, again, rose the Trans-Alai range, greater than its northern namesake, and the impressive pile of Peter the Great range, amongst whose summits were the highest peaks in the Russian Empire. Further to the south, Pamir succeeded Pamir, in giant corrugations, to where a thin silver streak denoted the upper Oxus. Here again a narrow track indicated the third " way-through " this mountain world, the corridor by which passed all the learning and the art that India gave to China. Beyond this rose the stormy Hindu Kush, guardian of the North ; and beyond again a labyrinth of lesser ranges dropping to the Indus and the plains of Hindustan.

Turning north, the outlook was very different. The encirclement of the Farghana was completed by mountains, it is true, but they were less impressive and less famous than those to the south. There seemed to be no romance about them. They were not inhabited by mountaineers of ancient lineage, there were no sedentary cultivators tied to the soil by virtue of acquisition and reclamation. There were few ancient sites or time-worn ways. In other words, it was not " Central Asia," although it might be called a neutral zone between it and Siberia. And beyond the northern ring of mountains ?—vast horizon-bounded plains as far as eye could see and imagination carry one. First desert, then steppe, then downland, then cornland merging into the cold northern forests and tundras that border the Arctic Seas. The Syr is, indeed, the dividing line between two fundamentally different spheres ; as Baber remarked, it is " the extreme boundary of the habitable world."

Back in Andijan I found the busiest horse-bazaar

that I had yet seen, which is not to be wondered at since this is rail-head. And what a rail-head ! To see another train one would have to go up to the Turkestan-Siberian Railway, south to Peshawar or east to Pekin. I bought four horses of an excellent type, and hoped to be gone quick from the flies, and the heat, and filth of my caravanserai. This was, I suppose, the best the place could offer, and for ought I know had been honoured by all the great travellers who had passed this way, from Chang Kien onwards. Perhaps it used to be under better management, but at the time of my visit, its sanitation was nil, and its lack of privacy revolting. There was no reason to *look* " how wide also the East is from the West." I can live " native " in the wilds and enjoy it, but to attempt the same on the edge of civilisation is disastrous. The one redeeming feature was the fruit, which not only ripened earlier here than elsewhere, but was of a quality which well merited Baber's many allusions to its variety and excellence. I used to breakfast off green-tea, native bread, and little white figs, which were hawked round already skinned and iced. Apricots, peaches, pomegranates and melons followed during the day.

The inhabitants of this ancient capital of the Farghana, like those of most key-towns on trunk trade routes, were crafty, money-grabbing, pleasure-seeking and shockingly immoral. I was glad to leave for Osh, where the air was cleaner, the horses better and even cheaper. Here I completed my caravan and rode for Uskent—the last town in the eastern Farghana. The inhabitants of Osh must be possessed of a certain æsthetic sense, for they have deliberately utilised the natural beauties of the locality in their town-planning. Their eating-houses and tea-shops were built out on little piers overhanging the river, which flowed through the town. Here they could sit and enjoy the natural beauties of waterfalls and gushing torrents, and benefit by the cooler air which accompanied them. The " picturesque " was in marked evidence at every turn in the bazaars, and on every stretch of the river.

Between Osh and Uskent is lovely country, rather like the Canadian foothills of the Rocky Mountains. The altitude was about 4000 ft. and crops could be grown without irrigation. So it was not altogether surprising to come suddenly upon colonies of Russian peasants, who had emigrated to this distant corner of their Empire, and settled down permanently and apparently successfully. The rolling hills were one wide wheat-field, and typically-Russian villages nestled in the hollows, looking homely and prosperous. But the fact of them being here at all gave one much food for thought. They were an isolated community, living cheek by jowl with the indigenous native population, a population consisting of mixed races of purely Asiatic origin, and of a different religion. Below them on the plain was, perhaps not a seething, but a very numerous society of Moslem cultivators, who had been there always. Above them in the mountains, and on the plateaux, was another and possibly more incompatible element, the nomadic or semi-nomadic Kara Kirghiz, a race much more likely to resent the presence of incoming Russian emigrants, and one, owing to their Turkish-Mongol origin, more likely to be aggressive. Yet, all seemed to go well. There was no race-hatred and no religious antagonism between the two. The Russians did not look upon the " natives " as such ; they fraternised in a way I have never seen East and West do before. I racked my brains for an equivalent within the British Empire, but could not recall one. The fact remained that if this was a true example of how Russia deals with Asia, her future there is assured. Indeed, it appeared to me that the Russians had inherited that quality which certain ancient Asiatic invaders of the West had possessed in full measure, namely—" the necessary gift for all people destined to political predominance—tolerant assimilation."

Uskent had the atmosphere of a town from which glory had departed. It must have been a great place once, and was doubtless one of those walled cities of which Chang Kien spoke. I can hardly credit the supposition that Uskent had anything to do with Greek-Bactria, but its ruins do suggest an age and a prosperity even greater than it enjoyed in the sixteenth century, when it was acknowledged to be the most important town of the whole Farghana.* There is a fine Minar of tessellated tile-work, very like the Minar Katan, in Bukhara.

My forty rouble (£4) ponies pleased me, and as I rode along, enjoying their paces, after donkey transport, I recalled that the Farghana had always been famous for its horses, and that their excellence had been responsible for one of the greatest horse-raids in history. The possession of good horses was as vital to the early Empires of Asia, as the ownership, or control, of oilfields is to-day for the well-being of progressive States ; while for war-making they were as essential as tanks are now. The simple fact that

* See *Tarikh-i-Rashidi*, p. 320.

the Huns possessed more and better horses than the Chinese forced the latter to build the Great Wall, which, far from being a " folly," was one of the most stupendous and effective defensive works ever conceived and carried out by Man. Not having sufficient horses to compete in open warfare, the Chinese completely double-crossed their arch-enemies by rendering their own territory secure against aggression. But on the other hand they could not take the offensive without many more horses of an improved type. And so it happened that the Farghana, far away as it was, appeared in the Chinese Annals about two thousand years ago. Having first tried diplomacy and failed, the Chinese had to resort to force, and sent a military expedition to " acquire " what they needed. Thus, about 100 B.C., Farghana horses were driven off in large numbers to augment, and improve, the Chinese Imperial stud.

At first sight the Farghana does not give one the impression of being a horse-country ; but neither does Transcaspia for that matter, yet we are told that the Chinese penetrated so far in search of Turkoman horse-flesh. But may not the proximity of such renowned pastures as the Alai valley be the secret of the Farghana studs ? For the Alai, although a Pamir, is of a lower altitude than the type, but with a higher precipitation, consequently it has better pastures, in fact some of the richest grazing in all Central Asia.

Here I cut all ties with so-called civilisation—that is to say, with an existence in which one is entirely dependent on somebody else for everything. From now onwards I was absolutely dependent upon myself. I had four good ponies, two rotten servants, no guide, and my own wits. As I faced the main Farghana range I confess my spirits sank. The Russian 40 verst map, a marvel of production, covering a colossal area, is on too small a scale to travel by in mountainous country. It showed a pass, aptly called Suok —the cold—at the head of the Kara Kuldja valley, up which I was riding, which appeared to lead direct to the Ak Sai Pamir. But passes, in this part of the world, are not always as they appear on the map.

The Kara Kuldja seemed to be an important river. It is the head, or one of the heads, of the Kara Darya which is by far the largest tributary received by the Syr, from either bank in all its length, and is considered by some to be the main source of the Syr, and, in point of fact, it does, at certain seasons of the year, carry a greater volume of water than does the Narin, in spite of the latter's far greater length. For the Kara Darya drains, with its tributaries, the Yassi and the Tarz (Tara or Taz), the whole of the east and south-eastern corner of the Farghana ; that is to say the entire Farghana and Farghana-Alai ranges feed it, and these being under perpetual snow the water supply never fails. We found this to our cost for the river had to be crossed and recrossed many times. In some places it flowed through a wide shingly bed, broken up into many channels, which could be forded with circumspection ; in others the geological formation of the hills forced the river through some narrow chasm a few yards wide, and here the shepherds had built rickety bridges for their own use.

Cultivation extended beyond Uskent for a day's journey, above this there was a zone of rank vegetation, such as I had not seen before in Turkestan. The ponies ploughed their way through high grass and golden sorrel, which reached to their bellies. There were tangles of roses, and sweeps of senecios ; starwort grew by the acre, hollyhock, pyrethrum, columbine, flea-bane, asphodel, and poppies spangled the hill-sides, and all were smothered in a flutter of bright butterflies. There was not much tree growth, but in certain localities the valley bottom was choked with poplar, plane and giant walnuts. There were some birch, oak and apple.

This solved some bird problems for me. For instance, those Scarlet Finches (*Carpodacus erythrinus roseatus* Blyth), which I had noticed passing through the Samarkand valley at the end of April, obviously going farther north to breed—this was their breeding zone and they were here in numbers.. So were many other birds, the majority of which were new to me, but they were all in such a dilapidated state of moult that I did not bother to collect them.

At about 8000 ft. vegetation ceased in the face of the terrific and appalling disintegration which was going on all around. The hillsides were denuded of all growth, there being no holding ground for even a blade of grass. There must have been an everlasting movement of material in order to produce this state of affairs, snow-slide in spring, mud-avalanche and land-slip later, and slither of rock and shale going on all the time. The result was a scene as forbidding as it was dangerous. It was black, jagged, craggy, slippery, and cold. The little track which dared this confusion bristled with horrible possibilities, a drowning in the torrent, a burial under a land-slide, or just a dead halt, where it would be impossible to proc d

and equally difficult to retreat. In places the valley
bottom was choked with snow, the residue of earlier
avalanches, and this sometimes made the going easier.
But for the most part we spent our time climbing shale
slopes in order to avoid the chasm below, or following
the river to avoid the precipices above. My plain-
bred ponies were out of their element ; the baggage-
pony went down, dragged another with him, and both
rolled down a steep shale slope. Luckily they ended
up on soft ground and not in the river. But it took
me some hours to collect my scattered belongings,
and to mend the broken gear. The outlook was as
black as the hills around me, but " difficulty makes
desire," and I kept on towards the pass.

Such a place one would hardly expect to be
inhabited, but, as a matter of fact, nearly every
side-valley had an " alp " in its upper reaches, and
there, far away up under the snow-fields, were bright
green meadows which were dotted with the white
felt tents of the Kirghiz. If any of these were within
reasonable distance of my evening camp I would
send a man up there to procure sour-milk, junket
or cheese.

On the fourth day I began to doubt the wisdom of
going on, progress was so slow and so hard on the
ponies. But, at this juncture, a party of Kirghiz
came on the scene, ten of them, riding their little hill-
ponies, and each one carrying a leathern bottle of
kumiz as their sole ration for the journey over the
range to Kashgar. They passed me at a shuffle,
which exactly describes the action of their ponies as
they traversed the shale-slopes at an easy speed. They
hailed me, pointed upwards towards the pass, crying
the equivalent of " Excelsior," and were soon out of

sight. This was encouraging, so we proceeded till nightfall, when we lay down amongst the rocks, and the ponies had no feed.

Next morning, as we were loading up, who should appear but our friends the ten Kirghiz, riding their little ponies, and each one still carrying his bottle of *kumiz*. They came scurrying down the valley, as sure-footed as yaks, and seemed in no way disconcerted at their failure to make the pass. They told me that it was closed, and that I had better follow them along to the next one, the Sur-Tash, which was sure to be open. They passed on down the valley at what appeared to me to be break-neck speed. I was only too glad of a reasonable excuse to follow them, for I certainly could not have hoped to succeed where they had failed. The truth was that the way up the Kara Kuldja to the pass at its head is entirely at the mercy of the elements, and in the hands of Nature. This year's track might be obliterated by next spring's land-slides, and it is difficult to believe that it could remain intact over the upper part of the valley for any length of time. So I should put a query on the map after the word Suok and its altitude around 13,000 ft.

But the Kirghiz considered it worth trying as it would certainly have been a short-cut to Kashgar, had it been open. Having attained the Suok Pass and the Arpa plateau beyond, they would have had to cross another pass—over the Kashgar range—before dropping down to Chinese Turkestan.

A very confused mass of mountains lies at the head of the Kara Kuldja. Three ranges meet there, the Farghana, the Kashgar (as this south-western outlier of the Tian Shan is sometimes erroneously called),

and the Alai ; and the rivers run in several directions
—east to the Tarim, west to the Syr, and north to the
Naryn or upper Syr.

I was in no hurry to follow my Kirghiz friends
as I knew I could not keep up with them. So,
retreating down the valley, I found a convenient
summer encampment in a lateral valley, and spent
two days there resting my ponies and recuperating
myself on the native diet of fermented milk of mares.
I agree with Marco Polo that it is " a right good
drink," but the local brew must have been an
exceptionally strong one ; I found it pleasantly
intoxicating, but my servants, drinking deeper,
became incapable of rendering any service, until they
had slept off the ill-effects. Around my tent was
spread a perfect little garden of wild flowers—
ranunculus, pansies, omphaloides, gentians, forget-me-
nots, purple and yellow fumitory, orange erigeron,
alpine poppies, and many other varieties I could not
name. There were many birds, too, new to me, but
the Dippers were White-bellied, the same as those on
the high Hissar streams, and the Whistling Thrush I
found to range thus far northwards. It was a pretty
spot—a wide green grassy flat, flower-strewn, and
watered by innumerable little rills fresh from the
snows. There were the clusters of snug felt tents,
domed like bee-skeps, and droves of horses, flocks of
sheep, and herds of cows grazing over the hillsides.
The inhabitants were hospitable by custom, but
avaricious by nature. They kept open-house, the
evening meals being veritable Belshazzar feasts, but
they would quibble over threepence for a purchase.
The women, of course, were the worst ; a bargain
might be completed with the man, but should the wife

disapprove, the deal was off! I always found this with the Kirghiz, one never knew exactly where one was with them. No reliance could be placed upon them. Shifty, cunning, self-seeking in everyday life, one met a more generous and more likeable nature only when it came to companionship in travel, hardship or hunting.

The same strong type still endures : as of yore, " it is the women who do the buying and selling, and whatever is necessary to provide for the husband and household, for the men all lead the life of gentlemen, troubling themselves about nothing but hunting and hawking."

The approach to the Sur Tash pass was clearly marked out for me by the devastation caused by some thousands of sheep which had been driven over it recently from the plateau beyond. They had eaten off every living thing on a wide front. The shepherds who drove them were as primitive as their flocks, being clothed from head to foot in sheep-skins. In the Sur Tash valley was the first true forest that I had seen in Turkestan. It was only a patch, but they were " wild " trees—spruce—and were evidently the fringe of the Tian Shan forest zone, and therefore within its rain-belt.

The actual crossing of the pass was comparatively easy. Snow still lay (August) in the valley bottom, and we kept to it for preference, for the rock walls on either side looked most uninviting. The passage of the sheep had made a good hard track over the mile-long snowdrift which led up to the final climb, and though this last pull was stiff, the reward was great. For, from the crest of the pass, I got one of those views that only a country as vast as Central Asia can supply. Below and behind us was the Farghana, spread out like an old, mellowed Bukharan rug. The snowy crest of the Alai shimmered mysteriously high above the haze of the plain—cloud-like—baseless. To the south were regions of colour, as mountain succeeded mountain to infinity. But before us on the other side of the pass was something entirely new. No steep descent led down to the inevitable valley that usually greets the climber to the summit of a great divide. There was practically no descent at all. The rocks and the shale and the snow-fields ran down at an easy gradient to beautiful grassy slopes. The slopes spread themselves out into broader sweeps of undulating downland. A free country, easy-going, unhampered. I had reached the famous plateau pastures, which are a governing factor in the economic life of Central Asia.

Here scenery was designed on a colossal scale. The Pamir before me was the Arpa. I overlooked the whole of it, with the Arpa river winding like a silver thread through the midst. Beyond it, over a far distant horizon, I knew, but could not see, that the Arpa merged into the Chatir Kul basin, and that again into the Ak Sai—my destination. A boundless and inspiring landscape—High Tartary indeed.

Skirting the snow-fields that lay along the northern slopes of the Farghana range, we kept to the highest grass just under the shale and found the going good. Occasionally snouts of snow extended across our track, which showed that our altitude was about 10,000 ft. A few days ago I was sweltering in the heat, and living on semi-tropical fruit ; now I rode through drifting mist, icy wind, and rain, with the marmot's

HIGH TARTARY

whistle for my morning call, and hot tea the only
antidote to shivers. It was austere and exacting, and
the first evening proved it, for the one essential of life
at high altitude—fuel to cook on—was lacking.
Timberless countries and desert areas usually produce
something in the way of a scrub or a root which will
serve the purpose and boil a kettle, but these plateaux
did not ; and unless they have been habitually used
as grazing ground, even dung is denied one. But
such famous pastures as the Arpa can supply this
commodity in variety, and it is not long before one
becomes an expert in deciding the respective merits
of the droppings of horse, cow, sheep and camel.
Cow and sheep were the best, if dry and of a certain
age ; even when damp they were better than the
others, and this being the wet season they were always
my choice. The only thing that defeated us was a
fresh fall of snow ; then we had to go without cooked
food and hot drinks—a sore trial at this height, in a
land far beyond the reach of my native whisky.

Besides being a dividing line 'twixt wood and
dung fuel, the Farghana range is also a zoological
boundary between certain Central Asian species
such as the marmots. These offered a fair example
of two species of a widely dispersed genus just
overlapping, although their respective territories were
distinctly marked by a hard and fast line which in
this case was the Farghana range. All over the
Pamirs, and the Bukharan ranges, and indeed all the
mountains lying to the south-west of the Farghana
range, and on the south side of this range itself, the
Long-tailed Red Marmot (the *caudata* group) is the
only representative of its genus. Immediately one
passes north and east over this range the Short-tailed

Brown Marmot (*M. baibacina*)* appears, and eventually takes the place of the Red. But there is a zone where the two overlap. In the lower part of the Kara Kuldja valley the Red Marmot is found in small numbers, but higher up, at about 8000 ft., I noticed a few Brown, or partially-Brown, individuals in among the Red. On the Arpa plateau, around the Sur Tash pass, there are Red and Brown in the same colonies. But at the Kara Kul river the Red disappears entirely, and the Brown is found, in enormous numbers, all over the Chatir Kul basin, the Ak Sai and the At Bashi. The Brown Marmot gives one the impression of being the marmot of the high barren steppe-plateaux, the Red being typical of the richer alpine zone in precipitous mountains.

This intrusion of a Himalayan form into the Tian Shan mountain system is reciprocated by the latter extending its flora far beyond its natural home, to a point in the Yarkand river valley, which is Karakorum if not Himalayan.

There were no nomad encampments along my route but I passed great flocks of sheep that were being driven down to market on the plains below, and occasionally parties of Kirghiz, wayfarers like myself—men in company, on pleasure or business bent. Many carried falcons and I noted that these were always carried right-handed—not left, as in Europe—and yet the art originated in these parts.

Riding thus along the upper slopes of the Farghana range one had the whole undulating plateau in view,

* The specimens I brought back from the Ak Sai were described by Thomas as *centralis*, a new local (Western Tian Shan) form of the widely distributed *Marmota baibacina*.

but there was not a vestige of human life on it. The pasture had been eaten-up, and the nomads were now established in the highest valleys of the border ranges, where the grass was the richest, but the last they would get before winter drove them to lower altitudes.

The northern border range—the Jaman—contributes nothing to the Arpa river, for it is steep, sterile and rocky, so it may be said the Arpa has its origin in the Farghana range. Of its many sources there the largest and longest is probably the Kara Kul, which rises in that vertex whence spring those other rivulets destined to flow to the Tarim and the Aral Sea. At its head is the pass leading to Kashgar, the pass which my ten Kirghiz friends would have taken had they succeeded in crossing the Suok. So I turned my ponies up this valley to see what it might contain in the way of human and animal life.

On a landscape of emerald green, blue-black, and white—alpine meadows, shale screes, and glistening snow-fields—I came upon a Kirghiz encampment, and at the door of the first *yurt* stood a figure who hailed me from afar as if I was his long-lost brother. A little hill pony, sleek and plump, grazed on the succulent grasses, and the familiar *kumiz* bottle hung, empty, on the side of the tent, for its owner now dined daily, like a prince, on mutton and rice. It turned out that he was one of the party who had attempted the Suok Pass as a short-cut home.

At his invitation I pitched my tent nearby, and for the next few days I enjoyed Tartar hospitality, fed as they fed, on proper food instead of camp-fare, and hunted with them in the evenings. They were too lazy to hunt during the day, or perhaps they knew that the daytime was not the best time to pursue the shepherd's worst enemy—the wolf.

At these high encampments, surrounded as they were by a wild turmoil of hills, the flocks were at the mercy of the wolf-packs which infested them. Only constant hunting and harrying kept them at bay, and in spite of this it was quite common to find large packs of wolves lying within sight of the flocks around the tents. We hunted them with horse and hound, and they gave us as exciting a run as anyone could wish for, in fact it was far too exciting at first until one had become accustomed to one's mount—which refused nothing—and to keeping up the pace when the angle of the slopes was about 45°. The " meet " was fixed for the highest *yurt*, the one farthest up the valley, beyond which was the most likely ground to draw. The " field " consisted of six or eight of us mounted on their incomparable little hill-ponies, without which one could not ride a yard in such country. The pack was composed of three or four dogs of the long-haired greyhound type, something like the so-called Afghan greyhound, there being many varieties of that particular breed up here. The ponies breasted the steep shale slopes as if they were on the flat, slopes so steep that they crumbled away beneath each step, but the short shuffling paces of the ponies seemed to counteract the slip. Once we reached the top we rode over great rounded humps, on which the snow lay in broad drifts. It was strange ground to draw for wolves, and to me it seemed unlikely ; the Kirghiz, however, knew what they were about. They knew full well that the wolves followed the sheep, and that this particular desolation just below perpetual snow-line became their summer quarters, when the flocks were driven up to the highest pastures. We had not gone far before we rode right onto a pack (I believe *route* is the correct word) lying asleep on the shale, resting before their nightly raid on the sheep below. Here they spent the day, and well might they think themselves secure in such a wilderness of rock and shale, for indeed they were practically unapproachable.

Now the fun began. We played their own game on them, using the wolf's tactics of running down the quarry with the object of singling out a victim. As the hounds ran in the wolves moved off over appalling ground, and made for a stronghold of rock and crag, where no horse could live. But the Kirghiz rode hard to cut them off from their objective. This manœuvre turned the wolves towards the lower slopes, where the going was hell, but not suicidal. The slopes were so steeply tilted that the whole surface slid away as we crossed them, yet the ponies never made a mistake and seldom reduced their pace. Gaining confidence, I accustomed myself to the art of lying back with my head on my pony's tail.

After a " ski " down shelving rock and scree, slanting at a ridiculous angle, the dogs turned a single wolf out of the pack and quickly brought it to bay. Then the riders came up, and one man, throwing himself off his pony, slipped in behind the wolf and slit his throat.

A kill, and the disturbance of so large an area around the camp, did not prevent another night attack that very same evening. The camp dogs gave the warning of an attempt to reach the flocks, which showed that the wolves were a constant and serious menace. We hunted most evenings with varying luck, the constant harrying of the wolf-packs being almost as satisfactory as a kill, from the Kirghiz point of view.

It was tough hunting in cruel country, and it was evidently considered to be more of a duty than a pastime, an arduous and often risky business carried out largely in self-protection. The evenings, especially if we had been lured far afield by some pack more elusive than usual, were bitterly cold at this high altitude, so that the felted tents were all the more appreciated when we returned to them, while the lavish dishes of steaming hot mutton and rice were to be remembered by us for many a long week when reduced to very Spartan diet.

The predatory Wild dogs are also a menace to the flocks, but they are mostly confined to the forested zone at a lower altitude, and do not come up to these high barren plateaux (although they have been recorded from the forested zone on the eastern wall of the Pamirs). They, like the wolves, hunt in packs, but for some reason they pay more attention, and are more deadly, to wild game than to domestic animals. They seem to fear man and his belongings far more than do the wolves, although they are daring and savage enough when in pursuit of their prey. These Cuon (probably *Cuon javanicus jason* Pocock) hunting-dogs are wolf-like in appearance and tawny in colour : the Russians call them the Red Wolf to distinguish them from the Grey, although there is no generic relationship between them.

I wondered why the Kirghiz never used their trained eagles in the chase, since the wolf is one of their favourite quarries, but was told that they dislike using their hunting-eagles at this season. Eagles have great powers of fasting ; in consequence they are difficult to get into *yarak*—that is to say into keen flying condition, at any time, and more especially during the summer months, when the birds, being dull, often abscond. It is preferable to reserve them for the winter's sport, when they fly better. But another reason may be that, since their use is largely utilitarian, as a means of procuring good fur, their owners forego these risky summer flights when pelts are in poor condition.

The Golden Eagle must be fairly common in these parts, judging by the numbers one sees in captivity. Hawking with eagles (I use the word intentionally, for since falconers " hawk " with either falcon or hawk, I presume they " hawk " with eagles) is a favourite pastime of the sedentary people and the nomads alike. It is somewhat select in that it is only the yeoman farmers, Begs, Khans, and such-like, who can afford them. For although an eagle may be said to be worth a horse or two, a good one seldom comes on the market, for he is priceless. They are taken from the nest, of course, not caught on passage, but occasionally adult birds may be captured, for they can be easily ridden down when gorged on carrion. These will sometimes submit to training. In early stages they are wrapped up in a sheep-skin, in the same way as the Dutchmen use a sock—the lower portion of a worsted stocking, either of which making an ideal straight-jacket for the purpose. They are probably no more difficult to train and handle than a Goshawk, a bird of somewhat similar temperament and inclined to the same faults— sulkiness, for example. But they vary individually in character, some being easy to handle, others impossible to train at all.

Eagles are entered to fur only, which they clutch and hold.* They " bolt " or fly straight from the fist at the quarry. They cannot be " cast " as falcons are, nor thrown as short-winged hawks usually are, and always should be. When let fly, they do not mount aloft in order to stoop onto the quarry, therefore the actual flight is a somewhat dull show, neither impressive to watch, nor exciting to follow, apart from the actual " kill " ; the eagle just flaps along, and without apparent effort easily over-takes its victim. There is no thrill, no swift thrust up into the sky, and no sudden stoop earthwards. Having seen one flight you have seen the lot, there being little variation except in the nature of the quarry.

Herein lies the excitement of the chase, for the quarry consists mostly of foxes, gazelle, wolves, and, in earlier days, the Saiga antelope. It is said that a good eagle can kill a wolf unaided, but I have never seen it happen. Some authorities, Levchine for instance, declare that if a wolf is too strong, and goes off with the eagle still hanging on to it, the eagle is able to hold it with one foot and anchor itself with the other, until the wolf exhausts itself in the struggle ! Believe it or not, but one must remember that *smaller* birds of prey, such as Peregrines and Sakers, are habitually flown at gazelle in other countries. These Tian Shan wolves may be a trifle smaller than the Siberian or Tundra wolf, but the difference would scarcely be discernible to any but an expert eye.

Occasionally larger game, such as deer—hinds and

* According to Gordon and Bellew they are occasionally flown at herons and wild-geese ; and some writers say bustard.

BERKUT OR *KUSH*

calves for choice—form the quarry, but this can only happen when the deer inhabit suitable country, such as river-jungles on the plains, and not forests in the mountains. Generally speaking, however, larger game is not flown at, unless it is in conjunction with men and dogs, and then the eagle may be used to advantage. In these cases, however, it is not employed to kill, but to fluster the quarry, and so to bring it to bay and bag. Even as the Badawin are in the habit of flying their Saker falcons, succoured by greyhounds, to take ibex and gazelle.

The early accounts, and pictures, of eagles pulling down and killing unaided, full-grown stags, are, of course, " travellers' tales," embellished by an artistic imagination. In those dark days of ignorance there was little or no zoological discrimination ; " antelope and deer " of the books on this region prior to the twentieth century mostly referred to gazelle, and in some cases possibly to saiga. In like manner, " lions and tigers "—employed in the same lax manner as British boys use " blackbirds and thrushes "—might refer to any beast of prey or carrion feeder, not excluding cheeta and hyena. This makes identification difficult.

Roe-deer, especially the fawns, may form part of the wild eagle's diet, but they would not always be satisfactory quarry at which to fly trained birds, owing to the nature of the country in which they live ; however, in certain suitable localities they are a favourite quarry. On the other hand we do know that eagles are used at wild-boar hunts. They are certainly employed by the natives of the Tarim for this purpose, the eagle being used to bring the wild-pig to bay so that the hunters are enabled to close in and club the victim to death. In this case, obviously, the eagle has little more than a nuisance value, but it is sufficient to fluster the quarry to the extent of putting him at the mercy of unmounted and poorly-armed men.

The same applies to the " Haukes " which Anthony Jenkinson saw being used by the Tartars to take wild horses. This was " beyond the Caspian " in 1559. Presumably the " Haukes " would have been eagles, and the wild horses, the Kulan, or little horse-ass so numerous in those days in the region twixt Aral and Caspian. Jenkinson does not credit the " Haukes " with the killing of this unusual quarry, but notes correctly that they are used as an accessory, to bewilder the hunted animal—" The Haukes are lured to sease upon the beastes neckes or heads, which with chasing of themselves and sore beating of the Haukes are tired : then the hunter following his game, doeth slay the horse with his arrowe or sword ! "

Up here they call the eagle *Berkut*, a name which although of Turki-Tartar origin, seems to have passed into the Russian language. Pallas, a German, writing for Russians, distinctly states that the eagle was called " Berkut by the Tartars," and neither the Tartars, nor Baber three hundred years earlier, would have had to resort to the Slavonic language for a name for their own favourite bird *pour la chasse au vol*.

The settled Turki-speaking races call it *Kush* or *Kara Kush*—the Black eagle. The Chinese use the same adjective for our Golden eagle. *Kush* is literally the equivalent of our bird-of-prey, the place (Mews) where either falcons, hawks or eagles are kept during the moult being termed *Kush Khana*. The nomads

usually set them on blocks beside their tents, but I
have seen them being weathered on stunted poplar
trees. It has been suggested that the *Berkut* of the
north side of the Tian Shan and the *Kush* of the
southern side are different varieties, but this is not
so. The Golden eagle may not be one and the
same bird from the Hebrides to Kamtchatka, but
its variations throughout this wide range are very
slight. The Russians split their Russian Golden
eagles into four geographical forms, which can be
described (roughly) as Western, Central, Eastern and
Southern. The Southern form is distributed over the
whole of " our " Central Asia, all Middle Asia, in fact,
bounded by the Kirghiz steppes, the Altai and the
Himalayas. This bird is *Aquila chrysaëtos intermedia*
Severtzov (*daphanea* Menzbier), and this is the bird
which is caught up and trained as *Berkut* or *Kush*.
It is actually a trifle larger and darker than the other
forms. Some of the northern tribes, such as the
Kirei of the Altai who are great sportsmen, may use
their locally caught eagles, and these, according to
Russian classification, would be the variety they call
obscurior Sushkin (*kamtschatica* Severtzov). In earlier
times the Western race, *Aquila chrysaëtos chrysaëtos*, was
used as well ; for we know, from Pallas, that there
was a regular eagle-market at Orenburg, where, up
to the end of the eighteenth century, the local
Bashkirs traded young untrained birds from the Ural
mountains to the Kirghiz [Kazaks]. This is of
considerable interest. The Tartar invaders had
carried this purely Asiatic form of falconry with them
into Europe (if it had not been brought there by earlier
waves of Turanian immigrants), even as they had
introduced it into China ; and for a while Muscovite

Grand-Dukes and Chinese Emperors enjoyed alike the same form of sport. I call it purely Asiatic, because, although falconry had been in vogue in Russia since earliest historical times, I can find no record of the eagle being trained and used there, except by people of Asiatic origin, such as the Bashkirs, until *after* the Mongol invasion. It had doubtless been fostered and kept alive in Russia by that element of Turkish origin which was left behind there when the Mongol flood receded. The market at Orenburg was probably the last vestige of the declining sport as practised in Russia between the thirteenth and seventeenth centuries.* The custom gradually died out in both Europe and the Far East, ending where it began in the very heart of Asia. I have never seen, nor heard of, a trained hunting-eagle being used in Asia at the present day outside the limits of its original home. Although the Mongols used the eagle as a device on their battle-standards, we are left in doubt as to whether it was they, or their co-aggressors, the Turkish tribes, who were the principal exponents of the art. We do know, however, that it is only the Turkish branch of the Turanians who continue to practise it now.

* The single instance of eagles being brought from Orenburg to be flown at bagged wolves and foxes on the Tolstoi estates in 1856, would appear to have formed part of the Coronation celebrations on the occasion of the accession of the Emperor Alexander II.

CHAPTER VI

HIGH TARTARY—*Continued*

BUT to return to High Tartary and the Black, or Wild Mountain Kirghiz. They were a healthy-looking lot—and who would not be, living up here in this rarefied atmosphere, on a diet of sour milk? For those who were fit enough to survive, it was as near everlasting-life as could be. I benefited from it even during my short sojourn, and came to know the ecstasy of assured immortality. One felt very near to Nature, and very near to Heaven, lifted up as one was so high above the world below, surrounded by boundless horizons and bountiful skies. The desire of the poet who cried :

" O, all wide places, far from feverous towns,
   Great shining seas, pine forests, mountains wild,
   Rock-bosomed shores, rough heaths, and sheep-cropt downs,
   Vast pallid clouds, blue spaces undefiled,
   Room ! give me room ! give loneliness and air,
   Free things and plenteous in your regions fair."

was fulfilled within me.

When the wolves were not troubling us, I attempted to find the big wild sheep in company with these Kirghiz, but soon gave it up as a useless waste of time and energy. "Solo" should be the motto of the hunter of wild sheep ; indeed, the first essential towards success in this, the most exacting of all hill-stalking, is to be *alone*. To depend on a native hunter for eyes, ears and brain is a deplorable acknowledgment of inefficiency. Those who cannot rely on their own had better go away and try something easier. The extra labour and self-imposed difficulties, resulting from an ignorance of local conditions and lack of acquaintance with the game, are very soon refunded in the form of an intense enjoyment in solitude, and an exhilarating sense of independence. I confess that I have never got any real satisfaction from hunting, unless I have found, stalked, killed, and carried home the trophy I had set my heart upon, *unaided*. More than that, I require virgin country, and if possible a " new " beast, to satisfy me. This may sound like snobbery or bravado, but it is not. It is a legitimate indulgence in the exultation derived from self-reliance, which is a form of intoxication that agrees with some, but is poison to others. It corresponds to the mania of the mountaineer who prefers to find his own way up a difficult and dangerous peak, disdaining professional guides. There is in many men a special satisfaction in reliance on their own resources, and this compensates for the greater risk incurred. It is, I assure you, a grand tonic.

So I forsook my comfortable quarters in the shepherd's encampment, and went out into a region where maps were useless and guides would have been a curse. I wandered southwards into very high, very bleak country, until I was somewhere in the void that exists at the sources of the Tarz tributary of the Kara Kuldja, and the Suok sources of the Kashgar river, and was probably more often in Chinese territory than in Russian. Judging by the number of days I spent there, and by the amount of ground I covered on my hunting-pony and on foot, there must be an enormous area which is too high for domestic flocks, but not too high for wild sheep. This implies that there is a large expanse of shale, with a little grass, which, although not good enough to tempt the Kirghiz shepherds, is sufficient for wild-game during this short period (perhaps two months at the most), when they are pushed to the uttermost limits of their rightful domain. For the other eight or ten months the wild sheep have the whole place to themselves. Those members of the Forsyth Expedition to Kashgar in 1874, who went as far north as Chatir Kul, found large flocks of *Ovis poli* on the undulating plateau to the south of the lake, in the month of January, which shows that the sheep have, or had in those days, the run of the whole Arpa and Ak Sai Pamirs during the winter months. But for the rest of the year they have to be on the move, in retreat from the shepherds advancing with their flocks and herds.* It is the embarrassment caused by their presence that makes the hunting of wild sheep such a precarious and un-certain business, partly because the sheep are naturally more wary than usual, when man is in the vicinity— even if he does not harry them—and partly because they retire into the most inaccessible and difficult

---

* The annual movements of the great wild sheep of Central Asia, especially their winter migrations, are surprising. Far from being high-mountain beasts, they appear to be by nature creatures of the down-land of any altitude as long as it is safe. I have seen them on the low foothills of the central Tian Shan, practically on the plains of Dzungaria. For they are forced to resort to these low altitudes to find food, should their natural haunts be of such a nature that they are not blown clear of snow in winter. Sometimes these low grounds are open steppe rather than hill country. Ibex do not follow their example, for a goat can find a living where a sheep cannot. In certain remote and unfrequented places that I know of, you may find wild sheep living all the year round on very low hills, with no high ground to fall back on for safety. In some parts of the Mongolian Gobi, where they are seldom disturbed, they habitually frequent low hills, averaging 6000 ft. above sea-level, or 3000 ft. above the surrounding plain.

country. Difficult country means age-worn shale-slopes, rounded sky-lines, total absence of cover, and terrain over which it is often impossible to move silently and sometimes impossible to move at all—and the whole of it at a height of 10,000 to 12,000 ft., where life is not easy for man or beast. But the man who has once set his eyes upon these heavy horns knows full well that his desire will prevail. He may hunt alone up in these barren solitudes till the spirit fails and the heart grows sick, but he will never give in.

I spent much time and energy in trying to get specimens of these particular sheep, because they happened to be the link between the true *Ovis ammon poli* * of the Pamirs and their cousins of the Tian Shan, about which we knew very little. The early Russian naturalists had classed them all as *poli*; Severtzov giving them a range from the Pamirs all the way to Khan Tengri in the Central Tian Shan; and the first specimens to fall into British hands were classified as such. But eventually it was realised that these " Forsyth Expedition " examples were a variety of the true *poli*, and were named after that eminent Indian civil-servant and naturalist, A. O. Hume. This particular region was the habitat of *Ovis ammon humei* Lydekker. The Russians, however, still do not recognise this subspecies. But while it is true to say that this area was occupied by *poli* before they extended their range to the Pamirs (see Sushkin)

---

* It is interesting to follow the slow stages by which these great sheep have become known to the West. *Ammon*, first seen and reported in 1253-4 by Father William—the Franciscan Friar of Rubruck in French Flanders—did not receive a name until 1758. *Poli* was recorded, though *not* seen, by Marco Polo in 1273, but six centuries elapsed before it was *rediscovered* by Burnes, in 1834, and the first specimen retrieved by Wood in 1838 enabled Blyth to name it in 1840.

it is wise to reflect that this relates to ages and ages ago.

After many fruitless days of hard hunting, during which period I saw only small flocks of ewes, I eventually reached the sanctum of the old gentlemen. It was as remote and secluded a retreat as any I had ever encountered, and I am sure I could not find my way back to it again. There did not appear to be a main ridge or watershed to the range, and there were no landmarks ; it was a confused jumble of very high, very worn mountains, and the streamlets flowed north, south and west in the course of a day's hunt. It was this featureless wilderness of shale and snow that the old rams had taken as their own for this brief period of the year. And they had it to themselves—except for me. Even at this early date in August I was hampered by snowfalls, and on two occasions had to retreat to lower ground. But late one afternoon I spied two old rams before they saw or scented me, and one of them paid the penalty.

It was a short stalk and a long shot, success depending on negotiating a loose scree noiselessly. When that was safely accomplished there was no further possibility of a nearer approach, and I lay at a distance of 250 yards from the prize I had come so far to win. So near and yet so far. But the satisfaction was great. Was I not in the presence of the so-called " heraldic beast of Central Asia," and how many men have lain alone as near as I was to him ? Alone, at 12,000 ft., in a region where, as I knew with secret satisfaction, I was the very first of my birth and breeding to hunt. Alone in the death-like silence of that vast uplift of rock and snow—I might as well have been hunting undreamt-of monsters on Mars or the Moon. For the setting of the scene and the feelings it aroused in me, I might have been Prehistoric Man crawling on his belly to within close range of the Mammoth.

There was a rare grassy strip between the sterile shale slides, half in sun and half in shadow, and on it fed those two wondrous beasts. They were vast : their heads seem to weigh them down—such was the length and the girth of their twisted, gnarled horns. I lay there—it may have been an hour—hypnotised by the primeval scene, vainly hoping that they might feed towards me, but they only fed away in the opposite direction, and the distance widened. They were never at rest, but always on the *qui vive*, looking round and sniffing the breeze ; yet they might have been a hundred miles from any danger. Then the shadows lengthened, and I knew it was to be now or never. But before the climax was reached, the anticlimax set in, and I had the same revulsion of feeling that I have had on previous similar occasions. I had succeeded in my quest, what more ? Must I break the silence that was gold ? Must I kill ? What was the treasure compared with the hunt ? Why not go away and cry quits ? Yet they were fair game ; they were old—far past their prime. Next winter, or the winter after, they would be caught in some snowdrift, and suffer a horrible death from wolves. But I would kill in a second ; and instead of a nameless grave, and their great horns lying to rot by wind and weather, they would live for ever ; their magnificence would be the wonder and awe of multitudes in some far western city. They were fair game indeed, for when I looked along my sights I realised that the betting would be about 100 to 1 on a miss. Sheep on shale, at that range, are never conspicuous, but when there is the shimmer of sun rising off it they are hardly discernible.

However, a single shot left me in possession of a trophy which now gazes down on you and me from its pedestal in the Natural History Museum at South Kensington.*

During these days spent in the chase, I had obtained some stupendous views of the surrounding regions, views not allowed to the ordinary traveller who is relegated by circumstances to the orthodox routes, which perforce follow the easiest lines through difficult country. Even as in England it is the shooting man and the hunting man who gets the best of the scenery, and thereby develops an " eye for country." My diary records—" I got some of the biggest views I have ever set eyes on. I was in the midst of a vast creation of mountains ; as far as eye could reach they extended north, east, and south—ranges of rock and shale, ranges of shale and snow ; beyond were open plateaux and then more ranges. I could see Chatir Kul, a turquoise dot on the tawny steppe. I could see the Ak Sai plateau, and beyond that again the ranges that border it on north and east. I could see where the mountains began to drop towards the deserts of Chinese Turkestan, and I could see where they rose as eaves to the Roof of the World."

This was a lot to say of innermost Asia, where Nature is built on such a colossal scale, and where everything is immoderate and abnormal. The effect on one is an abiding sense of helpless inferiority and

---

* And this in spite of Hitler's recent efforts to unseat him ; for although he blew out the Bird Gallery on the ground floor, my sheep on the first floor escaped unscathed !

insignificance ; indeed I know of no better corrective
to any tendency towards self-importance !

Chatir Kul had been a landmark to me for many
a day. At times it appeared to be quite close, but it
was actually thirty or forty miles away, as I found to
my cost when I set out for its more salubrious climate,
at a mere 11,000 ft. above sea-level, in order to dry
my skins. The lake basin, which is self-contained, is
separated from the Arpa on the one hand, and the
Ak Sai on the other, by almost imperceptible water-
sheds. The lake itself has that cheerless appearance
common to most of these high, wind-swept, exposed,
plateau tarns ; the shores are saline and there is little
attraction beyond its population of wild-fowl. The
surrounding area carried more and better pasture,
judging by the numbers of Kirghiz who had remained
on here with their innumerable flocks and herds—
camels, sheep, goats, cows and horses—when all
their kith had removed to higher ground.

The direct and only route passable for wheeled
traffic between Kashgaria and the northern steppes
by way of Naryn, here passes round the west side
of Chatir Kul, and thence skirts the western spurs of
the At Bashi range. The old road followed the east
side of the lake. This must have always ranked as a
major line of communication between north and
south. There is a significant reference in the *Tarikh-i-
Rashidi* to a great caravanserai, built by the Moghul
Khan Muhammad early in the sixteenth century, in
the vicinity. It was said to be of vast proportions,
and stone built, but I think that in an unsettled
region such as this, where ruined sites are rare, the
importance and dimensions of this one may have
been exaggerated. But still it has given its name,

Tash Rabat, to the pass and the locality where it is situated.

Marmots, like the Kirghiz, preferred this locality to others. They were all of the Short-tailed Brown species, which, by the way, are not nearly so vociferous as their Red cousins. But still the air was full of their whistling, and this, together with the animated shore-line with its Grey Lag Geese, Ruddy Sheldrake, and many Waders, contrasted strongly with the silent, birdless plateaux I had just vacated. A few days in the neighbourhood might have been well spent, but my food supply was all but finished and I had to prepare for eventualities. My great stand-by, on this sort of journey, was one of my own concoction, namely, all sorts of dried fruits and nuts—apricots, raisins, plums, walnuts, and almonds—mixed and pounded into a solid lump. The resulting mess was compact, indestructible, and a very sustaining diet. But even this supply was now finished. The local Kirghiz were not helpful, so I rode south to the Turugart pass, leading to Kashgar, where there was said to be a temporary trading-post, and I hoped to buy flour—at a price. At the entrance to the pass, which is but a col leading off the plateau down to the plain (the plateau being over 11,000 ft. and the pass under 13,000 ft.), I found a group of *yurts*. One of them was the biggest I had ever set eyes upon, and in it sat an old Tartar with his bales of trade goods stacked around him. He looked like some giant spider lying in wait for victims to enter his web. He caught me. In spite of an hour's haggling, he extorted the utmost, knowing full well that I was starving, and was not going to leave without my flour.

There was a small Russian frontier-post here, garrisoned by a few soldiers. They inspected me.

They made no comment and asked no questions, but the incident had results : thereby hangs a tale.

With full saddle-bags I returned to the bleakness of the naked Chatir Kul, and then headed east to the Ak Sai plateau. Although I now had a small reserve of food for myself and my men, feeding the ponies was still a problem. The upper end of the Ak Sai was destitute of fodder and almost waterless. No doubt at the right season there was good grazing, but in August it was a stony barren waste, so I hurried on to the border-ranges on the south-eastern side where there was some nourishment to be found. This was my ultimate goal, for I decided that neither time, money, nor animals would last out for a journey further east. In a way, the handicap was a blessing ; for however delightful the forested valleys of the Tian Shan, around its culminating peaks of Khan Tengri may be, they are better known than these wilder and less attractive ranges, and so less useful for my purpose.

The ranges of Kok Kia and Kok Shal do not appear much in literature—they are side-tracked, and therefore a refuge for all wild-life. In fact, I would place this region high in my (private) list of unknown hunting-grounds, the sort of place I should like to be able to go to every August, in preference to Scotland ! It would take a lifetime of Augusts to know it well, and I should be able to hunt a different area every autumn for the best years of my life. At about thirty-five years of age I would have to go slow, and at forty to give it up altogether, for I defy anyone over that age to do any good on that particular ground. It was cruel going for man and beast.

The Ak Sai plateau, as already pointed out, drains into Chinese Turkestan. The river is known as the

Tauskhan when it has broken through the bordering ranges and reached the plain, but up here it is called Ak Sai; it has three main tributaries—the Terek, the Kok Kia and the Mudurum. The actual area of Russian territory drained by these rivers is very considerable—the County of Yorkshire would drop into it quite easily. The whole of it is above 10,000 ft. in altitude, and the surrounding ranges run up to 17,000 ft.; not very high, be it noted, but for that very reason they are of that characterless desolation which makes a safe sanctuary for wild game.

There is another factor which renders this retreat so favourable for the same purpose. Although harried on the north by nomadic tribes with a taste for hunting, they are not so molested from the south, where there is a wide zone of less inhabited country. On this, the Chinese flank of the watershed, parallel ridges and outliers, actually higher than the frontier range, protect it. Also this region, being outside the rain-belt, is not so frequented by nomads, nor is it likely to be developed, as Russian territory may be; for even if enthusiasts succeed in " growing strawberries on the Pamirs," it is unlikely to be attempted here.

I found the Kirghiz in occupation of all the lower valleys of the Kok Kia, but they were an ill-mannered lot, and none too pleasant to deal with. They were independent to the point of insolence, and I put this down to their living on a frontier, which gave them a freedom of movement denied to others. They could snap their fingers at Moscow and Pekin in turn, and run with the hare or hunt with the hounds just as they pleased. Younghusband had come up against this same tribe, on the Chinese side in 1887, and noted their churlish truculent nature; in fact on his trans-continental journey covering some three thousand miles, and involving contact with a variety of race and religion, they were the one black spot in human nature which he encountered. These were the tribes who took advantage of the first World War to make trouble in the rear. When all the Russian men had been called-up to fight, these rascals descended from their plateaux onto the pleasant and peaceful colonies in Semirechia, and wreaked their vengeance on the remaining, unprotected, population of old men, women and children. They destroyed, and robbed and killed to their hearts' content, and finally carried off into slavery any women they pleased. For years afterwards Russian fathers were seeking their abducted daughters amongst the nomad encampments on the Chinese side of the mountain frontier.

I was glad to see the last of them, and to gain freedom from the human element in the vast and delightful solitudes of the Kok Kia. This was a country after my own heart. There was no fear of running into anyone. Once only, in three weeks, did I meet strangers, and on that occasion it was a band of Kirghiz who had to ask me the way !

The wilderness of shale and snow was topped by the most terrific, serrated outcrops of naked rock, which shot up skywards as if conscious of the fact that they were indeed the boundary line between two great Empires. They were a great feature, and in some way excused the anomaly that the international frontier did not here follow the true watershed, which would have made the Ak Sai plateau Chinese instead of Russian, but chose the more significant battlements of the Kok Kia. This emphasises the rather peculiar type of drainage for which the Tian Shan is famous, namely, rivers which lead a double life and have several aliases. The Ak Sai river, for instance, is also the Kok Shal and the Taushkan. Its original home is a mountain-girt plateau, where spasmodic pastoral life alone exists. It then disappears into a gorge; but when it reappears, at a much lower altitude, it creates a settled zone of great fertility. The two zones are completely separate, and there is little or no inter-communication between them. Other examples of this type of valley are the Kum Arik, which creates the oasis of Aksu, and the Yulduz sources of the Kara Shahr.

When I had got clear of the last Kirghiz encampment, and had moved on a couple of days' journey into the Kok Kia, I found game. First of all ewes, and then rams, of the true *Ovis ammon humei* type, with some remarkably big ibex on the crags above the open sheep-country. These ibex were not of the same calibre as the giants of the central Tian Shan, but they were very big for a region where the feed was not super-abundant. I witnessed one old fellow through my glass scratching his backside with the tip of one horn, and he seemed to exert no effort whatsoever in order to reach his posterior.

These ibex should belong to the variety named *Capra sibirica merzbacheri*; but I reject this fine splitting of the Asiatic Ibex into so many local races. I cannot believe, for instance, that there are four recognisable local varieties in the Altai, a comparatively small region, and one very similar throughout its entirety. Nor could I guarantee to distinguish three distinct types in the Tian Shan, although I have examined many hundreds from widely separated localities. The genuinely distinct geographical races are probably not more than three—Himalayan, Tian Shan and Altai.

Some Russian zoologists (C. C. Flerov) go further, and assign all these Asiatic ibex to *two* specific groups, *sibirica* and *sakeen*, the line of demarcation between the two being the River Irtish ; all those to the north and east of the upper course of this river are *Capra sibirica sibirica* Meyer, all those to the south and west are *Capra sibirica sakeen* Blyth. The former group includes *lydekkeri, altaica, fasciata, hagenbecki,* and *lorenzi*; to the latter belong *almasyi, merzbacheri, alaiana, trans-alaiana, wardi, dauvergnei, pedri* and *filippii,* but all are considered unstable local races, and some are founded on particularly untrustworthy and insufficient data. I think this particular area could produce specimens indistinguishable from *alaiana, almasyi* and *merzbacheri.*

These Kok Kia ibex horns ran up to fifty-three inches. There were many old heads lying in the river bottoms. I counted ten or twelve to a mile. They were mostly old bucks or seven-year-olds. Their characteristic, if any, was their thickness in relation to their length—which was not very great according to local standards. Many had that great outward twist which is a special feature of the Tian Shan ibex.

But the snow came down again and buried the fuel and drove me out of my seclusion. So, retreating to lower altitudes, I crossed the Ak Sai plateau to have a look at the At Bashi range on its northern side. Here I found many nomads, but no sign of game. Yet in Severtzov's day it abounded in wild-life,* so I surmised that the Kirghiz must have either increased in numbers, or moved in from other districts. There was certainly not room for both man and beast on the At Bashi during the summer months, but in

* Earlier still, in the sixteenth century, the Moghul chieftains used to hunt the wild-ass on these Pamirs.

winter, when man has departed, the wild sheep might come in. It is a narrow range with no back to it, while the valley of the same name on its northern side is the favourite winter-quarters of Kirghiz from all over this area, and I do not believe that they would leave in peace any game, such as sheep, during that period when they have little to do except hunt. But there are ibex, which survive for the simple reason that the Kirghiz are loth to hunt except on horseback.

When the weather cleared I made for the Kok Kia once more ; but it was now a race against time, worn-out ponies, reduced rations, and tired men. I pushed deeper into the range, found a veritable hunter's paradise, and after several hard, but fruitless days, succeeded in my quest.

The recounting of stalks, long or short, is apt to bore, but this particular one was so unusual that I will risk it.

At very great range I spied through my glasses the great curling horns of a giant ram. He was alone and apparently asleep, but in an impregnable position on the top of a little isolated grassy knoll. I could see nothing except the horns, but presumably they were attached to a beast, for it was not a likely place in which to find a pair of derelict horns.*

---

* Derelict horns of ibex are usually found in the valley bottoms and in the streams, where they have been deposited by time, wind and weather. Sheep horns, on the other hand, are nearly always to be found *in situ*, where their owners died, the very nature of the country in which they live forbidding any or much movement after death. Those Golgothas, which one occasionally comes across, where horns lie in hundreds, are nearly always in places situated close under escarpments, where deep snowdrifts would be likely to accumulate, and therefore to become traps for unwary or hard-driven beasts. Wolves are probably the main causes of sheep being killed in numbers in certain definite localities, such as these.

He was solitary and therefore might be a monster, for the chances were that he was a very aged ram, who, being worsted in a fight to maintain supremacy, had retired to a lonely but more peaceful existence away from the herd. I had met such a one in the Altai, and he had obviously removed himself from his fellows—and the ladies—because he was so ugly. A battle-royal had damaged his nose so badly that a large scab had grown over the wound, and the resulting disfigurement entirely justified his action. Fighting had spoilt his beauty and so he lived alone.

The knoll was so isolated that there was no possible means of getting within shot of the beast, until one arrived there, literally on top of him. In due course I reached the flank and, with infinite care, crept up it. With even greater care I raised myself the last few feet, and finally the last few inches. As the grassy summit came slowly into view, I realised that there was nothing on it ! But I saw to my astonishment that there was another knoll, *exactly* like this one, a little further on ; and there lay my beast. It *was* a ram, a monster—and he was fast asleep.

The distance was still too great to risk a shot, so I had to repeat my assault on position No. 2. This time I took even greater care, for I now knew for a certainty that, if only the wind remained friendly, I was about to meet " *Ovis poli* himself, face to face." In fact, I calculated that I should reach the crest of the knoll within a few yards of him—a unique experience.

I could hardly believe that my thumping heart would not wake him, as I crept up to where a solitary rock broke the skyline and gave some sort of cover. Otherwise the final approach was over the smooth

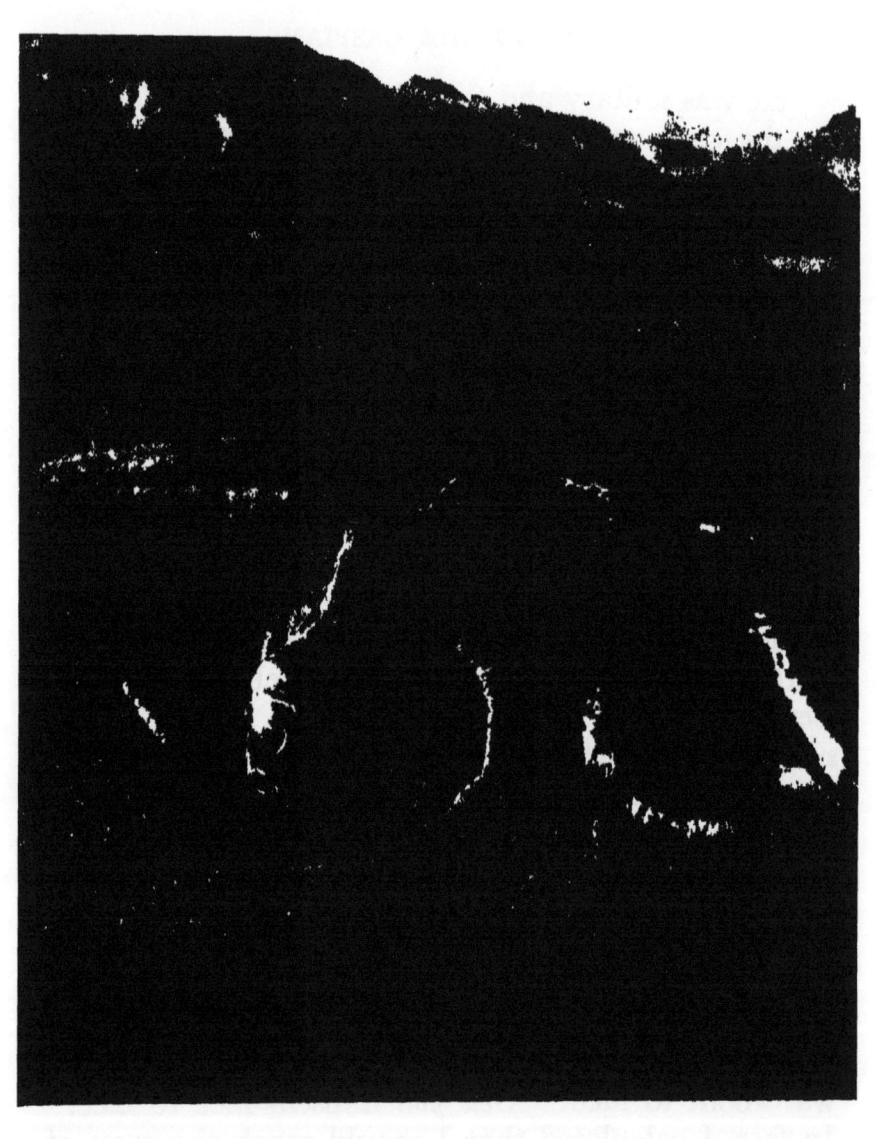

...FIGHTING HAD SPOILT HIS BEAUTY...

rounded curve of a sugar-loaf-shaped hill. I could have no warning at all of just when the top of his horns would come into view.

I was quite close to the rock, when the silence was broken by a sudden stamp ; a mighty pair of horns reared themselves above the rock—but I could see no more—the rock hid the rest of him from me, and all of me from him. The distance was about ten yards !

Our hearts stood still.

Trembling with anxiety, my eyes wet with sweat, I waited.

He took one step forward, exposed himself, and before he knew that Man was upon him, he died.

Not instantaneously though, for the range was so close my bullet drilled a tiny hole clean through him. He charged away and down the slope several hundred yards before he fell dead.

He was a fine specimen—a perfect one of his race. But some days later while scouring the hills for the very purpose, I picked up an old pair of horns which must be a record for the type—the Western Tian Shan race of *Ovis ammon*. In size of body they must be the equal of any recorded *Ovis poli* ; my measurements were forty-four inches at the shoulder, with a total length of sixty-eight inches.

For the sake of comparison I illustrate the three controversial wild sheep of this part of Central Asia, the examples being typical heads, not rare records in size, or abnormal in shape (see p. 254).

I made further expeditions on foot over the topmost Kok Kia, but they were in search of scenery, not game. On the map this area over which I climbed and hunted looks insignificant enough, yet it appeared to me a vast world to itself. Away beyond it were the landmarks by which I could orient my position. To the north rose the first ramps of the Kok Shal range, capped by three thousand feet of snow, running east as far as eye could see. The Kok Shal is no colossus—for these regions—but it has a peculiar grandeur, and a certain arrogance not usually possessed by ranges of far greater elevation. Its (southern) face is forbidding. Here at its western end, called Bos Adir by Severtzov, there are no grassy slopes or forests to relieve the monotony of its sixteen thousand feet of crag and skree and snow. It looked unassailable, and appeared to be proud of the fact that our little maps showed no means of crossing it.

Even from the high plateau to the north, the Kok Shal is impressive. Ellsworth Huntington—the only non-Russian traveller to have seen it from that quarter, thought it " the loftiest and most picturesque of the Tian Shan ranges. Here the mountains rise to a height of 16,000 ft.* and are high enough so that even in the relatively short time since their upheaval they have been carved into forms that are truly alpine. Below the snow-line large glaciers stretch out their moraine-covered tongues from immense U-shaped valleys, while at greater heights the summits of the range have been carved into sharp-edged triangular matterhorns."

The Kok Shal may be only an offshoot of the main Tian Shan, but it is not an unworthy one. Although it has a run of two hundred miles from its birth as a buttress of Khan Tengri, thrice only are its solitudes violated—twice by Man, who utilises the only two feasible passes across it, and once by Nature, who has carved a mighty chasm through its

* They run up to over 19,000 ft.

" . . . OUR HEARTS STOOD STILL . . . "

very heart in order to allow the waters of a vast drainage-area in the Central Tian Shan to escape to the plains below. This Kum Arik canyon must be one of the wonders of Central Asia. It may be twenty-five miles in length, with a fall of 3000 ft., and so far as I know has never been penetrated. The volume of water that passes through it may be gauged by the size of the area that it drains—a basin with a circuit of three hundred miles, the border ranges being mostly above the line of perpetual snow, and very heavily glaciated ; there are scores of glaciers—including some of the longest in the world, and in addition there are many transverse ranges within the basin which would rank as first class. The drainage from all these during the summer, quite apart from precipitation, which is also very heavy, must be colossal.

The idea that the chief glories of the Tian Shan lie within Chinese territory, that is to say to the east of the culminating point Khan Tengri, and that the Russian Tian Shan lacks interest and grandeur, is entirely erroneous. On the contrary, it is on the Russian side of the frontier, to the *west* of Khan Tengri, that the Tian Shan attains its maximum height and greatest beauty. The great amphitheatre which encircles the highest sources of the Aksu river, and those ranges around the head-waters of the Naryn cannot be surpassed by anything within Chinese territory. Moreover, I think I am correct in saying that there is a much larger area under perpetual snow, an excess of high summits, and a *very* great deal more glaciation in the Russian Tian Shan than in the Chinese section.

The Kok Shal appeared to be contiguous with the

Kok Kia. I sought the passage of the Ak Sai river from the plateau to the plain, but never discovered it ; nor did I see anything that looked like a gorge, or a break in the mountain barrier. And yet we know the Ak Sai river does pass between them. Nor did I ever hear by night the sound of imprisoned waters, such as one would expect to hear, where great rivers are hemmed in by narrow walls. Like its counterpart, the Kum Arik, this gorge is probably impassable. It must be of considerable length, for from the point where I saw the Ak Sai river, supplemented by the Mudurum, enter the mountain barrier, to the door-shaped opening where Merzbacher saw it issuing forth onto the mile-wide Kok Shal valley cannot be less than forty miles. The fall would be about 1500 ft. over this distance. These impregnable labyrinths of Nature have a peculiar fascination for me. There is another at the extreme eastern end of the Tian Shan (a miniature one compared with this, but none the less exciting because of its size), which I had the good fortune to be able to explore in mid-winter because the waters were frozen solid. In addition to the pleasure of penetrating a forbidden place, I was treated to the spectacle of perpendicular red rock-walls rising sheer out of blue and white ice, and of waterfalls transformed into gigantic icicles.

Westwards I could see for a good three-days' journey to the Farghana range. Chatir Kul still remained in view. The whole of the Ak Sai plateau was spread below me, backed by the At Bashi snows. On certain days this vast panorama was prolonged indefinitely, for great banks of cumulus clouds, hanging over the horizon, gave the impression of more and more mountain ranges, so that it was difficult to know where earth ended and heaven began.

To the south, into Chinese Turkestan, I could see nothing that indicated the low desert basin of the Takla Makan. Indeed one would not know, from this standpoint, that the Tarim basin existed at all, for all was mountainous and appeared to be even loftier than this frontier line on which I stood. This offshoot of the Kok Kia, called the Kara Teke, is in fact higher than its parent. It is a great mountain range and glaciated. There is very good grazing on it, and consequently there are wild-sheep, which should prove to be of interest, for they are an indeterminate race. They may belong to the so-called Aksu variety, since the two habitats are not far apart, and if so they should be an intergradation between *humei* and *karelini*. Or they might possibly prove to belong to that race which inhabits other southern extensions of the Tian Shan, such as the Kurruk Tagh, described on somewhat insufficient data as *Ovis poli adametzi* by Kowarzik in 1913. The Russians should have had the full data, for the naturalist-brothers Grzhimailo had collected for the Academy of Sciences at St Petersburg two specimens of what they considered to be a new species, in the same locality, as long ago as 1889-90.

It was during the last days of August that I met a solitary Hoopoe at 11,000 ft., southward bound. The following night a fresh fall of snow reminded me that I, too, had better be going, so I hastened to save my now starving ponies. Following the nameless valley to a point where it was lost in abysmal depths between steep rock-walls, I cut over the hills down to the Ak Sai plateau, where the climate at 10,000 ft. felt comparatively mild.

The nearest point where food was obtainable was the Russian town of Naryn, on the Naryn source of the Syr, some three or four days' journey away, and thither I hurried, as fast as my poor ponies allowed. The way led over the At Bashi range, or rather through a low col in it, for at this eastern extremity the mountains merge into the plateau, and little or no climb is needed to cross them.

This range, it must be remembered, is the true watershed between the Aral and the Tarim basins, the political boundary between Russia and China taking a more direct line, but not the natural watershed as its frontier. Nature's frontier is the more immutable, for it marks a definite climatic and floristic zone. On crossing the At Bashi range I left behind me the now herbless plateau, and in a few steps descended to flowers, thickets, and forests. The change was welcome, for we were dog-dirty, lice-ridden, and wet to the skin. At the first pine trees we encountered I ordered a halt, pitched camp, and then—like children—we lit the biggest possible bonfire. After four fuelless weeks our enjoyment was great; tree trunks were piled high on the fire, and at long last we became warm and dry.

I had always looked on ravens as solitary, unsociable birds, but here they seemed to be gregarious, for I counted a flock—if that is the right word—of no less than twenty-seven circling over my camp. Carrion must have been the cause for such a gathering; they cannot resist it, and like the vultures, call each other to the feast.

The upper reaches of the At Bashi valley are very

lovely, reminding me that this was but the fringe of similar country extending eastwards for hundreds of miles. The Heavenly Mountains are well-named. They exercised a great influence on my future wanderings, and I was not content until I stood on those far-off spurs of the Karlik Tagh, where the great range dies away into the Gobi desert, having sampled its beauties over a distance of fifteen hundred miles.

The head of the At Bashi is a dead end ; but the central valley is historic ground. It has ever been a meeting place for nomad clans in winter, and has an air of settlement. There are " kraals " for cattle, semi-permanent crofts, and hay is cut and stored for winter use.

I rode into Naryn to find that the local police were on the point of sending out the second posse of native scouts to catch me ! It transpired that the Russian picket at the Turugart Pass had reported an Englishman in disguise (my old sheep-skin coat) wandering about the Ak Sai. The police at Naryn had promptly despatched their native *Jigits* to arrest me and bring me in. But they had failed to find me. My peregrinations in and around the Kok Kia had been such that I had eluded my would-be captors, not by fell design, but by sheer luck. Their consternation was great when I arrived at their headquarters of my own accord. But my sincerity did not save me from being put under house-arrest until my identity was proved, and my permits scrutinised by the authorities at Tashkent. A few days of enforced detention did not worry me. I slept off a certain over-tiredness, and ate my belly-full of bazaar dainties ; but after that time hung heavy on my hands. Also my lodgings were filthy. and my heart was in Samarkand. The local schoolmaster befriended me, and I was permitted to visit him. He happened to be a keen naturalist and in his compound I found a lot of material to interest me. There was a litter of horns from the neighbouring mountains, and although the exact localities were not to be relied upon, there was much to be learnt from them. I noted yet another obvious local variety of *Ovis ammon*, which was neither Hume's nor Littledale's, nor Karelin's, nor Polo's. It came from the north, which is, of course, the locality assigned to the so-called *heinsi* (Severtzov). It was evidently a smaller type of wild sheep, as one would expect from the lower altitude of its habitat. The ibex were well represented and although there was nothing to compare with the giants of the Central Tian Shan, a fifty-three-inch head was not to be sniffed at. The roe-deer, on the other hand, ran large, and were magnificent. Twelve to fourteen inches was a normal head, and fifteen-inch horns were not uncommon. These came from the headwaters of the Naryn and the sources of the Kum Arik. There were some fine Wapiti, but nothing above fifty inches; they lacked that last ten inches which makes the Tian Shan Wapiti the finest trophy in the world. There were captive eagle-owls and young snow-leopards.

The schoolmaster was a good fellow, with an insatiable appetite for knowledge, far in advance of his upbringing and education—one of those " Russians tense with the quest for truth, which maddens manhood and saddens youth." I promised to bring him to the notice of European collectors, and did actually put him in touch with several museums. But even the bond of science did not save him from official suspicion ; for fraternising with a stray Englishman was frowned upon, even if there was a mutual scientific interest. So much for international jealousy, race-hatred, or whatever the disease is which afflicts mankind and hinders progress.

From what I saw of the township of Naryn it somewhat resembled a trading post in the Canadian North-West in early days, with Kirghiz in place of Indians. It differed in that it has an historic back-ground, for the place must have figured largely in Tamerlane's campaigns into Moghulistan, lying as it did on the direct road between the two rival spheres of influence—Khokand and Kuldja.

Naryn is actually at the four cross-roads, and in a region of so few roads this carries much weight. It lies on one of the few north to south crossings of the Tian Shan fit for wheeled traffic,* thus connecting the settlements of Semirechia with the oases of Sinkiang. But it also stands on the only east to west route. All Tian Shan trade bound for the Farghana goes through here, all bazaar goods intended for the mountain tribes come up this way.

After many days news came that I was free to travel where I wished, so I set forth on my return journey to Samarkand down the Naryn valley. My ponies were poor, and the country I traversed was poorer, therefore I could not hurry. Passing hordes had eaten the country bare, while advancing ones were trying to find nourishment, for I was by no means the only traveller on the road ; long lines of

* This point illustrates the extent to which the Tian Shan is a natural barrier across middle Asia ; for in all its length from Tashkent to Hami, a distance of twelve hundred miles, there are but three passes of this category.

camels laden with pelts and felts, droves of horses, flocks of sheep, and herds of cattle crowded the narrow track, all streaming down to the bazaars of the plains, before the passes became difficult or finally closed for the winter.

The short-cut to Uskent and rail-head at Andijan leaves the Naryn valley at the point where the Alabugha enters it, and follows up this river to the well-known Yassi pass over the Farghana range, the Alabugha being the lower course of the Arpa. A short way up this valley I camped one evening beside a ruined site—an old fort or stronghold, built at a point where the valley bottom is impassable, and therefore strategically well situated.. It must have been the fort built by one of the Moghul Amirs, which was said to stand " on the summit of a hillock at a place called Alabugha, and its ruins are still to be seen."

My pace was so hampered by the lack of fodder that it was no less than eight days from Naryn before I finally climbed to the top of the Yassi, and beheld below me the friendly, fertile Farghana.

I had been " out " fifty days, covered roughly eight hundred miles on horseback, fired two cartridges, and brought back two valuable trophies.

He that bloweth not his own trumpet is as a grasshopper without legs.

CHAPTER VII

SNOW-WHITE BELKI

BELKI, or Snow-White, first came into my life on the outskirts of a Siberian village on the upper reaches of the Yenisei river. He was helping to round-up some cattle, at which game he displayed such unusual intelligence that I bought him immediately, for the equivalent of ten shillings. He was a pup of six months, pure white, with prick ears and beady black eyes ; he had lovely lines, and gave promise of being perfectly proportioned when fully grown. As I was about to start on a long journey, and there was to be no return, I took the precaution of tying him up.

In due course our caravan set forth, down the long straight street of log-built houses, and thence out into the virgin forest beyond. This was nothing new to Belki, for it was his own country. There were no new smells to excite his curiosity ; he knew them all —from squirrels to bears—for he came of a long line of hunting-dogs, his forebears having been used by successive owners to help in the chase of fur-bearing animals. It was not long before he became one of our party, and learnt the routine of the day's work—the breaking up of camp at dawn, the long day's march, the snug camp—with dinner—at dusk, and night under the stars. And so through two long years of continuous travel good dog Belki, either heading the caravan or following it, accompanied us in spite of many vicissitudes from Siberia to the frontiers of India ; through the forests and across the steppes, over rivers swollen by flood in spring, or frozen solid in winter, up mountain ranges that seemed to reach to Heaven, across plateaux where little lived, over deserts as wide as oceans. Two long years of such varied life that few men, and fewer dogs, have ever been permitted to experience and enjoy.

But enjoy it he did. He revelled in the nomadic existence, the ever changing scenes and new surroundings. Most dogs have a home of their own, but this dog had none—unless it was half Asia. He marched serenely ahead of the caravan into unknown country just as if it all belonged to him, exhibiting neither fear nor imprudence, for in a tight corner he showed extraordinary sagacity. Alone with the caravan he was master dog, but when we came to nomad encampments with their packs of savage sheep-guards, or Chinese cities full of the riff-raff of the canine world, he was definitely the under dog, and he had to use his wits in order to survive.

The first six months of Belki's life with the expedition was spent in his own glorious world, a realm of forest and river, of lake and meadow. But even here he had new experiences, one of the most important being his introduction to a completely new scent. Ranging ahead of the caravan one day he suddenly got wind of something which interested him very much, something which he had never smelt before. He followed it up until he found it was a herd of reindeer, and then proceeded to round up as many as he could manage. The commotion brought upon the scene some strange beings, clad in reindeer-skins, and riding upon reindeer, looking remarkably like something out of the prehistoric world as they emerged from the forest. These were the forest-dwelling Uriankhai who live at the sources of the

"BELKI"

great Yenisei, and whose whole existence centres round their reindeer-herds by which they subsist. We were in search of them, and it was Belki who found them.

All this forested region was virtually a homeland to Belki; the shock came when he left luxuriant Siberia and entered sterile Mongolia. He had to accommodate himself to an entirely new environment. At first he hated it. The gravelly steppe was uncongenial to his feet—so used to grassy meadows. The dazzling landscape was unlike his sombre forests. On the high plateaux, where it was always cold even in mid-summer, he was quite happy, but when we descended to lower altitudes his troubles began. He could not endure the heat. If at dawn he foresaw a grilling day's march ahead of him, he would accompany the caravan until he found a convenient and suitable nook, such as a shady place behind, or even under an overhanging rock, and there he would lie-up in comfort during the heat of the day. When camp was pitched and dinner was ready Belki, sure enough, would come cantering up, having followed us by scent or by instinct across perhaps twenty miles of what, to him, was enemy's country.

He attached himself to the camp rather than to me personally. I would go off for a long day's hunting, or perhaps be away for several days, without a moment's anxiety about him, knowing full well that he would be at the door of my tent to welcome me on my return. But if I called him to me he would go with me wherever I went, even if it entailed hard riding ten hours a day for a week. He made friends with everyone we came in contact with—Russian, Mongol, Kirghiz, Chinaman and Turk. Yet he retained his own wild independence. For instance, nothing would induce him to use the shelter of my tent ; even in the coldest and most inclement weather he preferred to sleep outside. He revelled in the snow ; thirty degrees of frost meant nothing to him ; he still refused protection, made a snug bed for himself and slept soundly. I never discovered whether this posting himself on guard, as it were, was for my safety or his own, or for both of us.

He must have had a dash of the wild wolf in him, even as " Huskies " are intentionally kept impure, in order to retain certain characteristics, or as continental sheep-dogs are crossed occasionally with wolves. For Belki had a strange streak in him, which showed itself in peculiarities which I have never seen in any " domestic " breed.

After seven months of travel he entered into his own climate again, for winter came, and it was as cold as his own Siberia. The rivers were frozen solid, snow lay deep over the whole vast Asian landscape, the thermometer sank to far below zero. Belki now thoroughly enjoyed life. By this time he had become an expert game-finder and retriever ; at pheasant and duck-shoots he proved himself invaluable ; indeed had it not been for Belki the British Museum would lack many specimens which they now possess. One of his best efforts was the finding, and killing, of the rare Sarmatian Polecat, the only one I ever procured. Nothing came amiss to Belki—rats, mice, moles, or voles—elusive small mammals that we seldom saw and which were difficult to trap. All were added to the collection, and for all these Belki should receive the thanks of the zoologists who wanted them. At pheasant marauds he surpassed himself, for the Central Asian wild pheasants love impenetrable jungles of berberis ; shooting without a dog was sheer waste of time and energy, but dog and gun together could outwit them. Whole series of skins of the Mongolian pheasants now in museums are largely due to my Snow-white Belki.

If Belki could tell his own story he would probably say that he thoroughly enjoyed his trip across Asia, excepting for the other dogs he met on the way. Looking back, I am at a loss to know how he survived the ordeal. For in that country all dogs are guardians of the caravans, or of the flocks, or of their master's homes, and their duty is to slay any stranger—man or dog—that comes too near. Anyone unmounted runs the risk of a severe mauling by dogs of an enormous size and very savage temperament. Every encampment, therefore, was a danger to Belki, and every new town we entered was a new hell to him. But he was equal to most occasions, and quickly learnt that the safest place when in danger was under my horse's nose. By taking up this position he knew he was safe from attack in the rear, and that no enemy could get to close quarters because of my whip-lash. Thus he would stalk along serenely, although surrounded by a savage pack of strangers all eager to tear him to pieces. I remember killing only two dogs for his protection in all those twenty months of travel.

The second year of our wandering brought very much the same sort of existence to Belki. He travelled a thousand miles with us in Chinese carts, or rather *we* used them while *he* kept to the high-road, sleeping under the carts at night even in fifty degrees of frost. But he did not like the crossing of the deserts in midsummer, when it was so hot that we only moved by night, and slept, or tried to sleep, during the day. This was for him almost the last straw, for he got sore feet from the grilling ground-heat of the gravelly steppes. We tried carrying him in a sack on the camel-bales, but he hated it, so I made some little boots for him out of soft raw-hide leather. But it was no use ; he always kicked or tore them off.

Eventually the caravan came to rest under the walls of the city of Kashgar. Our work was ended. This was the edge of civilisation for here we found a British Consulate, the first we had encountered. From Kashgar the route led over the Himalayas and down to India, so I decided to leave Belki in his own country, knowing he would never survive the heat of Hindustan. He was therefore bequeathed to the Consulate, whose spacious and lovely garden was not at all a bad place for a dog to end his days.

The caravan eventually set out southwards on its last lap, a mere eight hundred miles, over several passes of 17,000 ft. and one of over 18,000 ft., before reaching the Vale of Kashmir. But even this strenuous ride could not drive the thoughts of Belki out of my mind. I missed him terribly, and was conscious of a feeling that perhaps (unintentionally) I had let him down. Doubtless I knew subconsciously what had happened in Kashgar after our departure. It took many months for the news to reach me, but this is what occurred. When Belki discovered that the caravan—*his* caravan —had gone without him, no bolts or bars would keep him prisoner. He escaped and tried to follow us. Out of the safety of the Consular compound, into the maze of alleys and streets of the great native city he raced, hopefully but vainly trying to find us. What he endured, and what horrible experiences he went through we shall never know ; but he eventually found his way back to the Consulate in an exhausted, torn, and heart-broken condition. He had loyally done his duty, he had tried to follow his friends ; but now, thanks to the kindly treatment of the Consular staff, he accepted the inevitable and settled down. But I feel that for the remainder of his life he really lay waiting for the caravan, and listening for the sound of its bells.

CHAPTER VIII

PHEASANTS

My second winter in the heart of Asia was spent largely in another valley, eight hundred miles east of Samarkand, namely the Ili. This locality is even more remote from the ameliorating influence of the sea, and consequently has a far more severe climate than that of the Zarafshan.

The Ili valley, although of no special economic or strategic value, is definitely a landmark in Middle Asia. From the early days when it was a favourite camping ground of Mongol chieftains, down to the nineteenth century when advancing Russia came up against a static China, the locality has been well to the fore in the history of the Central Asian border-lands. But since the valley lies at right angles to all natural lines of communication, and itself leads to nowhere, its ownership is not a matter of vital importance either to Russia or China. But had the Muzart Pass, at its head, been an easy one instead of a very bad one, the frontier might have been adjusted to the advantage of the Russians. As it is they share it between them, Russia retaining the fairway across the plains and the lower rich agricultural lands, and China its less productive but far more attractive upper half.

The Ili valley is divided into three very distinct zones ; the lowest portion is desert-bound and of little account, its upper reaches are mountain-locked, inaccessible and unproductive for the most part, while its middle course is well-favoured and of great potential value. To the Mongols, when they first emerged from Mongolia, it must have appeared a land of promise—sheltered, watered and pastured on an extravagant scale. So the Chagatai heir of Jenghis Khan settled on the best of it and made it his permanent encampment.

I made it mine for the worst of one winter.

At the end of November there was a series of snowstorms, accompanied by a sudden ominous drop in temperature. By the first week in December the Ili river was frozen stiff, and the whole land was frost-bound. Snow would occur every ten or twelve days, not the big slow-falling flakes of the English scene, but a steady, continuous, relentless fall of minute particles of frozen snow, which lay, or drifted, according to where it fell, in sheltered valley or stormy steppe. The immense landscape of endless plain and gigantic ranges lay under a glistening white mantle, unbroken, save where black lines of dead vegetation denoted the river courses, or dark blue shadows on the mountains showed where precipices and ravine allowed no snow to lie. Always a land of immensity, it is seen at its best in mid-winter, when no dust-haze hides, and all its matchless grandeur is revealed. The intervening periods between the snowfalls were brilliant and sunny, but the temperature dropped to zero and then far below it. So long as the air was still the fifty degrees or so of frost were not felt, but if the wind blew, man could scarcely face the elements. Across the landscape moved occasional natives, Kalmuk and Kirghiz, wrapped in great sheep-skin coats, and wearing fox-skin headgear ; or Chinamen in quilted jackets and quaint but most serviceable ear-caps. For the most part the inhabitants had gone into winter quarters, hibernating like the marmots, and would not be much in evidence until the following spring. Groaning ox-waggons gave place to silent sledges ; the camel-caravan disappeared from the scene ; tumult died in the bazaars of Kuldja, trade centre of the Ili valley.

Bird-life, as might be expected, was scarce at this dead-end of the year. Had it not been for certain hot springs in the vicinity of the town my larder would not have been so well supplied with duck, and, but for a letter from Lord Rothschild requesting a series of skins of the local pheasants, I would never have seen the upper tributaries of the Ili river. And until the traveller has seen the Tekkes, the Kunges or the Kash he does not know the Central Asian border-lands, nor the intrinsic beauty of the Celestial Moun-tains. For it must be remembered that the southern flanks of the Tian Shan bear little resemblance to its northern face. The one belongs to the desiccated heart of Asia, the other pertains to the temperate southern borderlands of Siberia, and gathers its loveliness from the moister climate.

The local pheasant of the Ili valley is the one known to us as the Mongolian, and, in spite of its isolation in so distant a region, is more familiar to us in Europe, indeed, than the original Colchic introduction from the Eurasian borderlands. Unlike the majority of those many forms of the true pheasant which inhabit Middle Asia, the range of the Mon-golian is a wide one. It does not live in Mongolia, by the way, but that is neither here nor there, for geography is no concern of ornithological nomen-clature. Yet geography, or rather an acquaintance with the physical features of the Asiatic continent, should, in my opinion, enter into the problem of the classification of this particular species. Glance at a map of Asia showing the land surface features, and note the broad arid belt which extends across it from the Caspian to the Pacific, and note especially how it is intersected by strips and zones of fertility and vegetation. The first thing that strikes you is the lack of continuity of any one feature over any wide expanse of country. A desert, a lake, a great river valley, a range of mountains, a belt of sand-dunes, a zone of intensive cultivation, steppes, reed-beds, salt-encrusted mud, prairies of high grass : such is the Asian scene, which the true pheasants have chosen for their abode. It stands to reason that the homes of most of them are far apart and isolated one from the other, although some of them are semi-detached ; for pheasants are very particular as to their haunts. This picture should explain why the Colchic pheasant of the Caucasus does not continue in its pure form throughout the five thousand miles of its range into China.

Treating the subject broadly, and avoiding the difficulties raised by the recent creation of innumerable new forms, which are unlikely to stand the test of time, we can follow the various subspecies of the Colchic pheasant beyond the Caspian by a quick survey of the principal river basins. The Caspian marks the limit of *Phasianus colchicus*, and of its three or four Caucasian forms. There is no suitable accommodation for pheasants nearer than the Atrek valley in north-eastern Persia, and here they turn up as *persicus*. The next possible pheasant localities, well separated by mountains from the former, are the valleys of the Tedjen—lower course of the Hari Rud—and the Murghab, two indivisible pheasant haunts, occupied by *principalis*. Beyond the Murghab is a formidable desert barrier and having crossed it we come to the valley of the Oxus. So far the pheasant haunts have been more or less segregated, and there has not been much chance of interbreeding. But the Oxus valley presents us with another complication, for the great river flows through a thousand miles of almost continuous pheasant-country. This used to be the home of Severtzov's pheasant, *chrysomelas* (how much more suitable would have been the synonym *oxianus*!), but since the day of that great Russian naturalist two other forms have been recognised, Zarudny's pheasant on the middle Oxus, and Bianchi's on its upper reaches and tributaries. More recently still keener-eyed ornithologists have split these again into four more subspecies, making seven in all in one valley, where interbreeding is uncontrolled, and consequently the belts of inter-graduation must be very wide.

The Oxus is isolated from the next river valley—the Zarafshan—where we have already hunted its own special form of pheasant, but it is not so separated from the neighbouring great pheasant haunt—the Syr, for both rivers flow into the same Sea of Aral. Consequently there is a broad belt along the eastern shore of Aral where the two subspecies, *chrysomelas* of the Oxus and *turkestanicus* of the Syr, meet, overlap and interbreed. But *turkestanicus* holds its own over eight hundred miles of the Syr valley, from Aral up into the Farghana, where two local forms have been considered by Buturlin and Dementiev to be worthy of names—*triznae* of the Naryn and Kara Darya valleys, and *kvaskovski* of the Gulcha.

To continue the story eastwards. The bulk of Middle Asia beyond the Syr, wherever suitable ground occurs, is the home of the Mongolian or Kirghiz Pheasant—*mongolicus*. The basins of the Chu and of the Ili, with Lake Balkhash as a vast natural preserve, the Dzungarian lakes, the valleys of the Borotala and the Manass, and the far away Upper Irtish, all these are included in its wide range. Over this area the type seems to remain constant, with the exception of those on the extreme southern fringe, where an ill-defined, and perhaps indistinguishable local form has been separated under the name *semitorquatus*.*

The only point where *mongolicus* may extend into Mongolia is in the Kobdo region. Here around the shores of Atchit Nor and Kara Usu, and along the river connecting the two lakes the local pheasant is *hagenbecki* ; but some authorities consider this form to be more closely related to the Manchurian *pallasi* than to the Mongolian.

The Tian Shan, being a sufficient barrier to pheasants wandering out of their respective zones, makes Chinese Turkestan a little continent to itself inside a continent, and there, in complete seclusion, reside Shaw's pheasant and *tarimensis*.

* The Russian (Buturlin and Dementiev, 1937) classification of these pheasants is entirely different from ours. For instance, all the local races between the Aral Sea and the Altai are grouped under *semitorquatus*, thus—*Phasianus semitorquatus turkestanicus* of the Syr, *P. semitorquatus branti* of Semirechia, *P. semitorquatus semitorquatus* of Dzungaria. *Mongolicus* is applied to the trans-Altai races. But the complexity of the problem is shown by the fact that in one locality reputed to be the habitat of *mongolicus*, some of the pheasants I collected were indistinguishable from those obtained in *semitorquatus* territory, while others were intermediate between *mongolicus* and *turkestanicus*. See Appendix II.

There are many other varieties farther east, but they do not come within the scope of the present volume.

Broadly speaking, every river system throughout Middle Asia has its own pheasant ; and as most of these rivers flow in self-contained basins, and are cut off from each other by the type of country in which no pheasant could live, the pheasant population of each separate habitat may well be expected to acquire special characteristics, and therefore to differ slightly from those in the next—the Atrek and the Murghab, for example. On the other hand, there are cases where there is no such segregation and therefore inter-breeding must take place, as in the case of the Oxus and the Syr.

It must be remembered, too, that many of these pheasant haunts, which are *now* completely cut off from each other, and therefore out of danger of any chance interbreeding taking place, were not always thus secluded. For instance, the Zarafshan and the Oxus were once connected, and so were their pheasants. Of lesser antiquity may have been the connection between the Murghab pheasants and those of the Oxus. The outlets of the Oxus and of the Syr into Aral were, not so very long ago, much closer to each other. The valley of the Chu linked up with the Syr. Thus, as Kinnear says, " The whole question of the races of *Phasianus colchicus* is very complicated, as so much interbreeding takes place." Very much more interbreeding took place between some of the forms in days long gone by ; and, by a strange turn of the wheel of Fate, *will take place again*, for there are irrigation schemes projected, and in active operation, which will reclaim wide areas, and thereby join up the habitats of forms at present disconnected.

In its wild state the pheasant inhabits a great variety of country. We have already chased him over the tamarisk-covered sand-dunes of the lower Zarafshan, where the birds had never seen a tree in the whole course of their existence. In other places they frequent vast reed-beds, which are half under water at certain seasons ; again in others they keep almost entirely to the cultivated areas. But they love above all the jungles, thickets, and poplar forests which line the rivers where they debouch from the mountains. On the lower Ili the vegetation is such that the pheasants are more or less secure from any interference, but on its upper tributaries the " coverts " are good and the sport excellent.

So I set out one winter's morn, accompanied by a native servant, my good dog Belki, and one spare horse laden with food, cartridges and blankets. We rode sixty-five miles in two short winter days in order to reach the valley of the Kash, a major right affluent of the Ili. Going was good over hard snow—Belki made light of it—and at dusk on the second day we presented ourselves at the door of a mud-built hovel belonging to a Turki colonist. Where else could one do such a thing and be sure of admittance and even a welcome from complete strangers ? But such is Oriental hospitality in contrast to Western that we got more than we asked for. Horses were stabled and fed, the one small room already occupied by my host, his wife and a small child, was placed at my disposal, food was provided, and eventually we all lay down to sleep. This was my shooting-lodge for the time being.

The Kash is a fine river, typical of the wet belt of the Tian Shan, and carries an enormous amount of water. Here it flows through a wide steppe valley, bordered on both sides by mountains, and cut off from the Ili by a barrier of rugged hills, through which the river has carved a fine gorge ; its seclusion is complete. On this account, too, it is somewhat more sheltered and therefore warmer than the main valley ; and this, accentuated by the swift-flowing character of the river, accounts for the fact that in mid-December the Kash was not entirely frozen. High ice-banks lined the torrent, which made it impossible to cross ; in fact the only feasible crossings were in those places where rocks had caused the ice to jam, and a narrow natural bridge had been formed by the blocks freezing together. The river banks were fringed with a zone of woodland, thorn scrub, berberis thickets, and reeds. The trees were elm, birch and poplars which attained a great size, and gave my pheasant " shoot " an almost English aspect. Many a bit of the far-away Kash valley might have been in the woods at home. A mile-wide strip of this game-haunted jungle gave me plenty of room to shoot over.

There is little intrusion on the part of man. A few villages higher up the valley, and some nomad encampments across the river did not interfere with me. The only other sign of human life was as interesting as it was unexpected—namely, a large Lama monastery. I learnt eventually that the Kash valley was one of those areas which had been allotted to the heroic survivors of that Kalmuk tribe, which migrated *en masse* from the banks of the Volga back to the land of their origin, in 1771, and whose epic story is the subject of De Quincey's Essay, *Revolt of the Tartars.*

If I judge aright, their descendants live " in clover." This Nilki lamasery is their tribal centre, and it was the first indication of Buddhism that I met beyond the Caspian. From here eastwards this religion was paramount, and the Mongol type predominated.

The altitude of the valley was higher than that of any pheasant-haunt that I had encountered to date. It was from 3000 to 3500 ft. above sea-level, but perhaps the sheltered nature of the valley compensated for this. However, pheasants go higher still ; they are certainly found up to over 5000 ft. in certain narrow sheltered valleys, where, in spite of a heavy snowfall, there is a plentiful food supply in the way of berries.

The next morning I called up my beaters—one man and my dog—and as soon as the sun was well over the ridge, started to shoot the " home " coverts. We hunted through the tree belt, and then out on the river bank, where the country was more open, and where islands on the many-channelled river made ideal ground to work. Very beautiful on a frosty morning were these islands in the sun. The colours were white and gold, with the black tracery of elm and poplar. The river must be a magnificent torrent in summer, judging by the water-worn boulders that now stood high above the ice, and is probably unfordable over most of its length. Even now, in its semi-frozen state, it was impossible to cross in safety, for the ice-bridges seldom spanned its whole width.

The islands were covered with long grass, thorn scrub, and berberis, which no doubt formed the very safe and completely inaccessible breeding haunts of the pheasants in spring. But now they were exposed to attack, for we could cross over to most of them on the ice. It was here that we found the bulk of the birds, feeding on the berries of Pallas' Scarlet Thorn, *Cratægus sanguinea.*

The fact that they were on the islands, away from their real home and refuge—the thickets and jungles on the river banks—provided an opportunity not to be missed. With the assistance of my two beaters I organised impromptu drives, which were aided by the fact that the birds always flew—when put up off these insular feeding grounds—in a bee-line for the nearest jungle. I stood on the ice betwixt the two, the dog hunting the thickets which the man could not penetrate. When, at the end of these little drives, two or three, and sometimes even six or seven, gorgeously plumaged birds lay dead on the snow, I thought that this was indeed the real thing, and laughed at the idea of an army of beaters and all the other paraphernalia of a " shooting-party."

Where this method was impossible I had to resort to merely walking them up, but found that the quickness with which these wild birds sprang, and the speed they attained on the wing made the shooting quite worthy. Indeed, this trait in their character struck me so much that I carefully weighed and measured a series of cocks and hens in order to compare them with average English pheasants. All my birds were December killed and in fine condition, and the result of forty specimens weighed and measured showed that, although about the same in size as the English hybrids, the wild Mongolian does not run so heavy in weight. This explained why they were able to " get away " so much quicker than birds I had been accustomed to, and, what is more,

to fly high and strong even when not compelled to do
so by trees or vegetation. I saw birds, which my dog
put up on one side of the river, cross to the other bank,
a distance of a couple of hundred yards, at a height
which made one ache to be underneath them. They
were " screamers," and yet there was nothing to
make them fly like that. As far as my experience goes,
this is not the case with birds that have their abode
in the reed-beds and on the plains. There they fly
low on all occasions, and do not trouble to fly far
either, for their safety is in the swamp where man
cannot follow, and their refuge is on the ground.
The bulk of Central Asian pheasants in their natural
haunts have never seen a tree, much less a woodland
of considerable area containing high trees. But here—
and it was the first time I had seen it—the pheasants
went up to roost. At a quarter to five every evening
the valley resounded with the " cock-cock " of the
birds as they took up their quarters for the night.
This gave the native hunter his chance, for, creeping
through the undergrowth, he could hardly fail to bag
a bird at each shot from his ancient muzzle-loader,
the birds being very loth to fly when once off the
ground and settled for the night. Cockshut time
proved to me the truly incredible numbers of pheasants
that inhabited the locality. In the daytime, too,
during the winter months, the pheasants spend a lot
of their time off the ground, high in the thorn trees,
feeding on the berries which form their chief article
of diet. If it were not for this winter reserve of frozen
berries, which, by the way, the Chinese call " pheasant
food," the birds would be in a bad way. As it was,
all the birds that I killed, in spite of a month's duration
of snow-covered ground and hard frost, were very fat

and in the finest condition. I opened as many as thirty crops, and found all of them full of this berry, and little else besides. But they have to work for their keep ; they were busy feeding during the nine hours of daylight.

During the first day I shot twenty-six birds, and at dusk retired to the native house, where I spent most of my time devising a method by which I could keep my specimens out of harm's way. There were cats to be outwitted and the child, who would pull out all the long tail feathers. Eventually I resorted to the expedient of hanging my game out in the open, on an inaccessible branch, where it froze and thus saved me the trouble of skinning immediately those that I intended to keep as specimens.

Another day I shot through the more densely-timbered country, where I found pheasants wherever there were berries. Hares simply swarmed—the whole lepine population of the surrounding hills being concentrated into this confined food-belt for the winter. This caused Belki's undoing, for he had not been " broken " to fur ; very much the reverse, he was heir to all the instincts left to him by a long line of ancestors " *trained* " to fur. Consequently, although the hares were a poor substitute for sable, and squirrel, he felt it his duty to bring some to bag. The hare is regarded as a cat, or of the same tribe, by the natives, a classification we do not repudiate by calling him " Puss." They are banned as food, for they are, in point of fact, very foul feeders.

This great concentration of game, both fur and feather, attracted all the birds of prey into the same zone. The native falconers, or their retainers, took advantage of this to catch the passage hawks. I stumbled one day on to an old man, hidden in a booth of brushwood, who was waiting at one end of a long string. At the other end of the string, out on a clearing in the jungle, was the trap, which reminded me so much of what I had read of the hawk-catchers in Holland that I examined the contrivance more closely. The net, of very fine cord but of a large mesh, was hung on thin wands arranged in a circle, converging upward to a narrow mouth. Inside this was placed a captive pigeon, which the fowler in his hide could make flutter by pulling the string. The wild hawk would stoop at the decoy and become entangled in the netting, which would automatically fall in on him. Self-caught, as it were : there was no clap-net contrivance about it. Crude but efficient, for one had already been caught that day, and it lay there trussed up like a mummy in the booth beside the fowler. It ought to be a profitable business, if one had the patience, for the value of haggards is high. There was no butcher-bird to give the alarm, as the Dutchmen use ; nor was there any need of them for the whole valley was alive with hawks ; in fact, they probably caught too many of the sort they did *not* want. Those they chiefly required were Goshawks, Sakers, and Shikras, but their ambition was a Peregrine or a Gyr-falcon.

I never saw Peregrines in use by native falconers, although, of course, a Central Asian form, *babylonicus*, is here in a wild state and is trained. Nor did I ever see, or hear of, the celebrated " White Falcon," which presumably is a Gyr-falcon, a northern breed with a great reputation, and much in demand. They are rare, and like so many treasures are hard to come by. The Altai is their nearest home, but they are said also to nest in parts of the Tian Shan : they certainly come down here in the winter.

Although this species in general is confined to very high latitudes of the Northern Hemisphere, both Palæarctic and Nearctic, one form of Gyr-falcon is to be found in the highlands of Central Asia. This race, known as *Falco rusticolus altaicus* Menzbier (synonyms *Falco gyrfalco altaicus, Hierofalco altaicus, Hierofalco lorenzi* Menzbier), is resident over a small area along the north-western fringe of the Central Asian plateau, from the Altai to the Tian Shan—ranging further afield in winter. It might be considered a " Relict " of the glacial period.

The local Turki name, according to a reliable source (Skrine) is *toighun*, a word used, I believe, for a light form or albino of any species. But it is more widely known as *shunkar*, which, according to Pallas, is Bashkir-Tartar for Gyr-falcon, the same word appearing in Persian and Chinese literature. This name has been called " disputed," for the simple reason, I think, because it has been misapplied ; and the following may be the explanation. In old days, when the Gyr-falcon was less rare, and the art of falconry more in vogue, Oriental potentates were accustomed to receive their annual quota of these birds from the far north. *Shunkars* often appeared in the lists of presents sent by one great man to another. An Emperor of China bestowed them on Shah Rukh at Herat ; Muscovite Czars despatched them to London, Stambul, Tehran and Bukhara ; even the falconers of Hindustan received a few. Gyr-falcons must have been common in those days, and their fame wide-spread. Eventually, however, with a slump in the practice of the art of falconry and a decline in the supply of Gyr-falcons, the traffic in them to foreign parts died out. The Gyr-falcon became a rarity outside its natural home, *but the magic name endured* in Central Asia and became a synonym for any falcon that showed signs of being a little larger and lighter-coloured than usual. Thus it came about that the large pale falcon of the Saker type, which Henderson discovered, and Jerdon and Hume described from Chinese Turkestan in 1870, bore the native name of *shunkar,* or more precisely *kyzyl-chunkar* (Dementiev)—the Red Gyr-falcon, and this seems to be the origin of the Shanghar Falcon of ornithological nomenclature. This bird, however, is not a Gyr-falcon but a Saker, *Falco cherrug milvipes* Jerdon, or *hendersoni* Hume.* I sometimes wonder whether the identification of this Tibetan Saker with the famed *shunkar* is justifiable.

To return to the local falconers. I felt that the native methods of taking them were all rather backward and inefficient, but that, with a little more intelligence and the incentive of a better market, the whole business could be greatly improved. I cannot imagine a more suitable locality for the job. Seeing their methods made me wonder whether the art of falconry was as highly developed up here as it is in India and Persia. I doubt it. For instance, I never saw dogs properly handled as they should be to hunt in conjunction with hawks. When used they were run in packs, and not limited to a sporting and well-trained couple. On the other hand, the

* Opinion varies as to whether *milvipes* and *hendersoni* are conspecific or not. The most recent authority on the subject, Dementiev 1947, separates them, *hendersoni* being the resident Saker of the Tibetan plateau, and *milvipes* a partial migrant over the region north-east Mongolia—North China.

Central Asians should be pre-eminent at falconry. They live in ideal country, they own good horses and useful dogs, there is any quantity of game in great variety, *and* they have unlimited time on their hands.

Having finished all my cartridges I laid out my " bag " and found that I had got forty-one birds—sufficient for my purpose. The proportion of cocks to hens was twenty-seven to fourteen. This was satisfactory, for although I actually needed more cocks than hens I had not taken special trouble to secure them.

Packing the frozen carcases carefully in a couple of sacks, I left my servant to follow with them at his ease, while I rode ahead to Kuldja. It took me fourteen hours' hard riding ; but Belki had forestalled me—I found him waiting for his dinner.

CHAPTER IX

MONGOL AVALANCHE

LIKE an avalanche it came, and as unexpectedly. All seemed well in the world when there arose a cloud —" the size of a man's hand "—in the least expected quarter, away up on the remote bleak plateaux of north-eastern Asia. An observant witness, a spy, or an emissary of a foreign government, might have been conscious of a certain restlessness, of an atmosphere of tension, of a stirring amongst the tribes which roamed that vast pasture-land called Mongolia. " Tribal unrest amongst the nomads " might have been the report sent back to headquarters in the settled lands of China, India, Persia, Russia, and possibly middle Europe. But China continued to adorn herself with precious works of art—the Sung period was at its best. India thought herself as safe as ever behind her mountain ramparts—no undesirable outsider could possibly intrude upon her privacy. Persia, on the other hand, lay open to attack ; she heard rumours, had ample warning of what might happen : but nothing could have averted the catastrophe. Russia, such as she was before Muscovy arose, had had previous experience of what might be expected out of the East. It was seven hundred and fifty years ago that the Huns had ravaged her—a long time, it is true ; but one would have thought that such a terrible experience could never have been forgotten. Human memory, however, is surprisingly short-lived. Men return to the slopes of the recently-erupted volcano, as assuredly as they flock back to the alluvial deposits of a river which has just burst its banks and drowned a million of their fellows. Russia, lying as she did in the fairway, caught the hurricane full blast. Even middle Europe stood to arms, for it looked as if nothing could stop the human flood from swamping all Christendom. The cry, " From the terror of the Mongols, good Lord deliver us," rose from every cathedral, from every minster, from every village church in western Europe.

They were the cause of it all. . . The nomad herdsmen from bleak Mongolia, the children of the steppe, the slant-eyed, unsophisticated, leather-clad horsemen now out for world conquest. The horror had hung like a storm on the horizon of civilisation for centuries, but had not burst ; now it did burst, and with accumulated vengeance.

It is as difficult to account for these sudden, impulsive migrations of men, as it is to understand those of the lemmings or the sand-grouse, but one suspects that periodic high fertility, resulting in over-population in relation to their means of subsistence, has something to do with it. The Mongols may have increased to numbers that reached a figure far in excess of their means of livelihood ; or on the other hand their means of subsistence may have decreased to a point that made movement necessary. Or, again, the origin may have been more deeply rooted in the social evolution of the nomad tribes in relation to their settled neighbours. Perhaps it was the decadence of the latter rather than the strength of the former that gave the Mongols their chance ; for it is agreed that the Mongols were neither numerous nor powerful at the start of their career, although they became infinite, invincible, and remarkably efficient as they progressed. There were, indeed, probably several factors working together, which, reaching a climax, brought about the final explosion. But whatever the cause, the effect was that, in the early years of the thirteenth century, a movement germinated in northern Mongolia which was destined to have tremendous and far-reaching results. Although perhaps small in the beginning, it rapidly increased in size as it rolled westwards, gathering allies, mercenaries and collaborators in its wake, until finally it assumed alarming proportions. Then it became like a swam of ants, eating up everything that lay in its path. It was not human, for it betrayed no human emotion. It was without reason, for it consumed more than it could possibly digest. It advanced so far that it never recovered itself. It accomplished nothing, except that it satisfied its own desire, and, having done that, very soon evaporated.

In twenty short years the whole face of Asia was changed. Politically, the map from Poland to the China Seas had to be redrawn ; ethnographically also, for whole peoples had ceased to exist ; economically again, for many regions were so devastated that they have not even yet recovered from the passing of the Mongol maelstrom.

Jenghis swept into China and out again before opening the flood-gates and loosing his hordes on to the West. China presented natural difficulties to mobile warfare, but the West did not. Mongolia to Hungary was one clean sweep ; there were no obstacles and he took it in one gulp. The fertile valleys and great cities of Turkestan were a tempting and easy prey ; Samarkand and Bukhara fell at the first stroke. Merv and Khurasan carried the

avalanche onward to India, which was ravaged as
far as Lahore. The accumulated wealth of ages
was looted in a day, and as the Mongols swept
westwards, long caravans crawled eastwards laden
with booty—incredible booty.

If geography be the handmaid of history, let us
look at the Mongol Avalanche for a moment from
that aspect, for there is probably no better example
of it.

The actual land was the spacious plateau between
Siberia and China, which has been the breeding-
ground of all the wild races who, at different periods,
have swamped Asia and overflowed into Europe.
Huns, Mongols and Turks—all had their origin
there. It is a plateau averaging 3000 to 4000 ft. in
altitude, ribbed and flanked by mountain ranges,
which give sufficient water to form as perfect a
grazing-country as exists anywhere. Forested foothills, rich pastures, and perennial streams constitute
the main features of a region which to the average
person has the reputation of being largely desert.
Mongolia of the Mongols is really the borderland
of the desert interior called Gobi or Shamo; but
even this region has not the aridity attributed to it,
for it is mostly prairie supporting a partially nomadic
race. The Mongols, unlike other shepherd-people,
such as the Bedawin, are not forced to move continuously from well to well, from one scanty grazing
to another, always on the verge of starvation, always
at war with a relentless climate. In other nomad-
lands, like Arabia, the population probably exceeds
the limit that the land can support. In Mongolia
the population could be trebled, and there would

still be room to spare. One wonders, of course, what the conditions were like in the thirteenth century. It certainly would not require a Great Wall of China to keep out the fighting men of the present-day total population of about three million Mongols ; so one imagines that they were much more numerous then.

The rigorous climate, hot in summer, bitterly cold in winter, creates a tough people, inured to hardship, able to endure privation, but unable to withstand contamination by any form of luxury. We can get a good idea of what the Mongols looked like in old days from Chinese pictures of that date, from first-hand accounts of them by contemporaries of Jenghis' successors (we have none concurrent with Jenghis himself) ; or, in fact, a visit to Mongolia to-day would give one a fair idea of their general appearance at the time of their supremacy. For although the spirit has altered the type has not.

They were small, sturdy, squat men, thick-set and immensely powerful, bowed in the legs from generations on horseback, hard as nails, their yellow skin bronzed to the tone and texture of leather, remarkably hairless, and with little slit eyes. The women-folk were as adaptable as the men, suitable partners, and as hardy. Living entirely on the produce of their flocks and herds, their needs were few. Owners of vast herds of horses, they had unlimited transport at their disposal ; breeders of the best Bactrian camels, they had inexhaustible supplies of building material, for, apart from a few sticks, their tents are composed of felt made from camel and sheep wool. This invention, the *yurt* or felt tent, is unique in itself and peculiar to the Mongols, and it probably gave them a great

THE MONGOLIAN SCENE

advantage over their foes when they started to migrate. As Herodotus was quick to note of other Asiatic nomad invaders, the Scyths—" having neither cities nor forts, and carrying their dwellings with them wherever they go . . . how can they fail of being unconquerable? " The Mongols needed, and exhibited, the maximum degree of efficient mobility, and the *yurt* helped them to achieve it. Although a comfortable permanent abode adapted to a rigorous climate, well designed for a country which is exposed to every wind that blows, it is yet equally well-suited to the needs of a migrating people. Jenghis himself lived in a felt tent to the end of his days.

Or it may have been the horse—the little Asiatic Dun, rather than the *yurt* which gave the Mongols ascendancy over their neighbours. The place the horse has held in history remains to be written, but the Dun pony of Asia will figure largely in it, for it may have been the origin from which *all* " improved " breeds sprang. " The trail of the Dun horse always led to adventures. . . . Scythian, Hun and Tartar filled their native steppes until they were over-crowded. But for the Dun pony we might not have heard much more of them. When they tamed the pony the savages became barbarians, the little scattered tribes were welded into formidable hordes. And then they swarmed like locusts eating up the world."* Having unlimited reserves of horses (in place of tanks), their mobility was assured, while their range was only limited by the distribution of the pasture (in place of oil). They followed the grazing, their movements across Asia being directly influenced by this factor.

* Roger Pocock.

The Mongols were born fighters. They had imagination as well, and the invaluable gift of being able to assimilate the best ideas of the people they conquered. There is no doubt that the Mongol success was largely due to these qualities and not to weight of numbers. Their leader was a genius. His campaigns were carefully prepared and skilfully carried out. The regions he intended to over-run were systematically investigated beforehand. The Mongols made a point of learning all they could about their intended victims, and did actually acquire more information about them than *they* ever did about the Mongols. It was not overwhelming numbers, but sheer superiority of mind and method, plus unswerving determination, that carried them to victory. The Mongols had an ambition, and this they held in common—they had become obsessed with the idea that they should inherit the Earth ; the Western world, on the other hand, suffered from inertia, and was divided against itself. Another secret, perhaps the keystone of their rapid success, was their mobility—a mobility independent of a base. One mounted Mongol was a complete unit in himself. He lived on the country ; he needed no commissariat. Ten Mongols formed a troop, ten troops a squadron, ten squadrons a regiment, and ten regiments formed a *Touman*, or ten thousand independent, self-supporting, mounted men, able to act as one. Marco Polo realised their efficiency—" they are also more capable of hardships than other nations ; for many a time, if need be, they will go for a month without any supply of food, living only on the milk of their mares and on such game as their bows may win them. Their horses also will subsist entirely on the grass of the plains. . . . Of all troops in the world these are they which endure the greatest hardship and fatigue, and which cost the least ; and they are the best of all for making wide conquests of country." They were, indeed, the best and the toughest, as the following pages show.

By the way, it is interesting to note that Alexander the Great, who had played havoc with the Persian Empire, had made quick headway against highly sophisticated and well-organised kingdoms such as Egypt, and had even done quite well against great odds in Hindustan, was only once severely checked, and that was when he came up against the wild hordes of Central Asia. It will be remembered that he reached the Jaxartes (Syr Darya) and crossed it into their steppes ; but he very soon returned, having had the worst of it. Although he had succeeded in Asia Minor, Syria, Egypt, Mesopotamia, Persia and Bactria, against the vastness of Middle Asia and its nomadic myriads, he was impotent. If only his historian, Arrian, had told us something about this painful episode ; but for very good reasons Arrian kept a judicious silence !

This is roughly the background of the scene on which the curtain rose in the early years of the thirteenth century. Jenghis, of insignificant origin, had established his ascendancy over the neighbouring tribes, and began to look farther afield. The world, as he knew it, was limited by nomadic High-Asia, with its indefinite western horizon, and by Cathay— the rich region to the south, a land flowing with milk and honey, and full of loot. His ancestors had been in the habit of raiding in that direction since the beginning of time ; in fact, where else could the poor

THE GRAZING BELT

nomads raid ? China lay at their door ; the Great
Wall had been built fourteen hundred years before to
keep them out, and it still stood there—two thousand
miles of continuous propaganda—a broad hint to quit.

I have often wondered why Jenghis rode south into
China when he had been advised long before that
" the grazing was best in the west," but one supposes
that he could not resist such easily gained loot. He
required wealth, arms and the products of civilisation
which his nomadic world could not supply. He got
all that he needed without much trouble ; for China,
at that particular moment, was in evil plight. In four
short years Jenghis had dealt with China, in so far as
it suited him, and had turned his attention towards
the West—where the grazing was better.

From Mongolia westwards stretched a vast plain.
If the mountains of Middle Asia had run north and
south instead of east and west, had the Urals been
the Caucasus, history might have been very different.
But as it was the Mongols could ride unhindered by
natural obstacles, so long as they avoided the zone of
forest and swamp in the north and the mountain
barriers in the south, for between them is a fairway
five hundred miles broad. Through this trough
have flooded all those racial migrations and waves of
invasion which have had such a profound influence
on Europe. The Mongols came through it, too.
They let their horses follow their noses ; they took
the line of least resistance ; they swept the plains
where they found no obstacle ; they avoided the
regions where they would be at a disadvantage. And
for this very reason—because geography is the handmaid of history—Middle Asia became Tartary, and
Russia received her share of Mongol strain.

The ease of transport over this wide region is shown by the fact that the nomads did not even trouble to dismantle their otherwise movable dwellings. They carried their tents on wheels !

Æschylus told us about the " Wandering Scythes who dwell in latticed huts high-poised on easy wheels," and Ibn Battuta actually rode in one—" on the waggon is put a sort of pavilion of wands laced together with narrow thongs. It is very light, and it is covered with felt or cloth and has latticed windows." The Friar Rubruquis described one of these waggons as having an axle like a ship's mast, and it took twenty oxen to draw it. A thousand miles of open country separated the home plateau from the rich sedentary centres in the twin valleys of the Syr and Amu Darya. This was just right for Jenghis' cavalry, and the lines of communication were easily kept up.

As they moved westwards they left the plateau and entered the Dzungarian plains, equally easy to negotiate. To the south soared the Tian Shan ranges, to the north lay the Siberian forests. They kept between the two, avoiding the only mountain barrier that lay in their path by marching through the famous Dzungarian Gate to their *rendezvous* in the Ili valley. From here it was easy going right up to the banks of the Syr Darya, and there they entered upon what, to them, must have been an Eldorado.

They were now two thousand miles from their base ; but there was no fear of communications being cut, for Jenghis saw to that by annihilating all the inhabitants. He never risked trouble in the rear. The whole westward movement had now only taken twelve months. On reaching the Syr, Jenghis showed his cunning and executed one of the most brilliant pieces of strategy. Two great rivers and a sand desert lay between him and his goal—the twin cities of Samarkand and Bukhara. An age-worn route led onwards to both, but the nomad, with nomad instinct, gave it a wide berth. He was not going to be entangled and embarrassed by the intricate canal system and cultivation of the river valleys. He arranged a side-show to threaten his goal from that quarter, while he disappeared into the desert. With picked men, on iron rations, he made a forced march across the Kizil Kum desert, and took Bukhara in the rear. The rest was easy prey. He mopped up the hoarded wealth of the capital, Samarkand, and looked forward across the Oxus.

Beyond the Oxus lay Khurasan, bulging with riches and dotted with great cities, which had a special attraction for the destroyers. It must be remembered that this region over which Jenghis was striding was not the sparsely populated land it is to-day. Its now ruined sites were then busy cities, its deserts were fertile plains, and you may blame Jenghis for their destruction. Balkh, the great and prosperous " Mother of Cities," is now only a name on the map. Merv, once " Queen of the World," a centre of learning and of culture and of a vast agricultural district, has hardly yet recovered from Jenghis' visit. Herat (for much of present-day Afghanistan was included in the Khurasan) is not much of a place now, but it used to be the proud possessor of everything that denoted up-to-date luxury. Jenghis was responsible for its downfall, even as he was for the tragedy of the place usually referred to as Bamian ; but there he lost a grandson, so he had at least an excuse for razing that great city so efficiently that it has never reappeared. For the destruction of Nishapur he had no such excuse, but it suffered the same fate.

Jenghis, having finished off the remainder of the Khwarazm Empire, driven the Shah to exile and death, and collected his treasure, started with unsatiated appetite to form a scheme for eating up the unknown regions which lay farther west.

His spies had probably reported that Southern Russia held excellent grazing. So he continued his old policy of following the grass. Mongol horses were again the deciding factor in the campaign; where they could go Mongols could win. This first Mongol advance into eastern Europe was little more than a raid, but by it they established contact with the West, saw the busy ports on the Black Sea, heard of Poland and the Hungarian plains, and no doubt said: "Au revoir, but not good-bye." A greater effort would be made later, but before doing so Jenghis, now past his prime (he was over sixty), decided to return home. He must have travelled leisurely, for four years later we find him occupied in subduing a revolt in Tangut, in western China. Even at his ripe age he still had ambitions, his latest dream being to continue his conquest of China from this new base in the west. But he died in the effort.

The first crash of the Avalanche was over, but it was only the warning of something worse to follow. The Great Captain had gone, but he had started something which did not die with him. The ripple which had begun in a far-away Mongol encampment half a century before had grown to a wave. The wave, finding nothing to stop it, flowed on. As it flowed it grew larger and gathered strength, until it seemed to

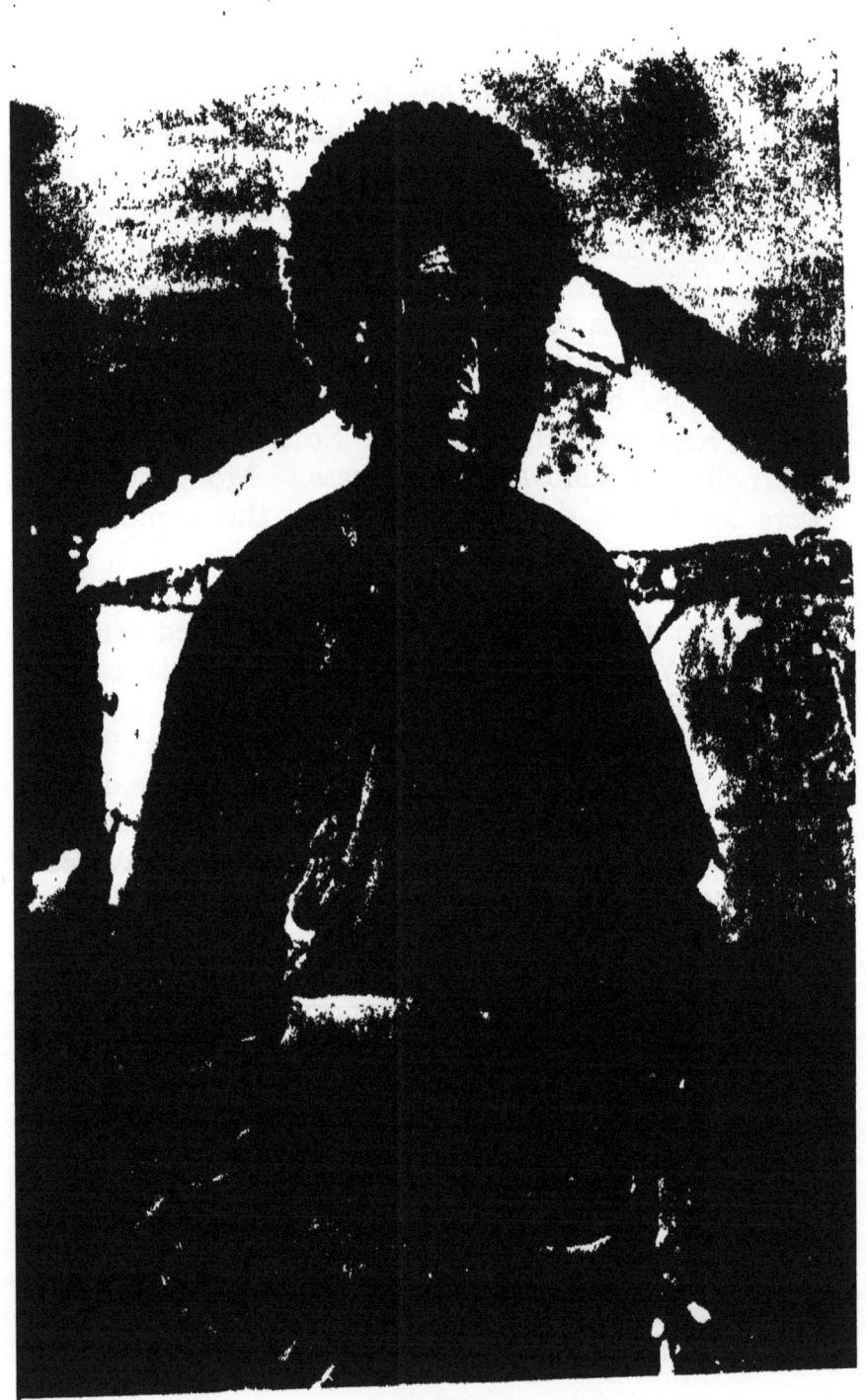

MONGOL TYPE

be beyond control. The Mongol wave was indeed, from its start, beyond human control.

Ogdai succeeded, and continued his father's good work, in that he concentrated on extending the already vast empire. So he sent off the great General Subutai to complete what had been left unfinished in the West. This time it was not a raid but a tornado that the Mongols brought into Southern Russia. Holy Kiev they burnt and pillaged. They entered Pest, and crossed the Danube, whilst another subsidiary force ravaged Poland. They watered their horses at rivers which flowed to the Baltic. They wiped out a combined German-Polish army at Liegnitz in Silesia, which meant that they were within two hundred miles of Vienna. Christendom trembled. At this moment (1241) Ogdai died, and his death was given as the reason for the halt and recession of the Mongol hosts. But it is more likely that the mountains and the forests stemmed the tide ; also they had come to the end of the grazing-lands. At any rate they retired and never returned.

Or was it, possibly, that the Mongols for the first time came up against something which was not Asiatic ? Muscovy had played a poor game, divided and disorganised she had hardly made a fight against the invaders. But the brave story of the trumpeter of Cracow tells us of how Middle Europe faced them. The young Pole who blew the trumpet —which it was his sworn duty to sound from the tower of Our Lady's Church every hour, day and night, until death, and which he continued to blow when the town was in flames and his fellow-citizens had all fled within the citadel—was the emblem of a different spirit. The Mongol conquerors gazed in amazement at him. " A Tartar below crouched to his bow, and drew back the arrow . . . the string whined. The dark shaft flew like a swift bird straight for the mark. It pierced the breast of the young trumpeter when he was near the end of his song—it quivered there a moment and the song ceased. But still holding the trumpet the youth fell back against the supporting wall and blew one last glorious note ; it began strongly, trembled, and then ceased—broken like the young life that gave it birth, and at that moment those below applied the torch to the wooden church and it, too, rose in flames to Heaven, with the soul of the youth among them." That was the spirit which the Mongols met when they reached the gates of Europe.

After a short interval—ten years—the third and last wave broke. Mangu was now Great Khan, and he had a brother, Hulagu, the biggest scourge of all. This time the Mongols concentrated on the Moslem world lying beyond the frontiers of Khwarazm. No doubt the spies had been busy in Mesopotamia ; and reported that Baghdad, then the religious capital of Islam, was well worth a visit. So Hulagu descended upon it, and although he exterminated the Assassins, of evil memory, he was responsible, not only for the sack of Baghdad (1258), but for the destruction of the vast irrigation system of Mesopotamia, and thus reduced its fertility to the waste that remains to this day. This was useless vandalism, unless it was a part of Mongol policy to suppress the sedentary races. Hulagu also executed the Caliph, swept on into Syria, and, but for the Mamluks, might have entered another continent—or was it again the lack of grazing, and not the Mamluks, that stopped the Mongol advance into Egypt? The horse again appeared as a dominating factor in Mongol history.

After this last crash there followed a period of calm which contrasted strangely with the tumult of the last forty-five years. Kubilai was elected Great Khan on Mangu's death in 1259, and he, being more interested in Chinese culture than in carnage, moved his capital from Karakorum to Cambaluc (Peking). There he built his " stately pleasure dome " and received homage and embassies from the whole world. Between them, the three generations had succeeded in building up the widest empire yet seen. It stretched from the Pacific to Middle Europe, from the Indian seas almost to the Baltic, from Siberian wastes to Burma.

Avalanche it was, in truth, for it had descended suddenly on an unready and unsuspecting world. Its immediate effects were entirely destructive, its ultimate result very far reaching. The Western world, divided against itself, was stirred into a new life, and incidentally became conscious, for the first time, that something existed beyond its narrow horizon, namely, the unimagined great new world of the Orient.

THE following story of what would appear to have been an English crown jewel is gathered from various sources. Firstly from *The Six Voyages of Tavernier*, the famous seventeenth-century traveller and jewel merchant, who acquired " the diamond ring on which are engraved the Arms of the King of England," and who sold it, or lost it, some years later on the Persian Gulf.

Secondly, from contemporary Embassy Archives,

now in the Public Record Office, and from the Finch Manuscripts, which show that the original owner of the diamond made great efforts to recover it.

Thirdly, from an altogether extraneous source, namely, the romantic, but probably largely fictitious story of one, John Campbell, a Scottish gunsmith in the employ of the Moghul Emperor Aurangzeb, who claims to have been given " a diamond as big as a pigeon's egg with the King of England's Arms cut on it." The manuscript of this tale (as told by Richard Bell) is in the British Museum, and has been already elucidated by Sir R. Carnac Temple in the *Indian Antiquary*. As far as I know no one has attempted to collate these accounts, or to sift the facts from the fiction. But, as will be seen from the following narrative, the problem remains unsolved.

CHAPTER X

THE KING'S DIAMOND

" Suddenly, as rare things will, it vanished. . . ."

ON the 27th of November 1663 there set out from
Paris a traveller whose name was already famous, for
Jean Baptiste Tavernier was on his sixth voyage to the
Orient. The great jeweller, since it is in the history
of precious stones rather than in the realm of travel
that his name will live, is worthy, without exagger-
ation, of a claim to greatness. Had he not already
carried into Asia the largest pearl* that ever came
out of Europe? Was he not the original owner of
that " extraordinary rarity " called Tavernier's Blue
Diamond, which, purchased from him by Louis XIV,
disappeared during the French Revolution, though
eventually a fragment of it reappeared and became
famous as the tragic " Hope." Moreover, he was
about to see, handle and weigh the " Great Moghul "
itself, the largest diamond known at that date.
Tavernier was certainly the first and probably the
only European to see it, for, unlike most famous
diamonds, the " Great Moghul " was short-lived ;
recently discovered (1630-50), it was soon to disappear
from human ken in the sack of Delhi by Nadir Shah
a hundred years later.

Tavernier may even have set eyes on that great

* After wandering about Asia for three hundred years, and being
owned in turn by Indian Rajahs, Persian Shahs, and Chinese Emperor,
this pearl is alleged to have passed into the possession of a French
religious institution, and to have been brought back to Paris. Its
adventurous career did not end there, for it narrowly escaped being
appropriated as Nazi loot during the German occupation.

Oriental talisman, the romantic Kuh-i-Nur, although he does not mention the fact, for its mere 186 carats might not have attracted his attention when seen in company with other giants. It was certainly in the possession of the Moghul dynasty. Unlike its rival, the " Great Moghul," this diamond had an authentic history dating back three hundred years, and a traditional one of fifty centuries ; moreover it was destined to live on indefinitely as part of the Regalia of English Kings.

Tavernier was shown the whole of the Moghul treasure. He held in his hand, he weighed, and he examined all the Emperor's priceless jewels, which was a favour never before manifested to any other European, all those indestructible wonders of infinite age, which had already been dominating factors in history, and which may still be controlling the destinies of men, when we have long departed.

On this, his sixth and last journey, Tavernier planned a grand tour of the great potentates of Persia and the Moghul Empire. During the short two years he had been at home, he had accumulated a stock of fine jewels and golden ornaments valued at about £30,000. We have no details of his stock-in-trade, but we do know that special mention is made of a " *diamond with the English Arms cut on it*," and therefore we may infer that this particular precious stone was worthy of notice. How he came by it we are not told, but it was without doubt one of the jewels pawned by Charles II during his exile.

Tavernier pursued his way slowly, but safely—in spite of many vicissitudes—across Europe, and eventually landed on the Asiatic shore at Smyrna. Here he tried to sell this diamond engraved with the English

Arms, but failed. So he moved eastwards, and presented himself at the Court of Shah Abbas II At the Persian capital of Isfahan he spent ten week and did good business, for he sold diamonds to the value of 3900 *tomans* or about £13,500, but he did *no* sell the diamond engraved with the Arms of the King of England.

The Shah happened to have in his possession a famous engraved diamond, so Tavernier showed him his stone, as an example of what European diamond-cutters could do, and although the intricate design of the Royal Arms of the Stuarts must have surprised the Shah, whose engraved diamond boasted only the comparatively simple Arabic script, we are distinctly told that he did not buy it.

Tavernier then set out for India and went down to Bunder Abbas on the Persian Gulf, in order to take ship for Surat. At that particular date the Dutch were so predominant in Persia and on the Gulf that the trade and prestige of the English East India Company were practically *nil*. This is an important point when considering what happened to Tavernier at Bunder Abbas. There was a resident English agent, Mr Stephen Flower, and also a Dutch agent, one Hendrick van Wijk, both of whom tried to buy the engraved diamond. Then followed a very curious incident. Tavernier lodged at the Dutchman's house, and as he was about to embark on a Dutch vessel for India, the English agent entrusted to his care despatches " which had arrived express from England to deliver to the President at Surat " : they had come through Aleppo, having been forwarded by the Consul Lanoy. There were also included in the packet a number of private letters for other residents in India.

Now a rumour had already reached the outposts on the Persian Gulf that war had been declared between England and Holland ; and the Dutch, being less well advised than the English, were anxious to learn the truth. It was obvious that the Arab, who had just arrived by the desert route from Aleppo, bearing the packet for the English agent, had brought the news. So the Dutch agent—van Wijk—by a clever ruse, removed the packet of despatches and letters from Tavernier's wallet, substituting another of similar shape and size, but containing only blank papers. In that wallet was also a single diamond, and this disappeared with the despatches.

Tavernier passed on to India, and delivered his charge ; but when the fraud was discovered, the displeasure and ill-feeling towards Tavernier became so great that he went in fear of his life. In fact, the episode ruined his Indian venture. He sold his jewels, it is true, to the Great Moghul and Shaista Khan, but then set out for home. On reaching Bunder Abbas, he found van Wijk already gone to his account—" It is rare to see treachery go unpunished," he remarks with satisfaction—" the plotters all died miserably." He proceeded to Paris, passing through Isfahan and Stambul. No further mention is made of the " diamond with the English Arms cut on it " until he reached the latter city, but there, when cross-questioned by the English Ambassador—Lord Winchilsea—who had instructions to recover the diamond at all costs, Tavernier declared he had sold it to van Wijk. In a despatch from the Consul at Aleppo to Lord Winchilsea, the transaction appears in a different light ; van Wijk is reported as having " got it into his possession and prevented Flower from obtaining it." " Got it into his possession " sounds suspicious, and if the Dutchman had been· so unscrupulous as to pilfer the private correspondence of his guest, perhaps he had no qualms about diamonds, especially as he knew the English agent was trying to outbid him. We know there was a single diamond in the wallet that contained the despatches, and it *might* have been the diamond engraved with His Majesty's Arms. Anyway, this particular jewel passes out of " Tavernier's travels " at Bunder Abbas in April 1665 ; sold, according to him, to the Dutch agent, on whose death later in the same year it was alleged to have been " sent to Batavia to the Dutch General Massugre (Maatzuiker) and his Council."

If this be true, what is the explanation of the strange story which follows ?

In the month of August of the year 1670, there might have been witnessed the most unusual spectacle of two way-worn European travellers—a Scotsman and a French priest—accompanied by an Arab guide, emerging out of the wilderness called the Syrian Desert, onto the outskirts of what was then the great and famous city of Aleppo.

Now, in the seventeenth century, Aleppo ranked as the third most important city of the Ottoman Empire. The Empire itself, although just past its zenith, ranked high in world power, holding the Christian West in complete contempt, and retaining that superior attitude towards it which made it difficult for the two to meet. Sultan Muhammad IV reigned at Stambul—or rather his Grand Vizier Kiuprili, functioned most successfully for him—and his frontiers extended from the Danube to the Persian Gulf, from the Black Sea to the Sudan. The Turks, in fact, commanded the Gate to the Orient, which at that moment was the goal for which western nations were striving ; they were therefore able to dictate their own terms to Europe. Aleppo was the Guardian of this Gate, and that is why the city ranked so high, and why its name was famous.

Incidentally, it was also the reason for there being a prosperous English colony there. For, in spite of the fanatical hatred that the Turks had for infidels, the English had been successful in maintaining more or less friendly relations with the Porte, which resulted in the establishment of a trading concern called the Levant Company. The principal emporium of the company was at Aleppo, and, in the days of which we write, the depôt there was at its prime.

And so it happened that one August day at noon there appeared before the entrance of the great Saracenic Khan, which served as a compound wherein dwelt and worked all the members of the Levant Company's staff, the aforesaid Scotsman— the Capuchin priest having betaken himself to the hostel of his own Order.

The " factory," as the trading community was termed, was at its mid-day meal, for the whole staff, Consul, Vice-Consul, Chaplain and clerks messed together. The stranger, admitted to their hospitality, was called to join them at dinner, where he made himself known as John Campbell, homeward-bound from India, having come by way of Persia and Baghdad.

The sumptuous repast must have been welcomed by Campbell for he had been in the desert for many months, while the safety of his surroundings, after the perilous way he had followed, filled him with a sense of complete security. Yet, as he sat down to eat, his hand unconsciously crept beneath his garments to feel that the packets were there. It had become a habit with him—that making sure of the little packets, sewn into the lining of his old coat, and the big one slung on a leather thong round his neck, and others secreted about his person, so that none could be taken from him except over his dead body. Alas, they were no longer there, only those hidden in his boots—they were still there, and safe now, within the walls of the British Consulate. For this bold adventurer had been carrying on him precious stones of great value, amongst them being a famous and historic diamond. He had attempted to carry them across eight hundred miles of lawless land ; a land where all life was held cheap, and where the life of a Christian dog was accounted of no value at all.

Campbell ate as a man half-starved, but by degrees good food and excellent wine loosened his tongue and he began to tell his story. His hosts, by this time, were eager listeners, for it must be remembered that the " factory " at Aleppo was the farthest outpost of the Levant Company ; beyond lay the Great Desert, and although they traded with regions still farther east, yet none ventured thither. The Consular staff, the resident merchants and their clerks made the best they could of life in Aleppo and its vicinity ; indeed, it was considered a great achievement when, a few years later, some members of the community penetrated the desert and rediscovered Palmyra, only one hundred and thirty miles away.

To these men sitting round the table, therefore, the advent of Campbell caused somewhat of a thrill.

They were well accustomed to the arrival of the great caravans, which came at intervals from Baghdad and Basra, armed, escorted, and well able to pay for their safety by much *baksheesh*; and occasionally a European came under their protection. But for a solitary individual to emerge safely from that, to them, horrible and hostile wilderness was a miracle. Attention was riveted on the rugged, travel-worn figure as he began to tell his tale.

" I, John Campbell, formerly gunsmith to Aurangzib, Emperor of the Moghuls, am here to-day by the grace of Almighty God, for seldom has any man passed safely through such perils as have befallen me.

" For some years I served the Shah Jahan, father of Aurangzeb, at Delhi as gun-founder. Now, the Emperor was at the war with Sivaji, the Maratha rebel, who was champion of his nation's independence, and I was sent to the wars, and remained two years fighting for the Moghuls. Indeed, we took twenty-eight castles from the Hindus.

" When at length Shah Jahan grew old his four sons fought amongst themselves for his throne. At that time I was with the youngest son—Murad Bakhsh—who raised an army of 150,000 horse, 150 great guns, and 20,000 elephants. But Aurangzeb defeated his brother and put him to death. So I served Aurangzeb for six years, and during this period I chanced to be in Agra, when the said rebel Sivaji and his son were there—first as guests, and later as prisoners. It was I who saved this young prince, Sivaji's son, and hid him in my own house until opportunity occurred, and then smuggled him out of the city, hidden in a large basket of sweetmeats ; three baskets of sweetmeats I sent out, but in one of them was hidden the prince. For this service I received many gifts from King Sivaji, and amongst them was ' *a diamond as big as a pigeon's egg with the King of England's Arms cut on it. Many diamond merchants from France, Holland, and other countries had been sent to India to purchase this diamond, but money could not procure what love did.*'

" I was in India for about ten years and when at last I obtained leave to return home, I went down to Surat, and, in company with a Capuchin brother took ship for Muscat, and thence to Bunder Abbas in Persia. From here I went to Shiraz and Isfahan, where the King Sulaiman rewarded me richly, for I cast shells for his guns and mortars. I also sold to him a bezoar-stone which expels poison. Leaving Isfahan in company with the French priest and two diamond merchants of Paris, we passed on to Tabriz and Kirkuk, eventually, after great privation and sufferings, reaching Baghdad. I stayed in Baghdad a month but had not the patience to wait longer for the Aleppo caravan, so the French priest hired an Arab guide and obtained security by his wife and four children, that this guide would bring us safe to Aleppo. The French diamond merchants fell sick and remained in Baghdad, but when they heard of my plan they tried to persuade me from it. They knew I had a charge, and also a diamond (the King's diamond), which they themselves had hoped to acquire but failed. The Capuchin priests also tried to dissuade me, saying that anything I left with them would be conveyed safely to whatever place I should choose, and warned me on no account to travel with valuables without the protection of a caravan. I denied that I had anything, and they replied, ' If you have, it will be the cause of the loss of your own life and the lives of all those who are with you.'

"So we set forth from Baghdad and reached the town of Ana on the Euphrates. We had not left Ana two leagues when seven Arab horsemen came riding after us. They had only lances, so I stood to them with my pistols. The priest cried : 'For God's sake take care : if we resist, they will kill us.' The guide said he had acted as guide to four diamond merchants and two priests who went this way a few years before, but by firing a pistol which wounded an Arab, they all lost their lives by having their heads cut off. I told the guide if he did not fight, he would be the first to be killed—by me. I told the priest to fight, but he said it was against his religion to fight. They both ran away to the enemy. When the robbers saw they could not prevail against me, they let the priest and guide go and disappeared ; but the priest knew they would return later, and advised me to bury my valuables, or give them to him. So I took my things out of the padding of my saddle, and gave the priest some, and some I kept myself. When the priest saw them, he cried, 'These will be the death of both of us.'

"I gave him :—

3 diamond strings with crosses.	A green stone.
2 bezoar-stones to expel poison.	12 sapphires.
2 great diamonds.	4 diamond rings.
A blood stone.	3 rubies (special).

"I kept myself :—

A great diamond with the King's Arms on it.
8 other great diamonds.

" These I packed ' in a little purse and tied them about my members ' ; others I hid in my boots.

" About an hour later we saw fourteen horsemen coming. They surrounded us, shouting, ' We have now got guns ; fire if you dare. If you fire a shot, or shoot an arrow, you are dead men.' The priest cried, ' Do not shoot.' They then ran in on me and stript me naked, all but my boots (which saved me something). They were all muffled up ; I could only see their eyes. Some few dollars I had about my middle they presently eased me of, and, stark naked, made me lead my horse to a valley. I did not go fast enough, so one of them gave me a push with the butt end of his lance, which put me on my nose. In my fall he spied the purse, and snatched it away. They then parted my things ; the dresses of honour given me by Aurangzeb and the Shah Sulaiman, and other valuables ; and cast lots amongst themselves who should have this and who that.

" They likewise stript the priest, and set us both down to cut off our heads. The guide said, ' My wife and children are pawn for the priest, cut off the head of the other.' So they gave the priest his coat again, and set me by myself with a lance at my back and two swords over my head, saying, ' Take your leave of the world.' I begged them to allow me to say a few prayers, which they did, and in that time they took counsel, and mutinied amongst themselves. He who had taken the jewels from my members, said, ' Is it not enough we have taken his goods ; must we take his life also?—there is a God.' They made me come to them and fall down and kiss their feet, and gave me a camel-coat and pointed out the way. I would have returned to Babylon, but they would not allow us to go that way. We travelled on wearily and without food until, when nearly ready to die, we came to the Euphrates, and on it, by God's providence, were men on rafts going to Basra. So we sent the guide, who got from them forty cakes of bread, which lasted us until we reached the old city called Taiba.* We travelled fourteen days and nights ere we could reach it. We arrived at Taiba heart-broken, having neither food, money, nor friends. Here we had to pay ten dollars a head as tax, and for lack of it were thrown into prison. On the fourth day there arrived a merchant from Aleppo, who, on hearing of me, came to ask who I was. I said I was a Christian and an Englishman, so he advanced me the money needed, and I gave him a note for twenty-four dollars. We paid our head-money and started from Taiba towards Aleppo. On the way we met a party of Arabs, who fired at us before we came within shot of them. Sending in advance a young man-servant of the merchant who had lent me the money at Taiba, he arranged for our safety by paying two dollars a man, having nothing to lose but our horses. When within two leagues of Aleppo, I said to the priest, ' Now we are out of danger.' But the people where we lay had sent to the neighbouring Arab king, saying, ' For so much we will deliver two

* Campbell was taking the ordinary short-cut in use at that date between the Euphrates and Aleppo, travellers preferring to run the gauntlet of Badawin robbers rather than submit to the extortionate demands of the Riverine Arabs for safe conduct through their country. The route lay across the North Syrian desert, the ancient (but derelict) walled town of Taiyibe, Roman Oriza, being the only settled site that the wayfarer would encounter during the crossing. A detailed account of this old way appears in my Introduction to *The Desert Route to India*, Hakluyt Society's publication for 1928, Series II, No. LXIII.

Christians into your hands.' We had not gone far before we overtook a drove of laden oxen. Said the guide, ' Now we are out of danger, let us go ahead.' No sooner had we passed these market-people than I espied twenty horsemen coming down on us ; so, leaving my horse, I joined the crowd of market-people and got behind an old Arab woman for shelter. She called them rogues, and railed at them for hindering travellers. But I was carried to their king all the same, although I would not part with my old Arab woman. The king asked me who I was. I replied, ' A poor man, robbed of everything on my way from Babylon.' Said he, ' You certainly do not look like a rich man.' He caused the woman to search me. Finding nothing, he said, ' My luck is out. I wish I had met you before you were robbed. But where is your horse ? ' The woman said, ' The horse is mine ; I let him ride, he being so footsore.' At last we parted, so I gave the poor woman a dollar, which made tears start out of her eyes for joy.

" That is the end of my story, and that is why I appear before you to-day in such a ragged and weather-beaten condition." *

A few days later there came the French priest, asking for an interview with the Consul and the Chaplain. In the presence of these two, the priest produced the jewels handed over to him for safe-keeping, when Campbell divided up his hoard in the desert. Thanking the Consul for the services Campbell had rendered to him, he departed, leaving the jewels lying on the table.

* The full account, as narrated by Bell, is of course of much greater length than this brief summary.

There is no further reference to the diamond engraved with the King's Arms in Campbell's narrative. There was a jewel amongst those the priest handed over, which the Consul thought would be a fit present for his wife in England, and he bargained with Campbell for its purchase. Campbell complained that the Consul and the Chaplain " wheedled him out of his jewels." But there is no mention of the diamond we have followed so far, only to lose again.

Whether Tavernier's statement is true and the diamond went to Batavia, or whether Campbell's account is correct and the diamond ultimately returned in his safe-keeping as far as the Syrian Desert, where it was filched by Arab robbers, we shall never know. I am rather inclined to think Tavernier the liar, and to believe Campbell. It is almost incredible that Campbell could have invented the diamond with English Arms cut on it ; and it is quite inconceivable that there could have been *two*. Curiously enough, the occasion on which he says he was given it corresponds with the period during which the diamond had passed out of Tavernier's possession, and during which (except for Tavernier's statement) its exact location was not known for certain. Supposing that it had been *this* diamond which had disappeared when the despatches were stolen, Tavernier would have been only too ready to cover up the fact during his interview with the Ambassador at Stambul ; he therefore *said* he had sold it, whereas it had really been stolen by the Dutchman. The Dutchman, in his turn, having got hold of the despatches, was only too glad to get rid of such damning evidence as the diamond, so he parted with it to a local native dealer, who made his profit quickly by passing it on to India. Indian princes were always vieing with each other in the accumulation of easily-carried treasure. Sivaji himself had recently sacked Surat, and therefore had a vast store of loot which he was anxious to exchange into more portable bullion. So the diamond may have found its way into his treasury, only to pass out again the following year as a reward to the Scotsman, Campbell.

Of course an engraved diamond is so rare a thing that we may well doubt the existence of this one. It has been suggested, for instance, that it was not a diamond at all, but a white sapphire. But would an expert like Tavernier have been deceived by a gem which anyone can recognise as such? And would there have been such urgency about its recovery? Not only was the English Ambassador on its track, but continental jewellers of note were scouring Asia in search of it. Again, we have three independent references to the same object—the jeweller Tavernier, through whose hands it passed; the Ambassador, Lord Winchilsea, who had orders from his government to recover it; and the gun-founder, Campbell, who says he was given it as a reward. These facts only tend to whet our appetite for more information, but we have to go unsatisfied for there is nothing more to add.

One thing is certain, and that is—" *The diamond as big as a pigeon's egg with the King of England's Arms cut on it* " never came back to the land of its original owners.

APPENDICES

Synopsis of the various classifications

Mufloniformes.

LYDEKKER, 1898-1916.

Ovis musimon Pallas.
Ovis orientalis orientalis (= *ophion* Blyth).
Ovis orientalis anatolica Valenciennes.

Ovis orientalis gmelini Blyth.
Ovis orientalis isphahanica Nasonov.
Ovis orientalis erskinei Lydekker (status doubtful).
Ovis orientalis urmiana Guenther.

Ovis laristanica Nasonov.

Ovis vignei vignei Blyth.
Ovis vignei punjabiensis Lydekker.
Ovis vignei cycloceros Hutton.
Ovis vignei arkar Eversmann.

APPENDIX I

of the Genus *OVIS*, belonging to the Old World.

NASONOV, 1910-1923.
Ovis musimon.
Ovis ophion ophion Blyth.
Ovis ophion anatolica.
Ovis ophion armeniana Nasonov.

Ovis gmelini gmelini.
Ovis gmelini isphahanica.
Ovis gmelini erskinei (? = *orientalis*, see below).
Ovis gmelini urmiana.

Ovis laristanica.

Ovis orientalis orientalis Gmelin (? = *erskinei*).
Ovis orientalis dolgopolovi Nasonov. Eastern Elburz, Asterabad region.
Ovis orientalis cycloceros (= *varenzovi* Satunin). Kopet Dagh.
Ovis orientalis arcar. Region between the Aral and Caspian Seas.

Ovis vignei vignei.
Ovis vignei punjabiensis.
Ovis vignei (?) *blanfordi* Hume (? = *cycloceros* or *laristanica*).
Ovis vignei bochariensis Nasonov.

SUSHKIN, 1925	FLEROV, 1935	BOBRINSKOY, 1944
follows Nasonov.	considers *Ovis vignei* an Eastern race of *Ovis orientalis,* both being very close to *Ovis musimon.*	separates the Mufloniformes into three Species-groups viz. *Ovis musimon,* *Ovis ophion,* *Ovis orientalis,* (which includes the *vignei* group).

HARPER, 1945.

Ovis musimon.
Ovis ophion ophion.
Ovis ophion anatolica.

Ovis ophion armeniana.

Ovis gmelini gmelini.

Ovis gmelini isphahanica.
Ovis gmelini urmiana.
Ovis laristanica.

Ovis orientalis (? = erskinei).

Ovis vignei vignei.

Ovis vignei punjabiensis.
Ovis vignei cycloceros
 (*= blanfordi*).

Ovis vignei arkal (? = varenzovi
 and *dolgopolovi*).

Ovis vignei bochariensis.

General Distribution.

Corsica and Sardinia.
Cyprus.
S. Anatolia. ? extending N.E. towards Erzerum.
Around Mount Ararat and Lake Van.
Erzerum district (Type—locality unknown, status doubtful).
S.W. Persia, Isfahan region.
N.W. Persia, Tabriz region.
S.E. Persia. ? extending to Baluchistan (Type—locality unknown).
Central Elburz (*erskinei* ? Western Elburz).
Basin of the Upper Indus, Ladak to Chitral.
Punjab ranges.
Afghanistan, Baluchistan. ? extending into E. and N.E. Persia.
Region between the Caspian and Aral, Kopet Dagh, Eastern Elburz.
Eastern Bukhara, N. of the Oxus.

Argaliformes.
LYDEKKER, 1898-1916.

Ovis ammon ammon Linnæus.
Ovis ammon mongolica Severtzov (= *jubata* Peters).
Ovis ammon hodgsoni Blyth.
Ovis ammon kozlovi Nasonov.

Ovis ammon poli Blyth.
Ovis ammon severtzovi Nasonov.
Ovis ammon nigrimontana Severtzov.
Ovis ammon karelini Severtzov.
Ovis ammon littledalei Lydekker.
Ovis ammon humei Lydekker.
Ovis ammon, collium Severtzov.
Ovis ammon heinsi Severtzov.   E. Alexandrovski range.
Ovis ammon sairensis Lydekker.
Ovis poli adametzi Kowarzik.   Kurruk Tagh, E. Sinkiang.

Ovis canadensis nivicola Eschscholtz.
Ovis canadensis borealis Severtzov.
Ovis canadensis alleni Matschie.
Ovis ammon storcki Allen.

NASONOV, 1910-1923.   SUSHKIN, 1925   BOBRINSKOY, 1944
                                  follows   separates the
                                  Nasonov.   Argaliformes
                                                    into two
                                                    Species-groups,
                                                    Ovis ammon and
                                                    Ovis nivicola.

Ovis ammon ammon.   Russian Altai.
Ovis ammon mongolica.   Mongolian Altai.
Ovis ammon hodgsoni.
Ovis ammon kozlovi.   S. Gobi.
Ovis ammon dalai-lamæ Prjevalski (validity uncertain).
Ovis ammon jubata Peters (= *darwini* Prjevalski, = *comosa* Hollister).
Ovis ammon przevalski Nasonov.   Sailughem extension of Great Altai.

Ovis poli poli.
Ovis poli severtzovi.
Ovis poli nigrimontana.
Ovis poli karelini.
Ovis poli littledalei.

Ovis poli collium.
Ovis poli heinsi (probably extinct).
Ovis poli (?) *sairensis* (doubtful geographically and systematically).

Ovis nivicola nivicola (= *storcki*).
Ovis nivicola borealis.
Ovis nivicola alleni.
Ovis nivicola lydekkeri Kowarzik.
Ovis nivicola potanini Nasonov.

HARPER, 1945.

Ovis ammon ammon (= *mongolica*, = *przevalski*).

Ovis ammon hodgsoni.

Ovis ammon dalai-lamæ.

Ovis ammon darwini (= *jubata*, = *comosa*, = *kozlovi*).

Ovis ammon poli.
Ovis ammon severtzovi.
Ovis ammon nigrimontana.
Ovis ammon karelini (= *heinsi*).
Ovis ammon littledalei.

Ovis ammon humei.

Ovis ammon collium.
Ovis ammon sairensis.

Ovis nivicola nivicola (= *storcki*).
Ovis nivicola borealis.

Ovis nivicola alleni.

Ovis nivicola lydekkeri.

Ovis nivicola potanini.

General Distribution.

Russian and Mongolian Altai, also subsidiary ranges in N.W. Mongolia.

Southern Tibet—Ladak to Szechwan; Central Tibet—N.E. to Koko Nor.

N.W. Tibet—Kun Lun, Altin Tagh region. ? eastwards to Nan Shan.

N. China, Inner Mongolia, extending across the Gobi to S.E. spurs of the Altai. ? westwards to Nan Shan.

Pamirs.

Nurata Tau, S. Kizil Kum.

Kara Tau, N. of the Syr Darya.

Issyk Kul region, S. of the Ili River, North of the Naryn.

Dzungarian Ala Tau, and other ranges N. of the Ili River. Yulduz Plateau. ? eastwards to Hami.

S.W. Tian Shan, between the Pamirs and Khan Tengri, S. of the Naryn River.

Semipalatinsk region, west to Akmolinsk (probably extinct).

Ranges between the Dzungarian Ala Tau and the Upper or Black Irtish.

Kamchatka Peninsula.

Syverma Range, between the Lower Yenisei and Khatanga Rivers.

N.E. portion of Stanovoi Range. ? extending into the Chukchi Peninsula.

Verkhoyansk region, between the Lower Lena and Indigirka Rivers.

S.W. portion of Stanovoi Range.

Analysis of the foregoing.

1. *Ovis gmelini gmelini.* ? Type locality and validity.
2. *Ovis orientalis erskinei.* ? Validity.
3. *Ovis orientalis dolgopolovi.* ? Validity.
4. Kopet Dagh and Ala Dagh (Persian—Transcaspian frontier). ? Status of subspecies inhabiting—and to which group—*vignei* or *orientalis*—they belong.
5. Birjand region, E. Persia. ? Status of subspecies inhabiting ——.
6. *Ovis laristanica.* ? Range east and north-eastwards.
7. *Ovis ammon littledalei.* ? Range eastwards.
8. Dzungarian Altai, Baitik and Aji Bogdo ranges. ? Status of subspecies inhabiting ——. The range allowed to *darwini*, viz. from N. China to the S.E. spurs of the Altai, seems to be unduly wide, although Allen " can find no differences that could possibly be of value in distinguishing the sheep from these various localities." But there are still 500 miles of sheep country between the extreme known limits of *darwini* and *ammon*.
9. Nan Shan, and subsidiary ranges to the N.W. of Koko Nor. ? Status of subspecies inhabiting ——.
10. Barkul—Karlik Tagh. ? Status of subspecies inhabiting ——.
11. Aksu. ? Status of subspecies inhabiting spurs of the Tian Shan, north of ——.
12. *Ovis poli adametzi.* ? Status and range of ——.
13. ? Status of the subspecies inhabiting the wide area in N. and N.E. Tibet, where the ranges of *hodgsoni*, *darwini* and *dalai-lamæ* merge.

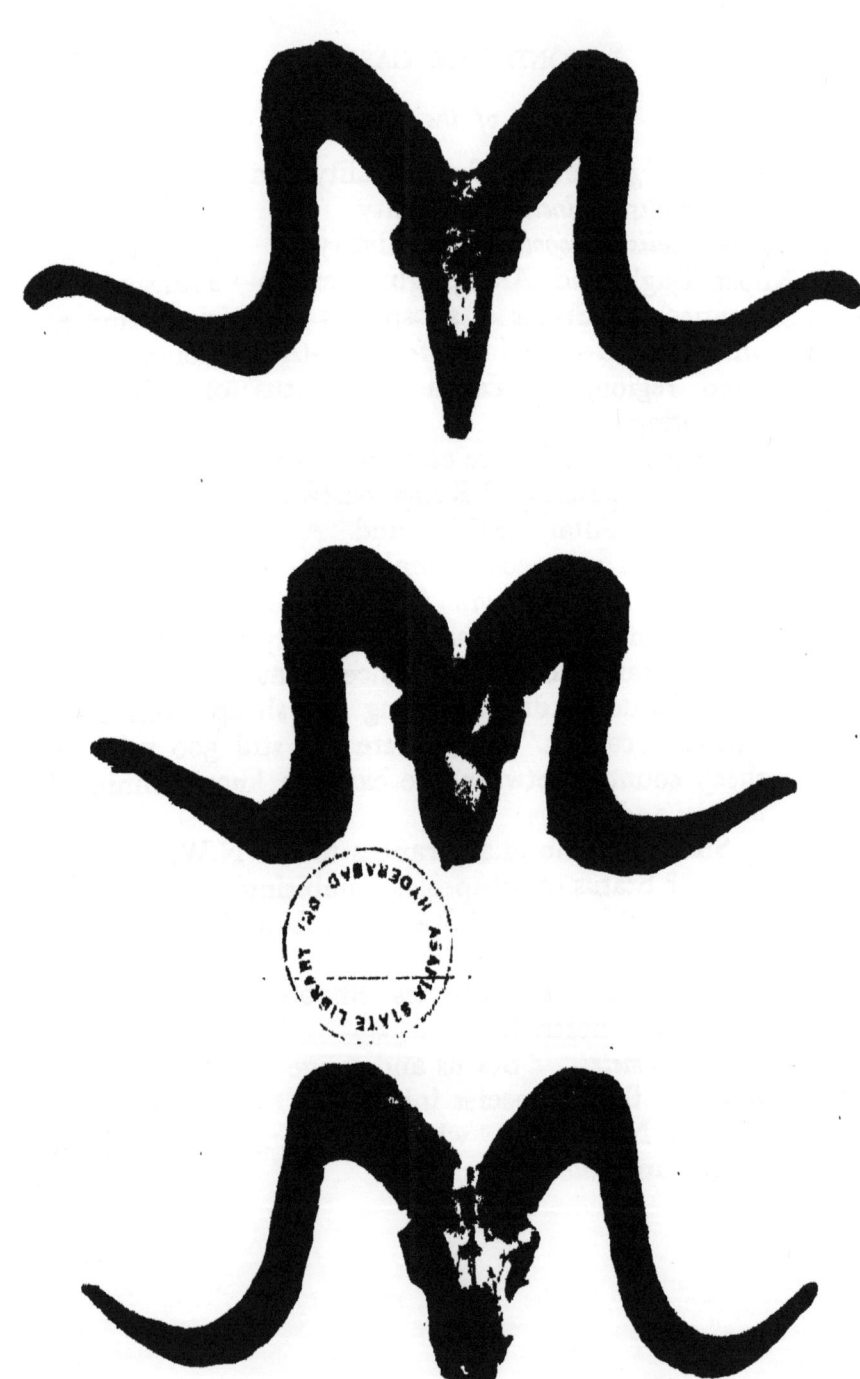

OVIS AMMON POLI.   OVIS AMMON HUMEI.   OVIS AMMON HEINSI

Synopsis of the various classifications of the True Pheasants of Central Asia and adjacent regions.

BUTURLIN, 1904-1908.

Phasianus colchicus colchicus.	West Transcaucasia.
Phasianus colchicus septentrionalis.	North Caucasus.
Phasianus colchicus lorenzi.	East Transcaucasia.
Phasianus colchicus talischensis.	South-west Caspian littoral.
Phasianus persicus.	South-east Caspian littoral.
Phasianus principalis typicus.	Murghab basin.
Phasianus principalis komarovi.	Tedjen basin.
Phasianus principalis zarudnyi.	Oxus, below Charjui.
Phasianus gordius.	Oxus, between Charjui and Kelif.
Phasianus tshardjuensis.	Oxus, around Charjui.
Phasianus zerafshanicus.	Zarafshan Valley.
Phasianus chrysomelas typicus.	Oxus delta.
Phasianus chrysomelas bianchii.	Oxus and its tributaries, above Termez.
Phasianus mongolicus typicus.	Semirechia and Semipalatinsk.
Phasianus mongolicus turkestanicus.	Syr Darya basin.
Phasianus mongolicus semitorquatus.	South Dzungaria.
Phasianus alpherakyi typicus.	Manchuria, Sungari Valley.
Phasianus alpherakyi ussuriensis.	Manchuria, Ussuri Valley.
Phasianus hagenbecki.	West Mongolia.
Phasianus shawi.	Kashgaria.
Phasianus tarimensis.	Tarim basin.

BEEBE, 1918-1922.

Phasianus colchicus colchicus.
Phasianus colchicus septentrionalis.
Phasianus colchicus talischensis.
Phasianus colchicus persicus.
Phasianus colchicus principalis.
Phasianus colchicus zarudnyi.
Phasianus colchicus zerafshanicus.
Phasianus colchicus chrysomelas.
Phasianus colchicus bianchii.
Phasianus colchicus turkestanicus.
Phasianus colchicus mongolicus.
Phasianus colchicus pallasi (= *alpherakyi* and *ussuriensis*).
Phasianus colchicus hagenbecki.
Phasianus colchicus shawi.
Phasianus colchicus tarimensis.

HARTERT, 1921-1922.

Phasianus colchicus colchicus.
Phasianus colchicus septentrionalis.
Phasianus colchicus talischensis.
Phasianus colchicus persicus.
Phasianus colchicus principalis.
Phasianus colchicus zarudnyi.
Phasianus colchicus gordius.
Phasianus colchicus zerafschanicus.
Phasianus colchicus chrysomelas.
Phasianus colchicus bianchii.
Phasianus colchicus jabæ.   Oxus, between Kelif and Termez.
Phasianus colchicus michailowski.   Region of Pamirs.*
Phasianus colchicus semitorquatus.
Phasianus colchicus turkestanicus.
Phasianus colchicus mongolicus.
Phasianus colchicus bergii.   Islands in Sea of Aral.
Phasianus colchicus pallasi.
Phasianus colchicus hagenbecki.
Phasianus colchicus shawi.
Phasianus colchicus tarimensis.

  * An insufficient and misleading " locality," but it can only refer to the highest reaches of the Oxus where pheasants occur, namely above the Chubek-Chayab crossing.

Peter's *Check-List of Birds of the World.* 1931-1934.

Phasianus colchicus colchicus.
Phasianus colchicus septentrionalis.
Phasianus colchicus talischensis.
Phasianus colchicus persicus.
Phasianus colchicus principalis.
Phasianus colchicus komarowii.
Phasianus colchicus zarudnyi.
Phasianus colchicus gordius (= *zarudnyi* ?).
Phasianus colchicus zerafschanicus.
Phasianus colchicus chrysomelas.
Phasianus colchicus bianchii.
Phasianus colchicus jabæ (status doubtful).
Phasianus colchicus michailowski.
Phasianus colchicus semitorquatus.
Phasianus colchicus turkestanicus.
Phasianus colchicus mongolicus.
Phasianus colchicus bergii.
Phasianus colchicus pallasi.
Phasianus colchicus hagenbecki.
Phasianus colchicus shawi.
Phasianus colchicus tarimensis.

BUTURLIN and DEMENTIEV, 1937.

Phasianus colchicus colchicus.	Rion, South-West Caucasus Pheasant.
Phasianus colchicus septentrionalis.	North Caucasus Pheasant.
Phasianus colchicus lorenzi.	Georgian Pheasant.*
Phasianus colchicus talischensis.	Talish Pheasant.
Phasianus persicus.	Persian Pheasant.
Phasianus principalis principalis.	Murghab Pheasant.
Phasianus principalis komarovi.	Tedjen Pheasant.
Phasianus principalis zarudnyi.	Lower Bokhara Pheasant.
Phasianus principalis gordius.	Kharnas (between Kerki and Kelif) Pheasant.
Phasianus principalis tshardjuensis.	Charjui Pheasant.
Phasianus principalis zerafshanicus.	Zerafshan Pheasant.
Phasianus chrysomelas chrysomelas.	Khivan Pheasant.
Phasianus chrysomelas bianchii.	Upper Bokhara Pheasant.
Phasianus semitorquatus semitorquatus.	Dzungarian Pheasant.
Phasianus semitorquatus turkestanicus.	Syr Darya Pheasant.
Phasianus semitorquatus brandti.	Semirechia Pheasant (= *mongolicus*).
Phasianus semitorquatus bergi.	Aral Pheasant.
Phasianus semitorquatus triznæ.	Farghana, Naryn and Kara Kuldja Valleys, Pheasant (= *turkestanicus*).
Phasianus semitorquatus kvaskovski.	Farghana, Gulcha Valley, Pheasant (= *turkestanicus*).
Phasianus mongolicus mongolicus.	Manchurian, Ussuri Valley, Pheasant (= *pallasi*).
Phasianus mongolicus alpherakyi.	Manchurian, Sungari Valley, Pheasant (= *pallasi*).
Phasianus mongolicus hagenbecki.	West Mongolian Pheasant.
Phasianus shawi shawi.	East Kashgar Pheasant.
Phasianus shawi insignis.	West Kashgar Pheasant.
Phasianus tarimensis.	Tarim Pheasant.

* The pheasant of Georgia is *colchicus* not *lorenzi*.

HARTERT and STEINBACHER, 1938.

Phasianus colchicus colchicus.
Phasianus colchicus septentrionalis.
Phasianus colchicus lorenzi.
Phasianus colchicus talischensis.
Phasianus colchicus persicus.
Phasianus colchicus principalis (= *komarovi*).
Phasianus colchicus zarudnyi (= *tschardjuensis* and *gordius*).
Phasianus colchicus zerafschanicus.
Phasianus colchicus chrysomelas.
Phasianus colchicus bianchii (= *jabæ* and *michailowski*).
Phasianus colchicus turkestanicus (= *triznæ* and *kvaskovskii*).
Phasianus colchicus mongolicus (= *semitorquatus*).
Phasianus colchicus bergii.
Phasianus colchicus pallasi.
Phasianus colchicus hagenbecki.
Phasianus colchicus shawi.
Phasianus colchicus tarimensis.

BIBLIOGRAPHY

ABBOTT, J. *Narrative of a Journey from Herat to Khiva, 1839-40.* 2 vols. London, 1843.

ADLER, H. E. Turkestan in transition, *Geographical Journal*, 1946, 230-235.

AITCHISON, J. E. T. *See under* THOMAS, OLDFIELD.

ALCOCK, A. W. *Report on the Natural History Results of the Pamir Boundary Commission.* Calcutta, 1898.

ALLEN, G. M. Bovidæ from the Asiatic expeditions, *Amer. Mus. Novit., 410,* 1930, 1-11.

ALLEN, G. M. *The Mammals of China and Mongolia. Natural History of Central Asia.* New York, 1938-40. Vol. xi, Part 1, 1938. Part 2, 1940.

ALLEN, G. M. Zoological results of the second Dolan expedition to Western China and Eastern Tibet, 1934-36. Part 3, Mammals. *Proc. Acad. Nat. Sci. Philadelphia, 90,* 1939, 261-294.

ANDREWS, R. C. *On the Trail of Ancient Man.* New York and London, 1926.

ANDREWS, R. C. *The New Conquest of Central Asia.* A narrative of the explorations of the Central Asian expeditions in Mongolia and China, 1921-30. New York, 1932. Vol. i. (This is the first, introductory, volume of the series entitled *Natural History of Central Asia,* extending to 20 volumes.) *See also under* ALLEN, G. M.

ANTONIUS, O. On the geographical distribution in former times and to-day, of the recent *Equidæ, Proceedings Zoological Society.* 1937, 557-564.

ATKINSON, T. W. *Oriental and Western Siberia.* London, 1858.

ATKINSON, T. W. *Travels in the Regions of the Upper and Lower Amoor.* New York, 1860.

ATKINSON, Mrs. *Recollections of Tartar Steppes and Their Inhabitants.* London, 1863.

ARGYROPULO, A. I. *See under* Russian Works.

BABER's *Memoirs.* Translated by Leyden and Erskine. London, 1826.

BAILEY, F. M. *Mission to Tashkent.* London, 1946.

BARGER, E. Exploration of ancient sites in Northern Afghanistan, *Geographical Journal,* 1939, 377-398.

BARGER, E. Some problems of Central Asian exploration, *Geographical Journal,* 1944, 1-18.

BARTHOLD, W. *Turkestan Down to the Mongol Invasion.* Translated from the Russian. London, 1928.

BEEBE, W. *A Monograph of the Pheasants.* London, 1918-22.

BEEBE, W. *Pheasants: Their Lives and Homes.* New York, 1937.

BELL, J. *Travels from St Petersburg to Diverse Parts of Asia.* 2 vols. Glasgow, 1763.

BELL, M. S. The great Central Asian trade route from Pekin to Kashgar, *Proceedings Royal Geographical Society*, 1890, 59-93.

BELL, R. *See* p. 277.

BELLEW, H. W. *Kashmir and Kashgar, etc.* London, 1875.

BENTHAM, T. *An Illustrated Catalogue of the Asiatic Horns and Antlers in the Collection of the Indian Museum.* Calcutta, 1908.

BERG, L. The Sea of Aral (Monograph on ———, in Russian). *Journ. Turkestan Branch Russ. Geo. Soc., 5,* 1908.

BERG, L. Note on the above, *Geographical Journal*, 1902, 503-505.

BIDDULPH, J. Letter from ——— regarding the wild-sheep obtained by the Forsyth Mission, in the Tian-Shan and the Pamirs, *Proceedings Zoological Society*, 1875, 157.

BIDDULPH, J. *See also under* GORDON, T. E.

BLACKER, L. V. S. *On Secret Patrol in High Asia.* London, 1922.

BLAINE, G. Falconry, *The Sportsman's Library.* London, 1936.

BLANFORD, W. T. Mammals collected by the late Dr Stoliczka in Turkestan, *Journal Asiatic Society Bengal*, 1875, 112 *et seq.*

BLANFORD, W. T. *Eastern Persia. The Zoology of the Persian Boundary Commission, 1870-72.* Vol. ii. London, 1876.

BLANFORD, W. T. Scientific results of the second Yarkand mission, *Mammalia*, Calcutta, 1879.

BLANFORD, W. T. List of mammalia collected by the late Dr Stoliczka in Kashmir, Ladak, Eastern Turkestan and Wakhan, etc., *Journal Asiatic Society Bengal*, 1878, 105 *et seq.*

BLYTH, E. An amended list of the species of the genus *Ovis. Proceedings Zoological Society*, 1840, 62-79.

BLYTH, E. *See also under* HUTTON, T.

BOBRINSKOY, N. List of printed works and of birds described by N. A. Zarudny, *Journal Turkestan Branch of the Russian Geographical Society*, 1923, 16.

BOBRINSKOY, N. *See also under* Russian Works.

BOGDANOV, M. N. *Description of Khiva Oasis and the Kizil Kum Desert.* Tashkent, 1882 (in Russian).

BONVALOT, M. *Through the Heart of Asia.* Translated from the French. 2 vols. London, 1889.

BRANDT, J. F. Zool. Anhang an A. Lehmann's *Reise nach Buchara und Samarkand, 1841-42.* St Petersburg, 1852.

BRETSCHNEIDER, E. *Mediæval Researches, etc.* 2 vols. London, 1888.

BROOKE, V., and BROOKE, B. On the large sheep of the Thian Shan, and the other Asiatic Argali, *Proceedings Zoological Society*, 1875, 509-526.

BIBLIOGRAPHY

Büchner, E. *Scientific Results of Prjevalski's Travels in Central Asia.* St Petersburg, 1888-94 (in Russian and German).

Burnaby, F. *A Ride to Khiva.* London, 1876.

Burnes, A. *Travels into Bokhara, etc.* 3 vols. London, 1834.

Burnes, A. *Cabool, etc.* 2nd edition. London, 1843.

Burrard, G. *Big Game Hunting in the Himalayas and Tibet.* London, 1925.

Burton, R. F. *Falconry in the Valley of the Indus.* London, 1852.

Buturlin, S. A. On the geographical distribution of the true pheasants, *Ibis,* 1904, 377-414. 1908, 570-592.

Buturlin, S. A., and Dementiev, G. P. *Analytic List of Birds of the U.S.S.R.* 4 vols. Moscow, 1934-37.

Buxton, P. A. *Animal Life in Deserts.* London, 1923.

Byron, R. *The Road to Oxiana.* London, 1937.

Campbell, J. *See* p. 277.

Capus, G. *Le Toit du Monde.* Paris, 1890.

Capus, G. *À travers le Royaume de Tamerlan.* Paris, 1892.

Carré, Monsieur. *Voyage des Indes Orientales.* 2 vols. Paris, 1699.

Carré, Abbé. The travels of the Abbé Carré in India, and the Near East, 1672-74, *Hakluyt Soc. Publ. Ser. II,* Nos. 95, 96, 97. Issued for 1947-48.

Carruthers, D. *Unknown Mongolia.* 2 vols. London, 1913.

Carruthers, D. Severtzoff's sheep from Russian Turkestan, *Field, 114,* 1909, 623.

Carruthers, D. The Near East. Central Asia. Upper Asia. *The Gun at Home and Abroad.* London, 1915.

Carruthers, D. On the birds of the Zarafschan Basin in Russian Turkestan, *Ibis,* 1910, 436-475.

Carruthers, D. *See also* p. 277.

Carpine, John de Pian. *See under Hakluyt Soc. Publ.*

Chaworth-Musters, J. L. Preliminary report of his recent journey in Afghanistan, *Proceedings Zoological Society,* 1946, 179.

Chaworth-Musters, J. L., and Ellerman, J. R. A revision of the genus *Meriones, Proceedings Zoological Society,* 1947, 478-504.

Childe, V. G. *New Light on the most Ancient East.* London, 1934.

Church, P. W. *Chinese Turkestan, etc.* London, 1901.

Clavijo, R. G. de. The embassy of ———— to the Court of Timour, 1403-06, *Hakluyt Soc. Publ.,* Ser. 1, No. 26. Issued for 1860.

Clavijo, R. G. de. *Embassy to Tamerlane.* Translated by Guy le Strange. The Broadway Travellers Series. London, 1928.

Cobbold, R. P. *Innermost Asia.* London, 1900.

Codrington, K. de B. A geographical introduction to the history of Central Asia, *Geographical Journal,* 1944, 27-40, 73-91.

263

CONOLLY, A. *Journey to the North of India, Overland from England, etc.* 2 vols. London, 1834.

COTT, H. B. *Adaptive Colouration in Animals.* London, 1940.

CUMBERLAND, C. S. *Sport on the Pamirs and Turkestan Steppes.* Edinburgh and London, 1895.

CURZON, G. N. *The Pamirs and the Source of the Oxus.* Revised and reprinted from the *Geographical Journal* for July, August and September 1896.

CZAPLICKA, M. A. *The Turks of Central Asia in History and at the Present Day.* Oxford, 1918.

DAVIS, A. P. Irrigation in Turkestan, *Civil Engineering*, 1932, 1-5.

DAVIES and STEIGER. *Soviet Asia.* New York, 1942.

DELMÉ-RADCLIFFE, E. *Notes on the Falconidæ Used in India in Falconry.* Southsea, 1871.

DEMENTIEV, G. P. *Systema Avium Rossicarum.* (Catalogue critique des Oiseaux de l'U.R.S.S.) Vol. i, Accipitres—Striges—Passeres. Paris, 1935.

DEMENTIEV, G. P. La fauconnerie en Russie, Esquisse Historique, *L'Oiseau et la Revue Française d'Ornithologie*, 1945, 10-39.

DEMENTIEV, G. P. Revision systematique des Faucons Sacres, *L'Oiseau et la Revue Française d'Ornithologie*, 1947, 9-22.

DEMENTIEV, G. P. Nouvelles données sur le Gerfaut d'Altai, *Falco gyrfalco altaicus* Menzbier, *L'Oiseau et la Revue Française d'Ornithologie*, 1947, 145-152.

DEMENTIEV, G. P. *See also under* BUTURLIN, S. A.

DE QUINCEY, T. *Revolt of the Tartars, etc.* In *Select Essays of Thomas de Quincey.* Vol. i. Edinburgh, 1888.

DINGELSTEDT, V. Irrigation, natural and artificial, in Samarkand and Bokhara, *Scottish Geographical Magazine*, 1888, 4, 642-654.

DOLAN, B. *See under* ALLEN, G. M., *also* SCHÄFER, E.

DRESSER, H. E. Notes on Severtzoff's *Fauna of Turkestan*, Ibis, 1875 and 1876.

DUMORE, Earl of. *The Pamirs.* 2 vols. London, 1893.

DUNMORE, Earl of. Journeyings in the Pamirs, etc., *Geographical Journal*, 1893, 385-411.

DURANTY, W. *I Write as I Please.* London, 1935.

DURANTY, W. *U.S.S.R.* London, 1944.

ELIAS, N., and Ross, E. D. *Tarikh-i-Rashidi. A History of the Moghuls of Central Asia.* London, 1895.

ELLERMAN, J. R. *The Families and Genera of Living Rodents, etc.* 2 vols. London, 1940.

ELLERMAN, J. R. *See also under* CHAWORTH-MUSTERS, J. L.

ETHERTON, P. T. *Across the Roof of the World.* London, 1911.

EVERSMANN, E. *Reise von Orenburg nach Buchara.* Berlin, 1823.

EVERSMANN, E., and JAKOVLEW [JACOBLEV], P. L.   *Embassy to Bucharia.*
Translated from the German. London, 1823.

FEDCHENKO, B. A.   Topographical sketch of the Zarafshan Valley,
Journal Royal Geographical Society, 1870, 448-462.

FEDCHENKO, B. A.   Geographical notes on the basins of the Oxus and
the Zarafshan, *Geographical Magazine*, 1874, 46-54.

FIELD, H., and PRICE, K.   Review of Soviet archæology, 1919-45,
South-Western Journal of Anthropology, 1947, 212-229.

FINCH, A. G.   *See* p. 277.

FLEROV, C. C.   *See under* Russian Works.

FORBES, R.   *Forbidden Road—Kabul to Samarkand.* London, 1937.

FORMOSOV, A. N.   Ueber die Säugetiere der Nördlichen Mongolei,
Folia Zool. et Hydrobiol. Vol. iii, 41-78. Riga, 1931.

FORSYTH, D.   *Report of a Mission to Yarkund in 1873.* Calcutta, 1875.

FORSYTH MISSIONS.   The first of the Forsyth Missions to Kashgaria,
1870, apart from Official Reports, gave us Shaw's *Visits to High
Tartary, Yarkand and Kashgar*, and Henderson and Hume's *Lahore
to Yarkand.* The second, and more important *Return Mission from
the Viceroy of India to the Amir of Kashgar*, resulted in a crop of literature by its various members—Gordon (incorporating Biddulph),
Trotter, Bellew, Stoliczka ; also Blanford, Scully and Sharpe on
the scientific results.

FOX, R.   *Peoples of the Steppes.* London, 1925.

FOX, R.   *Genghis Khan.* New York, 1936.

FRASER, D.   *The Marches of Hindustan.* London, 1907.

FRECHTLING, L. E.   Anglo-Russian rivalry in Eastern Turkistan,
1863-81, *Journal Royal Central Asian Society*, 1939, 471-489.

FUTTERER, K.   *Durch Asien.* Berlin, 1901.

GARDINER, —.   Abstract of a journal kept by —— during his travels
in Central Asia, by M. P. Edgeworth. *Journal Asiatic Society
Bengal*, 1853, 283-305.

GERARD, J.   Extracts from private letters of ——, written on journey
from Peshawar to Bukhara and Meshed, *Journal Asiatic Society
Bengal*, 1833, 1-22, 143-149.

GILBERT, C. M.   Life history of the golden eagle, *Jour. für Ornithologie*,
1934, 561-567.

GOLDSMID, F. J.   *Eastern Persia. An Account of the Journeys of the Persian
Boundary Commission, 1870-72.* 2 vols. London, 1876.

GOODWIN, G. G.   Mammals collected in Kazakstan, etc., *American
Mus. Novit.*, 1935, 769, 1-15.

GORDON, T. E.   Note on the Tian Shan wild sheep, *Proceedings Zoological
Society*, 1874, 425.

GORDON, T. E.   The watershed of Central Asia, etc., *Journal Royal
Geographical Society*, 1876, 381-396.

GORDON, T. E. *Roof of the World* (incorporating Biddulph's accounts). London, 1876.

GROVER, J. *The Bokhara Victims.* London, 1845.

GRIFFITH, W. *Journal of Travels in Assam, Burma, Bootan, Afghanistan and Neighbouring Countries, etc.*, posthumous papers, bequeathed to the Hon. The East India Co. Calcutta, 1847.

GRUM-GRZHIMAILO, G. E., and GRUM-GRZHIMAILO, M. Short report of the results of an expedition to the Alai region, by ——, *Bulletin Imperial Russian Geographical Society*, No. 20, 1885, 660-673 (in Russian).

GRUM-GRZHIMAILO, G. E., and GRUM-GRZHIMAILO, M. Sketch of the Pamir region, *Bulletin Imperial Russian Geographical Society*, No. 22, 1886, 81-109 (in Russian).

GRUM-GRZHIMAILO, G. E., and GRUM-GRZHIMAILO, M. Report on an expedition by ——, to the Pamirs, *Proceedings Royal Geographical Society*, 1887, 430.

GRUM-GRZHIMAILO, G. E., and GRUM-GRZHIMAILO, M Summary of a Journey by ——, in 1889-90 to the Tian Shan Oases and Lop Nor, *Proceedings Royal Geographical Society*, 1891, 208-226. Translated by E. D. Morgan.

Hakluyt Society Publications. *Early Voyages and Travels to Russia and Persia*, Ser. 1, Nos. 72-73, issued for 1885 (for A. Jenkinson).

Hakluyt Society Publications. *The Journeys of William of Rubruck and John of Pian de Carpine*, Ser. 2, No. 4, issued for 1900.

HANWAY, J. *An Historical Account of the British Trade over the Caspian Sea, etc.* 4 vols. London, 1753.

HALLER, C. *The Chase with Falcons and Hawks.* St Petersburg, 1885 (in Russian).

HARLAN, J. *Central Asia.* London, 1939.

HARRIS, A. *Eastern Visas.* London, 1939.

HARPER, F. *Extinct and Vanishing Mammals of the Old World.* New York, 1945.

HARTERT, E. *Die Vögel der Paläarktischen Fauna.* 3 vols. Berlin, 1903-22.

HARTERT, E. Addenda to above. 1923.

HARTERT, E., and STEINBACHER, F. Addenda and Corrigenda to above. Berlin, 1932-38.

HARTING, J. E. *Bibliotheca Accipitraria.* London, 1891.

HAY, R. G. Notes on the wild-sheep of the Hindu Koosh, *Journal Asiatic Society Bengal*, 1840, 440-443.

HEAWOOD, E. *History of Geographical Discovery in the Seventeenth and Eighteenth Centuries.* Cambridge, 1912.

HEDIN, S. *Through Asia.* 2 vols. London, 1899.

HEDIN, S. *Central Asia and Tibet.* 2 vols. London, 1903.

BIBLIOGRAPHY

HELLMAYR, C. E. Birds of the J. Simpson-Roosevelts Asiatic expedition, *Field Museum Natural History Publication*. Vol. xvii, *Zoology*. Chicago, 1929.

HELLWALD, F. VON. *The Russians in Central Asia*. Translated from the German. London, 1874.

HENDERSON, G., and HUME, A. O. *From Lahore to Yarkand, in 1870-71*. London, 1873.

HERRMANN, A. *Die alten Seidenstrassen zwischen China und Syrien*. Berlin, 1910.

HINGSTON, R. W. G. Animal life at high altitudes, *Geographical Journal*, 1925, 185-198.

HINTON, M. A. C. *Monograph of Voles and Lemmings*. London, 1926.

HOLDICH, T. *The Gates of India*. London, 1910.

HUDSON, A. E. *Kazak Social Structure*. Yale University Publication, 1938.

HUMBOLT, A. DE. *Asie Centrale*. 3 vols. Paris, 1843.

HUME, A. O. *See under* HENDERSON, G., *also* LYDEKKER, R.

HUNTINGTON, E. The mountains of Turkestan, *Geographical Journal*, 1905, 22-40, 139-158.

HUNTINGTON, E. *The Pulse of Asia*. New York, 1907.

HUNTINGTON, E. *See also under* PUMPELLY, R.

HUTTON, T. The wild sheep of Afghanistan, *Calcutta Journal Natural History*, 1843, 2, 514-521.

HUTTON, T., and BLYTH, E. On the ornithology of Afghanistan, *Journal Asiatic Society Bengal*, 1845-47.

JENKINSON, A. *See under* Hakluyt Society Publications.

JOHANSEN, H. Birds of Western Siberia, *Jour. für Ornithologie*, 1944, 1-105.
(Crows to Buntings : continuation not yet published.)

KASHKAROV, D., and KURBATOV, V. Preliminary ecological survey of the vertebrate fauna of the Central Kara-Kum Desert in West Turkestan, *Ecology*, *11*, 35-60. Brooklyn, 1930.

KASHKAROV, D., and LEIN, L. The yellow ground squirrel of Turkestan *Ecology*, *8*, 63-72. Brooklyn, 1927.

KENNION, R. L. *By Mountain, Lake and Plain*. Edinburgh and London, 1911.

KHANIKOFF, N. *Bokhara. Its Amir and Its People*. English translation. London, 1845.

KHOROSHKHIN, A. P. The Kizil Kum Desert. *Collection of Articles Concerning the Turkestan Region*, 1876 (in Russian).

KINNEAR, N. B. *See under* LUDLOW, F.

KOSSIAKOV, M. Journey in Karategin and Darwas, *Proceedings Royal Geographical Society*, 1886, 33-47. (This is the only account we have of Dr Regel's journey in Eastern Bukhara, Kossiakov being the topographer attached to the expedition ; notes on the zoology of the region were, however, contributed by Regel to the *Bull. Soc. Imp. Nat.*, Moscow, 1883-84.)

KOWARZIK, R. Etwas über die Arten der Wildschafe, und ihre Verbreitung. *Zool. Anzeiger, 41*, no. 10. 1913.

KOZLOV, P. K. *Mongolia and Kam.* St Petersburg, 1905 (in Russian).

KOZLOV, P. K. *Mongolia and Amdo, etc.* St Petersburg, 1923 (in Russian). ,

KOZLOV, P. K. German translation of the above. Berlin, 1925.

KOZLOVA, E. V. Birds of S.-W. Transbaikalia, N. Mongolia and Central Gobi, *Ibis*, April, July, October 1932. January, April 1933.

KOZLOVA, E. V. On the spring life and breeding habits of the pheasant (*Phasianus colchicus*) in Tadjikistan, *Ibis*, 1947, 423-429.

KRAFFT, H. *À travers le Turkestan Russe.* Paris, 1902.

KRIST, G. *Prisoner in the Forbidden Land.* Translated by E. O. Lorimer. London, 1938.

KRIST, G. *Alone Through the Forbidden Land.* London, 1938.

KUNITZ, J. *Dawn Over Samarkand.* London, 1936.

KUZNETZOV, B. *See under* Russian Works.

KUZYAKIN, A. *See under* Russian Works.

LAMB, H. *The March of Barbarism.* London, 1941.

LANSDELL, H. *Russian Central Asia, etc.* 2 vols. London, 1885.

LANSDELL, H. *Through Central Asia.* London, 1887.

LATTIMORE, O. *Desert Road to Turkestan.* London, 1928.

LATTIMORE, O. *High Tartary.* Boston, 1930.

LATTIMORE, O. The geographical factor in Mongol history, *Geographical Journal*, 1938, 1-16.

LATTIMORE, O. *Inner Asian Frontiers of China.* New York, 1940.

LECHE, W. Scientific results of Sven Hedin's journeys in Central Asia, 1899-1902, *Zoologie*, 6, 1-69. Stockholm, 1904.

LEHMANN, A. *Reise nach Buchara und Samarkand, 1841-42.* St Petersburg, 1852.

LEHMANN, A. *See also under* BRANDT, J. F.

LE STRANGE, G. *The Lands of the Eastern Caliphate.* Cambridge, 1905.

LEVCHINE, A. DE. *Description des Hordes et des Steppes des Kirghiz-Kaissaks.* Translated from the Russian. Paris, 1840.

LEWIS, E. (VESEY). *In Search of the Gyr-Falcon.* London, 1938.

LIPSKI, V. I. *The Bokharan Highlands.* 3 vols. St Petersburg, 1902-05.

LITTLEDALE, ST G. R. Across the Pamirs from north to south, *Proceedings Royal Geographical Society*, 1892, 1-35.

LITTLEPAGE, J. D., and BESS, D. *In Search of Soviet Gold.* London, 1939.

LODGE, G. E. *Memoirs of an Artist Naturalist.* Edinburgh and London, 1946.

LÖNNBERG, E. Birds as "Relicts" in Central Asia, *Ibis*, 1932, 625 *et seq.*

268

BIBLIOGRAPHY

LUDLOW, F., and KINNEAR, N. B. A contribution to the ornithology of Chinese Turkestan, *Ibis*, April, July, October 1933. January 1934.

LYDEKKER, R. *The Deer of all Lands.* London, 1898.

LYDEKKER, R. *Wild Oxen, Sheep and Goats, etc.* London, 1898.

LYDEKKER, R. *The Sheep and Its Cousins.* London, 1912.

.LYDEKKER, R. *Catalogue of the Ungulate Mammals in the British Museum (Natural History).* 5 vols. London, 1913-15.

LYDEKKER, R. *Catalogue of the Heads and Horns of Indian Big Game Bequeathed by A. O. Hume, C.B., to the British Museum (Natural History).* London, 1913.

MACGAHAN, J. A. *Campaigning on the Oxus.* London, 1874.

McGOVERN, W. M. *The Early Empires of Central Asia.* University of California, 1939.

MACHATSCHEK, F. *Landeskunde von Russisch Turkestan.* Stuttgart, 1921.

MAILLART, E. K. *Turkestan Solo.* Translated from the French. London, 1934.

MANNIN, E. *South to Samarkand.* London, 1936.

MARKOV, E. The Sea of Aral, *Geographical Journal*, 1911, 515-519.

MASON, K. Remarks on the Silk Routes, *Geographical Journal*, 1939, 395-397.

MAYDON, H. C. Eighteen varieties of wild sheep, *Field*, 25th December 1937.

MAYEF, N. Hissar and Kulab, *Geographical Magazine*, 1876, 326-330.

MEINERTZHAGEN, R. On the birds of Northern Afghanistan, *Ibis*, July and October 1938.

MERLANGE, G. Silk in the Orient, *Journal Royal Central Asian Society*, 1939, 65-76.

MERZBACHER, G. *The Central Tian Shan Mountains.* London, 1905.

MERZBACHER, G. Exploration in the Tian Shan Mountains, *Geographical Journal*, 1909, 278-288.

MITCHELL, R. The regions of the Upper Oxus, *Proceedings Royal Geographical Society*, 1884, 489-512.

MOLINEUX, H. G. K. *A Catalogue of Birds, giving their Distribution in the Western Portion of the Palæarctic Region.* Parts 1-3, 1930. Supplement, 1931. Eastbourne.

MORDEN, W. J. *Across Asia's Snows and Deserts.* New York and London, 1927.

MOREAU, R. E. Migration over the north-west part of the Indian Ocean, the Red Sea, and the Mediterranean, *Proceedings Zoological Society*, 1938, 1-26.

MORGAN, E. DELMAR. Geography of Central Asia from Russian sources. Supplement Papers, *Royal Geographical Society*, 1884.

MOURAVIEW [MURAVIEFF]. *Journey to Turcomania and Chiva*. Translated from the German. London, 1823.

MURRAY, J. A. Zoology of Baloochistan and Southern Afghanistan, *Indian Annals and Magazine of Natural Science, 1*, 1887.

NABOURS; R. K. The land of lambskins, *Nat. Geographical Magazine, 36*, 1919.

NASONOV, N. *Ovis arcar* et les formes voisines des moutons sauvages; *Bull. Acad. Imper. Sci. St Petersburg*, 1913, 7, ser. 6 (in Russian).

NASONOV, N. Les espéces des moutons sauvages du Turkestan décrites par N. Severtzov, *Bull. Acad. Imper. Sci. St Petersburg*, 1914, 8, ser. 6 (in Russian).

NASONOV, N. Über *Ovis severtzovi*, etc., *Bull. Acad. Imper. Sci. St Petersburg*, 1914, 8, ser. 6 (in German).

NASONOV, N. Sur la " perversion " des cornes des moutons sauvages, etc., *Bull. Acad. Sci. Russie*, 1919-21, 13, ser. 6 (in Russian).

NASONOV, N. *Distribution géographique des moutons sauvages du monde ancien*. Petrograd, 1923 (in Russian).

NAZAROFF, P. *Expedition to the Country of Kokand in the Years 1813 and 1814*. Translated from the German. London, 1823.

NAZAROFF, P. S. *Hunted Through Central Asia*. London, 1932.

NAZAROFF, P. S. *Moved On*. London, 1935.

NIKOLSKY, A. M. Materialien zur kenntniss der Wirbelthierfauna Nordost-Persiens und Transkaspiens, *Arb. D. St Petersburg Naturforschen-gesellsch*, 1886, 379-406 (in Russian).

NOACK, T. Die Haustiere und die Wildlebenden Säugetiere am Oberen Amu-Darja, *Zool. Garten. Frankfurt*, 1885, 153-155.

NOACK, T. Centralasiatische Steinböcke, *Zool. Anzeiger.*, 25, 1902.

NOACK, T. Steinböcke des Altaigebietes, *Zool. Anzeiger.*, 26, 1903.

OBOLENSKI, S. A preliminary review of the Palæarctic Sousliks (*Citellus* and *Spermophilopsis*), *Compt. Rend. Acad. Sci. U.S.S.R.*, 1927, 188-193.

OGNEV, S. I. *Mammals of the U.S.S.R. and Adjacent Countries, or Mammals of Eastern Europe and Northern Asia*, vols. i-v. Moscow, 1928-47 (in Russian).

OLEARIUS, A. *Relation de Voyage, etc.* Paris, 1639.

OLEARIUS, A. *Voyages and Travels of the Ambassadors Sent . . . to the Great Duke of Muscovy, and the King of Persia, etc.* Translated from the French. London, 1662.

OLUFSEN, O. *Through the Unknown Pamirs*. London, 1904.

OLUFSEN, O. *The Emir of Bokhara and His Country*. London, 1911.

OSTEN-SACKEN, T. Expedition to the Trans-Naryn country in 1867, *Journal Royal Geographical Society*, 1870, 250-268.

PALLAS, P. S. *Voyages en Provinces l'Empire de Russie et dans l'Asia Septentrionale*, vols. i-v. Paris, 1788-1793.

PALLAS, P. S. *Zoographia Rosso-Asiatica, etc.*, 3 vols. St Petersburg, 1811-31 (in Latin).

PAQUIER, J. B. *Le Pamir, etc.* Paris, 1876.

PARKER, E. H. *A Thousand Years of the Tartars.* London, 1924.

PAVLOVSKY, E. N. See under Russian Works.

PENNANT, T. *Arctic Zoology.* 2 vols. London, 1784-87.

PETERS, J. L. *Check List of Birds of the World.* 5 vols. Cambridge, Mass. 1931-34.

PHILLOTT, D. C. *The Baz-Nama-Yi Nasiri.* A Persian treatise on Falconry. 1842. Translated by —— London, 1908.

PONCINS, E. de. *Chasses et Explorations dans la Région des Pamirs.* Paris, 1897.

POUSARGUES, E. DE. Étude sur les Ruminants de l'Asie Centrale, *Mem. Soc. Zool. de France*, 1898, 126-224.

PRAWDIN, M. *The Mongolian Empire. Its Rise and Legacy.* Translated by E. and C. Paul. London, 1940.

PRJEVALSKI, N. M. *Mongolia, the Tangut Country, etc.* Translated by E. D. Morgan. 2 vols. London, 1876.

PRJEVALSKI, N. M. *From Kulja Across the Tian Shan to Lob-Nor.* Translated by E. D. Morgan. London, 1879.

PRJEVALSKI, N. M. *Third Journey in Central Asia, etc.* St Petersburg, 1883 (in Russian).

PRJEVALSKI, N. M. *Reisen in Tibet, etc., 1879-80.* German translation of the above, by Stein-Nordheim. Jena, 1884.

PRJEVALSKI, N. M. *Scientific Results of Journeys by* ——. 3 vols. St Petersburg, 1888-1912 (in Russian).

PRJEVALSKI, N. M. See also under BÜCHNER, E.

POCOCK, R. *Horses.* London, 1917.

POCOCK, R. I. Tigers, *Journal Bombay Natural History Society*, 1929, 33, 505-541.

POCOCK, R. I. The Races of *Canis lupus*, *Proceedings Zoological Society*, 1935, 647-686.

POCOCK, R. I. The Asiatic wild dog, *Proceedings Zoological Society*, 1936, 33-55.

POTAGOS, Dr. *Dix Années de Voyage dans l'Asia Centrale.* Paris, 1885.

PUMPELLY, R. *Explorations in Turkestan, etc.* Washington, 1905. Publication No. 26 contains (pp. 157-216) "A geologic and physiographic reconnaissance in Central Turkestan," by E. Huntington.

QUINCEY, J. W. *Chinese Hunter.* London, 1939.

RADDE, G., and WALTER, A. Die Säugethiere Transcaspiens, *Zoo. Jahrb. Abth. Syst.*, 1889, 4, 993-1094.

RANKING, J. *Historical Researches on the Wars and Sports of the Mongols and the Romans, etc.* London, 1826.

RAWLINSON, H. G. *Bactria.* London, 1912.

RAWLINSON, H.   A monograph on the Oxus, *Journal Royal Geographical Society*, 1872, 482-513.

REGEL, E. A. V.   For travels in the Tian Shan, 1876-80, *see* Petermann's *Mitt.*,1879, 376-384 ; also *Proceedings Royal Geographical Society*, 1881, 340-352.

REGEL, E. A. V.   Communication from —— to The Russian Geographical Society, on his journey to Karategin and Darwaz, in 1881. *Proceedings Royal Geographical Society*, 1881, 412-417. *See also* " Russian Pamir Expedition of 1883 " and map showing Regel's routes in Darwaz and Badakshan, *Proceedings Royal Geographical Society*, 1884, 135-142, 176, 479. *Also* Petermann's *Mitteilungen*, 1884, maps 4, 13.

REGEL, E. A. V.   For travels in Bukhara, *see under* KOSSIAKOV, M.

REINIG, W. F.   Beiträge zur Faunistik des Pamir Gebietes, *Wiss. Ergebn. der Alai-Pamir Expedition, 1928.* T. 3, Berlin, 1932.

RICHMOND, C. W.   Catalogue of a collection of birds made by Dr W. L. Abbott in Eastern Turkestan, etc. *Proceedings U.S. National Museum.* Vol. xviii. Washington, 1896.

RICKMERS, W. R.   Travels in Bokhara, *Geographical Journal*, 1899, 596-620.

RICKMERS, W. R.   The Fan Mountains of the Duab of Turkestan, *Geographical Journal*, 1907, 357-371, 488-502.

RICKMERS, W. R.   *The Duab of Turkestan.* Cambridge, 1913.

RILEY, J. H.   On Ground-Choughs, *Proceedings U.S. National Museum*, 1931, 27, article 15, 20-21.

ROCCA, F. DE.   Karatéghine and Darvoz, *Rev. de Géog.*, 1895, 24-37, 105-115, 179-188.

ROCKHILL, W. W.   *Diary of a Journey Through Mongolia and Tibet.* Washington, 1894.

ROCKHILL, W. W.   *Land of the Lamas.*   New York, 1891.

ROMM, M.   *The Ascent of Mount Stalin.*   Translated by A Brown. London, 1936.

ROOSEVELT, T. (Jr.), and ROOSEVELT, KERMIT.   *East of the Sun and West of the Moon.*   New York, 1926.

ROTHSCHILD, W.   On a new race of Ibex, *C. sibirica lydekkeri*, *Nov. Zool.* 1900, 7.

RUBRUCK, WILLIAM OF [RUBRUQUIS].   *See under* Hakluyt Society Publications.

Russian Works on Zoology and Ornithology :—
  Mammals of the U.S.S.R. and Adjacent Countries, or *Mammals of Eastern Europe and Northern Asia.* Vols. i-v. S. I. Ognev. Moscow, 1928-47.
  Mammals of the U.S.S.R. N. Bobrinskoy, B. Kuznetzov, and A. Kuzyakin.   Moscow, 1944.

Fauna de l'U.R.S.S. Vol. iii, new series no. 93. *Dipodidæ.* No. 4. B. S. Vinogradov. Moscow, 1937.

Fauna de l'U.R.S.S. New series no. 29. *Rodents.* B. S. Vinogradov, and A. I. Argyropulo. Moscow, 1941.

Mammals of Tadjikistan. B. S. Vinogradov, E. N. Pavlovsky, and C. C. Flerov. Moscow, 1935.

See also under BUTURLIN, DEMENTIEV, KASHKAROV, NASONOV, STEG-MANN, VINOGRADOV.

RYCHKOV, P. *Topography of the Orenburg District, etc.* 1772 (in Russian).

SALESSKI, P. Die Verbreitung der Paarhufer (Artiodactyla) in Westsibirien, *Zeitschr. für Säugetierkunde,* 1934, 9, 369-376.

SANDERS, J. H. *Tamerlane or Timur the Great Amir.* London, 1936.

SCHÄFER, E. *Unbekanntes Tibet.* Berlin, 1937.

SCHÄFER, E. *Dach der Erde.* Berlin, 1938.

SCHÄFER, E. Ornithologische Ergebnisse zweier Forschungsreisen nach Tibet, *Journ. für Ornithologie.* Sonderheft, May 1938, 1-349.

SCHOMBERG, R. C. F. *Peaks and Plains of Central Asia.* London, 1933.

SCHOMBERG, R. C. F. *Between the Oxus and the Indus.* London, 1935.

SCHOMBERG, R. C. F. Three journeys in the Tien Shan, 1928-29, *Geographical Journal,* 1930, 25-38.

SCHOMBERG, R. C. F. A fourth journey in the Tien Shan, *Geographical Journal,* 1932, 368-382.

SCHOMBERG, R. C. F. Peaks and passes of the Tien Shan, *Himalayan Journal,* 1932, 112-115.

SCHUYLER, E. *Turkistan.* 2 vols. London, 1876.

SCHWARZ, E. Zwei neue Lokalformen des Tigers aus Centralasien, *Zool. Anzeiger.,* 47, no. 12. Leipzig, 1916.

SCULLY, J. A contribution to the ornithology of Eastern Turkestan, *Stray Feathers,* 1876, 4.

SCULLY, J. On the mammals and birds collected by Captain C. E. Yate on the Afghan Boundary Commission, *Journal Asiatic Society Bengal,* 1887, 57, part 2, no. 1, 77-89.

SEREBRENNIKOV, M. K. Album Einiger Osteuropaischer Westsibiri-scher und Turkestanischer Säugetiere, II. *Zeitschr. für Säugetierkunde,* 1931, 6, no. 4.

SEVERTZOV, N. A. Journey to the Western Tian-Shan, *Journal Royal Geographical Society,* 1870, 343 *et seq.*

SEVERTZOV, N. A. *Travels in the Turkestan Region and Researches in the Mountain District of Tian Shan.* St Petersburg, 1873 (in Russian).

SEVERTZOV, N. A. Notes on some new Central Asian birds, *Ibis,* 1875, 487-494.

S

SEVERTZOV, N. A. The mammals of Turkestan, *Ann. Magazine Natural History*, 1876, *18*, series 4. Translated by F. C. Craemers.

SEVERTZOV, N. A. Notes on Severtzoff's *Fauna of Turkestan*, by H. E. Dresser, *Ibis*, 1875-76.

SEVERTZOV, N. A. On the birds of the Pamir Range, *Ibis*, 1883.

SHAKESPEAR, R. From Heraut to Ourenbourg, *Blackwood's Magazine*, June 1842.

SHAKESPEAR, J. How Sir Richmond Shakespear set free the Russian slaves at Khiva, *Journal Royal Central Asian Society*, 1921, *8*.

SHARPE, R. B. *Scientific Results of the Second Yarkand Mission*. Aves. London, 1891.

SHARPE, R. B. The Zoology of the Afghan Delimitation Commission. *Transactions Linnæan Society London*, 1889, *5*, series 2. Birds, 66-93.

SHAW, R. *Visits to High Tartary, Yarkand and Kashgar*. London, 1871.

SHITKOV, B. M. Ueber einer neuen Hirsch aus Turkestan : *Cervus hagenbecki* (= *C. bactrianus*), *Zool. Jahrb. Syst.*, 1904, *20*, 91-104.

SHITKOV, B. M. Über das Osttibetische Argalischaf (*Ovis ammon* subspecies ?), *Zoo. Garten.*, new series 8, 1936, 253-258.

SHITKOV, B. M., and SCHAUENSEE, R. M. DE. Zoological results of the second Dolan expedition to Western China and Eastern Tibet, 1934-36. Part 2, Birds, *Proceedings Academy Natural Science Philadelphia*, 1939, *90*, 185-260.

SHITKOV, B. M., and SABANEJEW, L. L. Über *Ovis heinsi*, etc., *Zool. Jahrb.* Jena, 1910.

SJÖLANDER, D. The distribution and habits of the Argali sheep of Central Asia, *Journal North China Branch Royal Asiatic Society Shanghai*, 1922, *53*, 131-157.

SKRINE, C. P. The Alps of Qungur, *Geographical Journal*, 1925, 385-411.

SKRINE, C. P. *Chinese Central Asia*. London, 1926.

SKRINE, F. H., and ROSS, E. D. *The Heart of Asia*. London, 1899.

SNIGIREWSKI, S. J. Beiträge zur Avifauna der Wüste Kara-Kum (Turkmenistan), *Jour. für Ornithologie*, 1928, 591 *et seq.*

SOUTHERN, H. N. The economic importance of the House Sparrow, *The Annals of Applied Biology*, 1945, *32*, no. 1, 57-67.

STEGMANN, B. *Fauna de l'U.R.S.S. Oiseaux*. Vol. i, no. 5 *Falconiformes*. Acad. des Sciences de l'U.R.S.S. Moscow, 1937 (in Russian).

STEIN, M. A. A third journey of exploration in Central Asia, 1913-16, *Geographical Journal*, 1916, 97-130, 193-229.

STEIN, M. A. *Serindia*. 5 vols. London, 1921.

STEIN, M. A. Innermost Asia. Its geography as a factor in history, *Geographical Journal*, 1925, 377-403, 473-501.

STEIN, M. A. *Innermost Asia*. 4 vols. London, 1928.

STEIN, M. A.   On ancient tracks past the Pamirs, *Himalayan Journal*, 1932, 1-26.

STOCKLEY, C. H.   *Stalking in the Himalayas and Northern India.*   London, 1936.

STOLICZKA, F.   Description of the *Ovis poli* of Blyth, *Proceedings Zoological Society London*, 1874, 425-427.

STRAHLENBERG, P. J. VON.   *An Historico-Geographical Description of the Northern and Eastern Parts of Europe and Asia, etc.*   Translation from the German.   London, 1738.

STRONG, A. L.   *Red Star in Samarkand.*   London, 1930.

STUMM, H.   *Der Russische Feldzug nach Chiwa.*   Berlin, 1875.

SUDILOVSKAIA, A. M.   Contributions á la connaissance des Migrations du *Syrrhaptes paradoxus Pallas*, *L'oiseau et la Revue Française d'Ornithologie*, 1935, 219-235.

SUSHKIN, P. P.   The wild-sheep of the Old World and their distribution, etc., *Journal Mammalogy*, 6, no. 3.   Washington, 1925.

SUSHKIN, P. P.   On Palæarctic Goshawks, *Proceedings Boston Society Natural History*, 1928, 1-39.

SWANN, H. K.   *A Synopsis of the Accipitres.*   London, 1922.

SWANN, H. K.   A review of the Gyr-Falcons of the Palæarctic and Nearctic Regions.   *Verh. des VI. Internationalen Ornithologen—Kongresses.*   Kopenhagen, 1926.

SWANN, H. K., and WETMORE, A.   *A Monograph of the Birds of Prey.*   London, 1924-30.

SYKES, C.   Some notes on a recent journey in Afghanistan, *Geographical Journal*, October 1934, 327-336.

SYKES, P. M.   *The Quest for Cathay.*   London, 1936.

SYKES, P. M.   *A History of Afghanistan.*   2 vols.   London, 1940.

TAVERNIER, J. B.   *See* p. 277.

TEICHMAN, E.   *Journey to Turkistan.*   London, 1937.

THOMAS, OLDFIELD.   The zoology of the Afghan Delimitation Commission (Introduction by J. E. T. Aitchison), *Transactions Linnæan Society London*, 1889, 5, series 2, Mammals, 55-65.

THOMAS, OLDFIELD.   On mammals collected in Turkestan by Mr Douglas Carruthers, *Ann. and Magazine of Natural History*, March 1909, 3, series 8.

THOMAS, OLDFIELD.   New mammals from Central and Western Asia, mostly collected by Mr Douglas Carruthers, *Ann. and Magazine of Natural History*, December 1911, 8, series 8.

THOMAS, OLDFIELD.   On mammals from Central Asia, collected by Mr Douglas Carruthers, *Ann. and Magazine of Natural History*, April 1912, 9, series 8.

THOMAS, OLDFIELD.   The geographical races of *Citellus fulvus*, *Ann. and Magazine Natural History*, 1915, 15, 422-423.

THOMSON, A. L. *Bird Migration.* London, 1936.

TIMKOVSKI, G. *Voyage à Péking à travers la Mongolie, 1820-21.* Edited by J. von Klaproth. 2 vols. Paris, 1827.

TROTTER, H. On the geographical results of the Mission to Kashgar under Sir T. Douglas Forsyth in 1873-74, *Journal Royal Geographical Society,* 1878, 173-234.

TRUBETSKOY, P. S. Bokharski Shtoporni Kozel (The Bukharan Markhor), *Priroda i Okhota,* 1910, 40-48 *(not seen).*

TURANIANS. *A Manual on the ——, and Pan-Turanianism.* London, 1918.

ULLAH, MIR ISSET. Travels beyond the Himalaya, *Journal Royal Asiatic Society,* 1812, 7.

VÁMBÉRY, A. *Travels in Central Asia.* London, 1864.

VÁMBÉRY, A. *Sketches of Central Asia.* London, 1868.

VÁMBÉRY, A. *History of Bukhara.* Second edition. London, 1873.

VIGNE, G. T. *A Personal Narrative of a Visit to Ghazni, Kabul and Afghanistan.* London, 1843.

VINOGRADOV, B. S. On a second species of Mongolian Jerboa of the genus *Salpingotus, Zool. Anzeiger.,* 1924, 61.

VINOGRADOV, B. S. A third species of Dwarf Jerboa, *Salpingotus thomasi, Ann. and Magazine of Natural History,* 1928, 1, series 10.

WARD, R. *Records of Big Game.* Tenth edition. London, 1935.

WALKER, C. C. *Jenghiz Khan.* London, 1939.

WHISTLER, H. Materials for the ornithology of Afghanistan, *Journal Bombay Natural History Society,* August, December 1944. April, September, December 1945.

WOEIKOW, A. [VOYKOV]. *Le Turkestan russe.* Paris, 1914.

WOLFF, J. *Narrative of a Mission to Bokhara.* 2 vols. London, 1845.

WOOD, H. Notes on the Lower Amu-Darya, Syr-Darya and Lake Aral, etc., *Journal Royal Geographical Society,* 1875, 367-413.

WOOD, H. *The Shores of Lake Aral.* London, 1876.

WOOD, J. *A Journey to the Source of the River Oxus.* With an essay on the geography of the valley of the Oxus by Colonel Henry Yule. London, 1872.

YATE, C. E. *Northern Afghanistan.* London, 1888.

YETTS, W. P. The horse : a factor in early Chinese history, *Eurasia Septentrionalis Antiqua,* 1934, 9.

YULE, H. *The Book of Ser Marco Polo.* Third edition. Revised by Henri Cordier. London, 1903.

YULE, H. The geography and history of the upper waters of the Oxus. *See under* WOOD, J.

YOUNGHUSBAND, F. E. A journey across Central Asia, etc., *Proceedings Royal Geographical Society,* 1888, 485-514.

YOUNGHUSBAND, F. E. *The Heart of a Continent.* London, 1897.

BIBLIOGRAPHY

ZALKIN, V.   On the taxonomic position of *Capra falconeri* in the U.S.S.R., *Comptes Rendus de l'Academie des Sciences de l'U.R.S.S.*, 1945, *46*, no. 5.

ZARUDNY, N. A.   The most comprehensive list (in English) of Zarudny's contributions to ornithology is to be found in H. G. Molineux's *Catalogue of Birds*, Part 1 and Appendix II.   The same applies to Menzbier and other important, but mostly inaccessible Russian sources.   For a more detailed list (in Russian) of Zarudny's publications between the years 1883-1918, *see under* BOBRINSKOY, N.

ZARUDNY, N. A.   Account of some sparrows of the species *Passer domesticus* (describing *Passer domesticus bactrianus* subspecies n.), *Journal Turkestan Branch of the Russian Geographical Society*, 1923, *16*.

ZARUDNY, N. A.   Birds of the Sea of Aral, *Journal Turkestan Branch of the Russian Geographical Society*, 1916, *14*.

ZARUDNY, N. A., and BILKEVITCH, S.   Birds of the Great Balkhan Mountains, *Journal Turkestan Branch of the Russian Geographical Society*, 1918, *14* (in Russian).

RELATING ESPECIALLY TO CHAPTER X

BELL, R.   The travels of —— (and JOHN CAMPBELL) in the East Indies, Persia, and Palestine, 1654-70, by Sir Richard Carnac Temple.   See *Indian Antiquary*, *35-37*, 1906-08, *passim*.   This is a copy of the original MS., in the British Museum, catalogued Sloane, 811.

BIRDWOOD, G.   *Report on the Old Records in the India Office*.   London, 1891.

CAMPBELL, J.   *See above.*

CARRUTHERS, D.   The desert route to India, *Hakluyt Society Publications*, 1929, *63*, series 2.

FINCH, ALLAN GEORGE.   *Historical Manuscripts Commission.   Report on the Manuscripts of* ——.   2 vols.   London, 1913 and 1922.

STREETER, E. W.   *Precious Stones and Gems*.   Fourth edition.   London, 1880.

STREETER, E. W.   *The Great Diamonds of the World*.   Second edition.   London, 1882.

TAVERNIER, J. B.   *Les Six Voyages de Jean Baptiste Tavernier, ecuyer Baron d'Aubonne, en Turquie, en Perse, et aux Indes, etc.*   2 vols.   Paris, 1676.

WOOD, A. C.   *A History of the Levant Company*.   Oxford, 1935.

INDEX

INDEX

INDEX

INDEX